CORPVS SPECVLORVM ETRVSCORVM

GREAT BRITAIN
1

THE BRITISH MUSEUM
FASCICULE I, ARCHAIC AND CLASSICAL MIRRORS
(EARLY TANGED & RELATED MIRRORS)

TEXT BY
JUDITH SWADDLING

DRAWINGS BY SUSAN BIRD

THE BRITISH MUSEUM PRESS

© 2001 The Trustees of The British Museum

First published in 2001 by The British Museum Press
A division of The British Museum Company Ltd
46 Bloomsbury Street, London WC1 3QQ

A catalogue record for this book is available from the British Library

ISBN 0 7141 1277 1

Designed by Martin Richards

Typeset in Bembo
Printed by Cambridge University Press

CONTENTS

THE CONTENT AND ARRANGEMENT
OF THIS FASCICULE

The mirrors in this fascicule comprise the archaic mirrors, nearly all of which are tanged, the earliest types of tanged Classical mirrors, and some problem pieces associated with these groups either in style or date but difficult to categorise, for example ancient mirrors with modern decoration or mirrors of uncertain origin. The format of this and the two British Museum fascicules of the Corpus Speculorum Etruscorum to follow concurs largely with the guidelines set out by the International Scientific Committee for the Corpus, but differs in one major aspect in that the mirrors are grouped within each fascicule according to type rather than in order of acquisition. It was felt that in this way the mirrors would more readily illustrate the development of Etruscan mirrors as shown by the British Museum's collections, and be of more assistance to the reader searching for *comparanda*. The groups are arranged with chronology in mind, but within the groups there is no strict attempt at chronology since absolute dating of Etruscan mirrors is for the main part too problematic, there being very few datable finds. The dates suggested for individual mirrors can therefore only be tentative. Since conflicting high and low dating systems continue to exist, as a less fallible means of dating, this fascicule follows the formula which we adopted for the first British fascicule to be published, *CSE* Great Britain 2 (Cambridge), in that the main phases of stylistic development are always cited, though it should be remembered that even these must have overlapped somewhat. The dates of phases for the early period employed in the British fascicules are as follows:

late archaic: later 6th – mid-5th centuries BC
early Classical: mid–late 5th century BC
Classical: late 5th – mid-4th centuries BC
late Classical: mid–late 4th century BC.
early Hellenistic: late 4th – early 3rd centuries BC
Hellenistic: 3rd – 1st centuries BC

The author has also abandoned the type of heading used in other fascicules, which attempts to describe the type of decoration, resulting in nearly all entries being entitled 'engraved mirrors'. This is of little descriptive help and in effect by no means all of the mirrors are engraved, as became evident during a technical study undertaken by the author together with members of the British Museum's Departments of Scientific Research (Dr P.T. Craddock and Dr D.R. Hook) and Conservation (Ms M. Hockey). The criteria for the different terms regarding decoration used within this fascicule are as follows:

engraved: this technique involves the actual removal of metal as a result of using a tool which is either V- or U-shaped in section

chased: using this technique metal is not removed but pushed up to either side of an incised line, made by hitting a chisel-type tool repeatedly with a hammer to propel it along. Sometimes this results in 'chattering', when the tool 'jumps' and fails to make a single continuous line

incised: this is a general term referring to either of the above techniques and is useful when it is no longer possible to discern which was used, either through erosion or polishing of the surface

punched: when a punch usually of spherical or circular design is struck with a hammer to stamp a design into the metal

The author and colleagues mentioned above have now published a paper on the subject of the technique of manufacture of Etruscan mirrors in general, in which it is argued that the vast majority of Etruscan mirrors were hammered and not cast to shape, an important step forward in the understanding of Etruscan mirror manufacture (see Appendix, and SWADDLING *et al.*

The layout of the illustrations mainly follows the guidelines set out for the Corpus, in that photographs and drawings illustrating the same view of a mirror are on the same page or on facing pages; wherever possible the obverse views are placed first, but occasionally the reverse precedes to prevent a photograph and drawing of the same side of a mirror not being seen at once. To save space the obverse of the mirror is often drawn only in part, where there is no decoration other than an extension motif. For consistency, all sections have the obverse uppermost as the mirrors would have been placed in antiquity. The centre point, a small depression often found on the back of mirrors and thought to be involved with apparatus used to steady the disc during polishing and/or decorating, is recorded in the text, but not usually in the drawing unless it is included as a feature.

THE HISTORY OF THE COLLECTION OF
ETRUSCAN MIRRORS IN THE BRITISH MUSEUM

The British Museum's collection of some 140 Etruscan mirrors is one of the world's finest and most comprehensive and includes mirrors representative of each phase of their production between the sixth and second centuries BC.

Over two-thirds of the Etruscan mirrors in the British Museum arrived during the two main phases of acquisition of Etruscan material, with the remainder being obtained individually. In the first phase came the rich assemblages either presented by or purchased from antiquarians and collectors of the 18th and early 19th centuries, principally, as far as the mirrors are concerned, Charles Townley and Richard Payne Knight, both of whom travelled and collected in Italy. Townley, of the distinguished Lancashire family, is famed for his superb collection of Classical sculpture, acquired by the Museum in 1805; some twenty Etruscan mirrors (including nos 11 and 34 here) were included among the Second Townley collection, bought from Townley's brother Peregrine in 1814. The collection of the wealthy numismatist and aesthete Payne Knight was assembled, mainly in Italy, in the late decades of the 18th century and early part of the 19th, but Payne Knight also acquired pieces in England and other European countries (seven Etruscan mirrors, including no.14). Further Etruscan material, including five mirrors, was acquired from Sir William Temple, who was British Ambassador in Naples for a few years during the early 19th century – again the bulk of his collection was acquired from southern Italy and Sicily, then the *Regno delle due Sicilie*. Some of the earliest Etruscan material in the Museum was among the collection of Sir William Hamilton, purchased by Act of Parliament in 1772. He had been British Ambassador in Naples from 1764 to 1800 and collected mainly from southern Italy and Sicily; only one Etruscan mirror was included, the well-known example with cast relief showing Herakles and Mlacuch (no.20). Indeed, some of the Museum's earliest acquired mirrors featured among the pioneering publications on the Etruscans. This particular mirror was first illustrated in 1723 when Thomas Coke published and supplied plates for *De Etruria Regali,* the great work of one of the earliest Etruscologists, Thomas Dempster. Together with nos 16 and 34, the Hamilton mirror also featured in J. Byres' *Hypogaei, or Sepulchral Caverns of Tarquinia, the Capital of Ancient Etruria,* published in London in 1842. The decoration of the well-published mirror no.34, showing Herkle and Menerva, has been called into question by recent examination, but it remains a fascinating if perplexing item.

The second phase of acquisition began with the vast exploitation of Etruscan cemeteries after 1828, the year in which a rich tomb was accidentally discovered near Vulci on the estate of Lucien Bonaparte, brother of Napoleon and Prince of Canino; the principality of Canino had been sold to him by the Pope in 1814. Many other tombs on his land were then located and opened up, with only the items of value being kept, the rest being sold on in the following years to a large number of museums and private individuals; three mirrors were acquired by the British Museum at one of Canino's sales in Paris (nos 1, 8, 13), while some other items coming through the hands of dealers, such as Dr Emil Braun, former Director of the Archaeological Institute in Rome, may also have originated from the same source (nos 21, 23, 25). The Campanari family of Tuscania similarly removed and sold the contents of numerous tombs, but also did much to introduce the Etruscans to the European public at large. The first Etruscan exhibition ever held in Great Britain was staged by Carlo Campanari in 1837, in a house in Pall Mall, London, where the rooms were arranged to resemble Etruscan tombs. The British Museum bought many of the items in this exhibition, and purchased further groups of material from the Campanari family until 1849, including at least eight mirrors.

The Pall Mall exhibition captured the imagination of the British public and it was shortly afterwards, between 1842 and 1847, that the Englishman George Dennis toured Etruria to compile material for his book, *The Cities and Cemeteries of Etruria*, first published in 1848. This was illustrated with evocative views of Etruscan sites sketched by Samuel James Ainsley, sometimes a co-traveller with Dennis, and who subsequently bequeathed most of his works to the British Museum. British interest in the Etruscans must have remained high, for between 1865 and 1884 the British Museum bought several large series of acquisitions including fifteen mirrors from the Castellani family, mainly from Alessandro Castellani (nos 18 and 24 here). The Castellani family specialised in reproducing and adapting ancient jewellery, but they also collected and traded in a wide range of other antiquities from Italian and Sicilian sites.

A third phase of acquisition is characterised by a smaller but steady flow of Etruscan items from a wide variety of sources, including groups from the collections of Sir A.W. Franks and Captain E.G. Spencer-Churchill (the latter including the fine mirror decorated with a scene of Peleus and Thetis, no.30).

Any known details of the recent history of each mirror are given in the catalogue entries, and lists of findspots, owners, donors, etc. are given in the appropriate indices. Unfortunately, relatively few mirrors entered the Museum with any firm indication of provenance. Mirrors marked 'Found unregistered' have been found in the Museum's reserves without any attached documentation – they may well have belonged to some of the older collections, though it has proved impossible to associate any of them securely. The registration system employing four units, e.g. 1837.6–9.96 (giving the year, month and day and running number of the acquisition), was not employed until about 1837, and even after this date some collections, such as that of Sir William Temple (1856), were not numbered in this way. Most of the objects acquired by the Department of Greek and Roman Antiquities before 1837 were given a registration number at the end of the last century by A.H. Smith, who worked through various lists of acquisitions and manuscript catalogues in order to compose a retrospective register.

ACKNOWLEDGMENTS

This fascicule has come to fruition over a number of years. I offer my sincere thanks to a number of friends and colleagues who have given assistance during this time. Firstly, my thanks go to fellow members of the International Scientific Committee for the Corpus of Etruscan Mirrors and to Massimo Pallotino†, formerly Director of the Committee, for discussing and authorising modifications to the guidelines for the Corpus (see p.5). Francesca Ridgway and Roger Lambrechts were diligent readers, offering valuable comments and constructive suggestions. For advice and encouragement, I am indebted to Sybille Haynes, Ellen Macnamara, Tom Rasmussen and Denise Emmanuel-Rebuffat. Others who kindly read and commented on earlier drafts are Dyfri Williams, Susan Walker and Susan Woodford. I have much appreciated the co-operation of Maristella Pandolfini of the Università di Roma for checking and providing valuable comments on the inscriptions, Etruscan epigraphy being a complex subject on which specialist opinion is always desirable. It was Brian Cook, former Keeper of the Department of Greek and Roman Antiquities, who originally suggested that I undertake the project, and I have enjoyed the opportunity to study material often of great aesthetic appeal and a rich source of information about one of the most fascinating of ancient peoples. Two colleagues whose work has greatly enhanced this fascicule are Philip Nicholls, by his skilled photography (the detail on many Etruscan mirrors is not easy to record on camera), and Susan Bird, whose inspired drawings I hope readers will enjoy as much as I. For discussion of technical matters I am indebted to Paul Craddock, who, together with Duncan Hook, provided the Appendix, and to Susan La Niece and Janet Lang for surface analysis and radiography respectively (all of the British Museum's Department of Scientific Research). I am most grateful for the detailed observations made by Marilyn Hockey, Department of Conservation, during her work on the mirrors. I thank editors Nina Shandloff and Laura Brockbank, and copy-editor Anne Marriott, for their patience and efficiency, and the designer, Martin Richards, particularly for successfully incorporating the innovations requested of him without losing the essential character of the Corpus. I extend warm thanks to Joan Edwards, a British Museum Society volunteer who has helped with routine tasks involved with the Corpus, and whose expertise in German has clarified points in a variety of German technical treatises old and new. Others whose help in a variety of ways I wish to acknowledge are Larissa Bonfante, Stefano Bruni, Adriana Emiliozzi, Bouke van der Meer, Candida Lonsdale, Glenys Lloyd-Morgan, Richard de Puma, Richard Nicholls and Helle Salskov-Roberts. Lastly, my appreciation goes to fellow curators in the Department of Greek and Roman Antiquities and my family for their support during the preparation of this fascicule.

Judith Swaddling
Department of Greek & Roman Antiquities
The British Museum
2000

TERMINOLOGY

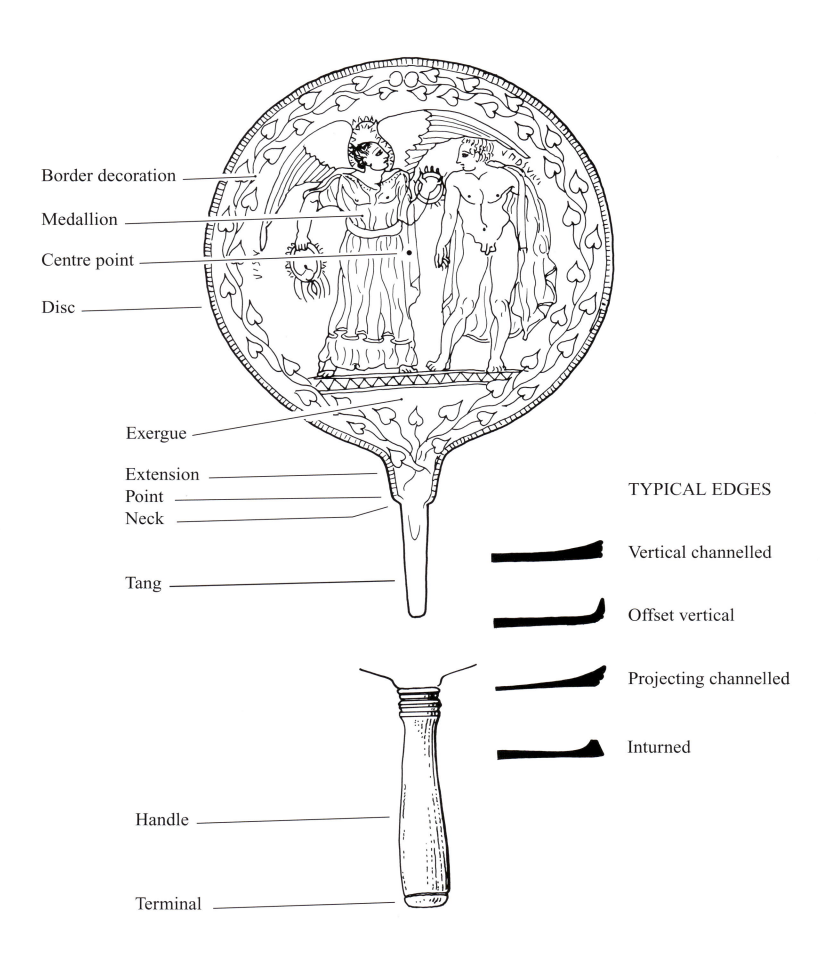

Border decoration

Medallion

Centre point

Disc

Exergue

Extension
Point
Neck

Tang

TYPICAL EDGES

Vertical channelled

Offset vertical

Projecting channelled

Inturned

Handle

Terminal

PART 1:
PLAIN MIRRORS AND MIRRORS WITH NON-FIGURAL DECORATION

1

Elliptical tanged mirror

GR 1837.6–9.96

Provenance. No recorded provenance, but purchased at the sale of part of the Canino collection in 1837 and therefore probably from Vulci. J. DE WITTE, *Description d'une collection de vases peints et bronzes antiques provenant des fouilles de l'Etrurie*, Paris 1837, p.132, lot no.298. The lot comprised six mirrors, 'sur lesquels on ne distingue plus les objets ... Un autre [= probably this mirror] a encore conservé son poli des deux côtés'. See also nos 8, 13.

Bibliography. Unpublished.

Material and condition. Bronze. Lower part of tang broken away and missing. Two holes were drilled through the tang in antiquity: that which seems to have been made first, nearer the disc, is well off-centre and penetrates at an angle, while the second, which coincides partially with the first on the reverse, goes straight through the metal and is slightly nearer the centre of the tang, being probably intended as a replacement. The purpose of the hole was presumably the attachment of a separate handle. *Obverse*. Very smooth, flat, shiny, largely uncorroded metal of gold-brown colour, with some pitting on the left part, partially filled with cuprite and bright green corrosion. At the centre a 'C' painted in white (for Canino). The tang and a small arc on the disc above it are rougher and coated with cuprite and green corrosion: this area was presumably covered originally by a separate handle with a rounded top. *Reverse*. The same type of corrosion appears on the tang, which seems to have been filed in antiquity with a coarse file; judging by the demarcation in the corrosion, the end of the separate handle was on this side contiguous with the rim of the disc. The surface of the disc where revealed is again very smooth and shiny, with a grey-black gleam much like tarnished silver, though the scientific analysis confirms that the metal is bronze. Extensive covering of warty green corrosion. *Edge*. Smooth, hard, black-brown metal.

Measurements. W. 15.2cm. H. 16.9cm. H. of disc 14.6cm. H. of tang 2.3cm. W. at neck of tang 1.8cm. Wt. 885g.

Type. Slightly elliptical mirror, flat on the obverse, very slightly thicker in the middle and rising again at the edge. At the top of the disc on the reverse the edge is acutely inturned but is elsewhere vertical. There is no centre point.

[figs pp.74–5]

Decoration. Plain on both sides and edge.

Technique. The very slight undulation and faceting of the reverse of the disc appear to represent traces of hammering. No similar markings appear on the obverse, which was probably worked more thoroughly to improve the surface. Around much of the edge of the disc there is a narrow strip of horizontal bevelling, as though the whole object has been scraped to and fro across a harder surface to level off the raised rim, so that when placed down the mirror would lie flat on its back. The disc appears to have been much too heavy for the tang and this no doubt resulted in the break at its base: at 885g, it is a particularly heavy mirror. A similar flat mirror with tang (but only *c*. 0.2cm thick) in the Rijksmuseum van Oudheden, Leiden (I 1965/11.10), has broken across the tang at the level of the hole (*CSE* The Netherlands, no.23). The present condition of the British Museum mirror indicates that it must have been superbly polished in antiquity.

Date. Late archaic. The closest parallel for this mirror in type, shape and section is one from the Arnoaldi cemetery, unfortunately not part of a *corredo* and therefore difficult to date with precision (Museo Civico Bologna, Inv. 16293, *CSE* Italia 1, II, no.3). The general type is found in tombs throughout the 5th century, most notably from the Certosa cemetery (*CSE* Italia 1, II, p.11, and nos 12, 13, 16, 18; cf. also two examples from the Giardini Margherita, nos 23, 24; for the type see also DE GRUMMOND *Guide* pp.174–5). MANSUELLI speculated on the local origin of these mirrors, considering Bologna, but ultimately decided it unlikely since mirrors are rare finds in tombs in the Felsinian area and those surviving were often repaired in antiquity, suggesting that there was no source of new mirrors close at hand (unless of course the workshop had gone out of production). He concluded their likely origin to be Etruria proper (*StEtr* 1941 pp.315–16). The mirror in Leiden mentioned above (see *Technique*), like this mirror, comes from Vulci: Tomb 148 in the Osteria necropolis. VAN DER MEER (*CSE* The Netherlands, no.23) dates it on the basis of the other tomb contents to 540–480 BC. Though a very fine object, the British Museum mirror may belong to this earlier period rather than the general 5th-century span allocated to its less monumental peers. There is a scattering of similar mirrors in various collections but all others so far published unfortunately have no provenance. Close in thickness (*c.* 0.4cm) is a disc in the Museum Bogaert-Wauters, Hamme, Inv. G.R. 465, of which LAMBRECHTS questions the identity, but it is hard to imagine its being other than a mirror, given the slight thickening at the rim and existence of the centre point, even though it lacks a tang (*CSE* Belgique 1, no.15). For other mirrors of the general type, see *CSE* USA 1, nos 29, 30 and 2, nos 2, 19, 36. An example in Bloomington, Indiana, Inv. 62. 117. 110 (*CSE* USA 1, no.40), is close, being flat and thick (0.4cm) but with a very slight extension.

2   [figs pp.76–7]

Circular tanged mirror

GR 1975.9–1.4

Provenance. Unknown. Found unregistered.

Bibliography. Unpublished.

Material and condition. Bronze. Mineralised and splitting away into layers around the edge at the top and to one side. Covered by matt green corrosion and cuprite with raised, warty areas particularly around the edge.

Measurements. W. 11.8cm. H. 16.3cm. H. of disc 11.5cm. H. of tang 4.8cm. W. of tang at neck 1.2cm. Wt. 329g.

Type. Circular mirror with thick flat section made in one piece with pointed tang. No evidence of centre point. Edge vertical.

Decoration. Plain on both sides. Edge too poor to reveal any decoration.

Date. Late archaic. The mirror is similar in shape and thickness to no.3, though it is overall smaller (see no.3 for comments).

3   [figs pp.78–9]

Circular tanged mirror

GR 1975. 9–1.5

Provenance. Unknown. Found unregistered.

Bibliography. Unpublished.

Material and condition. Bronze. Very corroded and covered by a thick layer of whitish mud which appears to be substantially bonded to the surface layer. One side, rough but fairly level, has had a small area partially cleaned to write on the registration number. The other side is badly mineralised and the surface of the disc is raised up by internal swelling. Beneath the mud and green corrosion on this side there is visible on the upper part of the disc an area of reddish orange and blue mineralised metal, and across this is an indentation about 2cm long apparently resulting from a blow with a chisel-like object. An irregular stain spreading up from the base of the disc indicates that the object has come into contact with liquid at some time.

Measurements. W. 13cm. H. 16.9cm. H. of disc 12.8cm. H. of tang 4.1cm. W. of tang at neck 1.3cm. Wt. 578g (includes mud bonded with encrustation).

Type. Circular mirror of thick, flat section made in one with a pointed tang. Edge rounded. No centre point visible.

Decoration. It is impossible to determine any decoration but judging by the type the mirror is likely to have been undecorated.

Date. Late archaic. In shape and size the mirror is very close to *CSE* USA 1, no.30 (Omaha, Nebraska), which is of unknown provenance and dated 475–425 BC, and *CSE* Italia 1, II, no.7, from the Certosa cemetery, dated 5th century BC and no.18, from the De Lucca cemetery, dated with its *corredo* to 450–400 BC. The weight and thick, flat section of the British Museum mirror indicate the early part of the 5th century BC. The close correspondence in the dimensions of the discs probably indicate a common origin in northern Etruria: another, very corroded mirror of the same type and dimensions comes from Vulci, from perhaps the Cucumella or S. Donatella necropolis (*CSE* The Netherlands, no.32, private collection 'Meer').

4   [figs pp.80–83]

Circular tanged mirror

GR 1867.5–8.379

Provenance. Unknown. Blacas collection (collection of Duke Peter Lewis John Casimir de Blacas): archaeological material from Italy assembled between 1816 and 1822.

Bibliography. Unpublished.

Material and condition. Bronze. Fair condition but most of the surface metal is covered by matt corrosion. *Obverse.* Extensive dark brown corrosion over red cuprite, with smoother bluish green layer across the upper disc. Rough striations in the area upper right indicate a past attempt to scrape off some of the corrosion. *Reverse.* Light golden metal partially visible near and on the rim, the rest of the disc and tang overlaid with areas of dark and light green corrosion. At some time in the past a small area to the upper right of the tang has been cleaned to write on the registration number. An old white label with blue lines remains attached to the tang, but no number is visible on it.

Measurements. W. 13cm. H. 16cm. H. of disc 13cm. H. of tang 3cm. W. of tang at neck 1.4cm. W. of hole in tang 0.4cm on obverse, tapering to 0.35cm. on reverse. Wt. 317g.

Type. Circular mirror made in one with forked tang tapering very slightly towards the base, in outline and section. The raised, vertical edge of the disc recedes to nothing on either side of the tang. Section of disc flat and fairly thick. A hole has been drilled off-centre two-thirds of the way down the tang. No centre point visible.

Decoration. Plain, apart from raised rim.
EDGE. Narrow channel adjacent to obverse.

Date. The mirror is close in shape and size to *CSE* The Netherlands, no.15 (unknown provenance), and to a mirror in the Museo Guarnacci, Volterra, from tomb III of the Guerruccia cemetery, whose *corredo* includes a scaraboid gem dated to the mid-5th century BC, *CSE* Italia 3, I, no.15. The shape and section of the British Museum mirror appear to indicate a fairly early date, perhaps 475–450 BC.

5 [figs pp.84–7]

Circular tanged mirror with extension

GR 1997.9–12.18

Provenance. Unknown. Formerly Museum of London; associated card label: 'Gould Collection. Bronze Mirror. Ancient Etruscan. Italy. 19'. Transferred in 1997.

Bibliography. Unpublished.

Material and condition. Bronze. *Obverse.* Disc has smooth dark green-black surface patina overlain extensively with thin matt greenish corrosion and traces of mud. Slightly pushed in at the centre from the obverse. *Reverse.* Matt green warty corrosion encrusted with mud. Circular white label on disc on which is written '19.' in faded black ink (see *Provenance*). Both sides of tang, extension and edge of disc have similar corrosion to the reverse.

Measurements. W. 14.9cm. Projected max. H. 22.3cm. Tang: H. 5.3cm. W. at neck 1.2cm. Wt. 245g.

Type. Circular thin mirror, made in one with a narrow extension set asymmetrically on the tang. The disc was perhaps originally slightly convex, but is now for the most part flat. Raised vertical edge. No centre point visible.

Decoration. Obverse and edge plain. No decoration visible on reverse.

Technical comment. On the reverse tool marks are clearly visible where the mirror was beaten out by hammering towards the edge. For a similar asymmetrically set disc see

CSE USA 2, no.45 (probably an ancient mirror with modern engraving); cf. also no.27 in this fascicule.

Date. Probably Classical. The mirror has little about it that is distinctive: thin, flat, lightweight mirrors of this kind with slightly tapering extensions and raised rims have often been attributed to the 4th century (e.g., *CSE* BRD 1, no.13; *CSE* Italia 1, I, no.27). Similar though slightly smaller and with a shorter extension is *CSE* France 1, III, no.28.

6 [figs pp.88–91]

Circular tanged mirror, with part of modern handle

GR 1814.7–4.1061

Provenance. Unknown. Found unregistered. Second Townley collection.

Bibliography. Unpublished.

Material and condition. Bronze. Good condition with mostly smooth, lustrous olive-green patina overlain here and there with a thin layer of brown corrosion. Several deep scores in the patination on both sides cut through the corrosion and must have occurred post-excavation. A stain at the base of the disc to the left of the tang indicates possible contact with liquid at some time. The tang has been vigorously filed away in modern times to narrow it and create an angle sloping upwards to the obverse and a bronze handle with matching recess has been soft-soldered on to it making a half-dovetail join. A rivet inserted from the obverse just beneath the collar of the handle, to secure the join, is made of brass. The handle itself is broken at the base and the rough broken surface bears traces of modern solder; this surface has a hole in the centre about 0.2cm across and 0.2cm deep where presumably a pin was fixed to hold the remainder of the handle, now missing.

Measurements. W. 15.5cm. H. 17.4cm. H. of disc 15.5cm. W. of tang at neck 1.0cm. Preserved H. of tang 1.8cm. Total preserved H. 16.3cm. Wt. 265g.

Type. Circular mirror apparently made in one piece with a tang; part of a bronze handle, as described above, adheres to the tang. The disc is flat on the reverse, and very slightly convex on the obverse. A small conical recess near the centre of the disc on the reverse may be the centre point.

Decoration.
EDGE. Adjacent to the beaded rim of the obverse is a plain band.

OBVERSE. At the base of the disc is a motif now difficult to decipher but apparently consisting of two addorsed spirals linked beneath by a series of curved lines, and with some kind of decoration extending outward to either side of the spirals.

REVERSE. Plain.

HANDLE. *Obverse.* Beneath a raised rounded cap at the top the handle is decorated by crossed lines forming a diamond pattern with a punched dot at the centre of each diamond.

Technical comment. See *Material and condition.* A radiograph clarified how the handle was attached and showed the brass rivet penetrating through it into the tang. Hammer marks around the rim on the reverse, where the mirror has been smoothed outward and 'dished' into the rim, are plainly evident. Radiographic examination report by Janet Lang, Department of Scientific Research, British Museum: Project rad6514, 12 December 1997.

Date. Early Classical. In section, shape and beaded rim the mirror is close to *CSE* The Netherlands, no.34, private collection 'Meer', ancient but with modern engraving, said to come from Orvieto. This latter is likened to no.14 here by VAN DER MEER (*CSE* The Netherlands, no.34), but no.14 is different in having a quite definite extension and is likely to be somewhat earlier. A date of perhaps 450–425 BC is likely for the mirror discussed here, which is thin in section, and distinguished by its very unusual handle. Another in the group, with just the usual tang, is *CSE* BRD 4, no.11, there dated early 5th century BC. The alien handle is of uncertain date, but the brass rivet indicates that it has been attached in modern times.

7 [figs pp.92–5]

Circular tanged mirror with extension with volutes

GR 1967.12–13.5

Provenance. Unknown. Found unregistered.

Bibliography. Unpublished.

Material and condition. Bronze, in fair condition though extensively pitted. Matt gold-brown appearance, the metal having at some time been chemically stripped of all patination save for small green patches above the centre of the disc on the obverse. The disc has been gouged on the obverse, below the centre, by a blow perhaps from a round-ended instrument, aimed from the direction of the extension, and to the left of this damage is a lesser vertical gouge about 5.5cm long. The first blow has pushed the metal up into a hump on the reverse. The damage appears likely to have been done in antiquity since there are no changes in the surface coloration of the metal, and the force of the blows indicate that they were deliberate.

Measurements. W. 14.5cm. H. 19.3cm. H. of disc 14.2cm. W. of extension at base of disc 3.6cm. W. across points of extension 2.6cm. H. of tang 3.3cm. W. of tang at neck 1.1cm. W. of tang at base 0.6cm. Thickness of tang 0.5cm. Wt. 344g.

Type. Circular flat mirror of even section and inturned edge with flat rim. The thick tang and the extension are cast on to the obverse, but on the reverse the fan-shaped upper part of the extension overlaps the disc without adhering to it (see *Technical comment*). The extension has 'corners' where it meets the tang. No centre point visible.

Decoration.
OBVERSE. There is a volute design on the extension, the centres of the spirals being marked by globules of bronze which could be the heads of rivets (see *Technical comment*); cf. no.28. The upper part of the motif extends outward along the rim of the disc but it is now difficult to decipher. Punched circles appear to either side.

REVERSE and EDGE. Plain.

Technical comment. The joining of the disc to the tang is complex and constitutes an elaborate repair rather than a deliberate variation on the norm. On the reverse the fan-shaped extension overlaps the disc without adhering to it, and in profile view a narrow slit is seen down the centre of the edge of the base of the 'fan' on either side; from there downwards the tang appears to be in one piece, and is particularly thick (0.5cm). On the obverse a slight change in the texture of the metal across the lower part of the extension, from corner to corner, indicates a horizontal join. The replacement tang, complete with fan-shaped overlap on the reverse, was clearly brazed on, but there was no attempt to secure a join between the fan and the disc surface. The globules of metal in the centre of the spirals of the extension motif look like rivet heads but there is no trace of them on the reverse, and they were probably simply decorative, a type of embellishment which was more frequently added in silver (e.g. no.28). The tang contains an unusually high amount of lead for an Etruscan mirror (16%: see Appendix). Radiographic examination report by Janet Lang, Department of Scientific Research, British Museum: Project rad6514, 12 December 1997.

Date. Late Classical. The distinctive shape of the extension is paralleled by three examples in the Vatican, *CSE* Vaticano 1, nos 9, 10, 20, all probably 4th century BC; none has a provenance, and all were in the Vatican collections by 1784. Although the join of the extension to the disc of the British Museum mirror has given it an unusual appearance on the reverse, its general similarity in size and silhouette to the Vatican mirrors may indicate a common origin, perhaps indicating a local fashion or a common workshop.

8   [figs pp.96–7]

Circular tanged mirror with vestigial extension

GR 1837.6–9.93

Provenance. Probably from Vulci. The Departmental register states that the mirror was purchased at the sale of part of the Canino collection, 1837, lot 298 (see nos 1, 13).

Bibliography. Unpublished.

Material and condition. Covered almost entirely with a perfectly smooth, hard, blue-green patina. On the reverse there are tiny patches where this is missing around the centre, and isolated wart-like nodules of corrosion. The lower edge of the disc and tang are overlaid with rough, dark brown corrosion, of which there are also traces near the upper rim. A white 'C' is painted at the centre, presumably for Canino. On the obverse there are similar nodules of corrosion and the rough surface of the tang has a brownish patina. A small label towards the upper left is inscribed in brown ink now difficult to decipher: it appears to read perhaps '37[?] Londres 13'; the first number could refer to the date of the Canino sale in Paris.

Measurements. W. 14.8cm. H. 19.0cm. H. of disc 15.0cm. H. of tang and extension 4.0cm. W. of tang at neck 1.2cm. W. of extension across points 2.0cm. Wt. 370g.

Type. Circular flat mirror with a short blunt-pointed tang and minuscule extension. The disc thickens a little towards the inturned edge. Two centre points.

Decoration.
EDGE. Square-beaded by punching with a tool that had a raised edge to either side of the beading which has created parallel grooves in the bronze.

OBVERSE. At the base of the disc are spirals bound together with a double band, each with a heart-shaped leaf on a stem emerging from the outer coil. A slightly asymmetrical palmette, with the large lobe flanked by three small lobes, each dotted at the end, rests on a double curved base over the bound coils. Opposing the curved base beneath the coils is another single curve. The design appears to have been carried out before the mirror was cut to shape and the edge beaded, as the lower edges of the motif are missing.

REVERSE. Plain.

Characteristics of the decoration. The decoration is chased; it is somewhat careless and lacking finesse. The palmette is comparatively faint, whereas the lines of the spirals and leaves are generally sharper and deeper, and were perhaps re-cut.

Date. Late archaic, about 475–450 BC. Cf. *CSE* Denmark 1, no.22, which is very close in shape and decoration of the obverse. Fake mirrors in Steinhorst (*CSE* BRD 2, no.34) and Orvieto (*CSE* Italia 4, no.33) have a similar motif. For a list of authentic parallels, see *CSE* Orvieto entry.

9   [figs pp.98–101]

Circular tanged mirror with extension

GR 1975.9–1.1

Provenance. Unknown. Found unregistered.

Bibliography. Unpublished.

Material and condition. Bronze. Generally poor condition, covered for the most part by a layer of raised, warty corrosion which has laminated away from the bronze around much of the edge, lifting the surface layer of metal with it, and a large area of the corrosion and original surface are now missing on the reverse (the missing layer was about 0.15cm thick, judging by the surrounding broken edge). Within this lacuna the metal is corroded green, with raised areas of patchy, black corrosion. On the reverse, shiny brown metal is partially visible beneath the dark red corrosion. There is pitting where a few of the 'warts' have come away, leaving rough black or green areas beneath the original surface.

Measurements. W. 16.6cm actual (part of edge missing on one side at horizontal diameter) or 16.9cm if restored. H. 24.0cm. W. of tang at neck 1.2cm. Wt. 618g.

Type. Circular mirror probably originally with offset projecting edge, and thick, slightly tapering, blunt-ended tang. It is impossible to know the original thickness of the disc and whether it tapered towards the rim, due to its badly corroded state. The straight-sided extension tapers down to a width only slightly more than that of the tang. The rim seems to have had a smooth, raised, horizontal surface, about 0.2cm wide, to judge by the better-preserved section on the extension. No centre point visible.

Decoration.
EDGE. Adjacent to the beading of the obverse is a row of tongues with internal concentric arches.

OBVERSE. The rim is beaded. The motif at the base of the disc and continuing on to the extension features a nine-lobed palmette, the lobes each with duplicate outline and emerging from a fan-shaped base with internal fan. To either side of the base double spirals extend along the rim of the disc. From the outer curl of each spiral extends a curved 'leaf'; around these 'leaves', the palmette and the spirals is a row of dots. Beneath the base of the palmette is a downward-pointing frond with six leaves to either side.

REVERSE. Due to the poor condition of the object it is now impossible to tell whether this bore any decoration.

Characteristics of the decoration. What remains of the decoration of the rim and edge is meticulous and regular. The motif on the obverse is cut deeply and carefully but the elements are somewhat asymmetrical, the double spiral on the right being stubbier than that on the left, which has an extra line along its central 'stem', presumably where the craftsman made a mistake; there are also two extra lines along the lower edge of the left-hand 'leaf'. Given the difference in quality between the decoration on the edge and rim and that of the extension, it could be argued that they were done by different craftsmen, or by one craftsman who was not quite so good at drawing the free-hand decoration of the motif as he was at carrying out punched decoration. Another possibility, as suggested elsewhere (see p.45), is that the mirrors were made and decorated in separate workshops.

Similar elements for the motif on the obverse can be found on *CSE* Italia 2, I, no.19, another mirror of similar type with beaded and tongued edge, and flat section which has spirals with outcurved 'leaves' and surrounding dotted line, while spirals with outcurved leaves also occur on the similarly shaped mirror *CSE* USA 2, no.37. The frond-like ornament is difficult to parallel, though a cruder, upright instead of inverted version of it appears on a mirror in Berlin, one of the works of MANSUELLI'S *Maestro dei Giocolieri*, and dated 525–500 BC, while a striking elongation of the motif goes all the way down the handle of a Praenestine mirror, *CSE* BRD 4, no.26 (the resemblance is clearer in the photograph than in the drawing). Another frond-like motif appears to either side of spirals on the obverse motif of a mirror made and found at Vulci, *CSE* Great Britain 2, no.8 (late Classical). A later variant of this is *CSE* USA 1, no.4, *c.*300 BC.

Date. The general shape, considerable weight and apparently thick, flat section of the mirror indicate a late archaic/early Classical date. Mirrors of this general type appear to span from the early 5th to the early 4th century BC, for example, *CSE* Denmark 1, no.10; the Eos and Memnon mirror, no.22; *CSE* USA 2, nos 5, 13, 37; *CSE* Great Britain 2, no.23, combining also the beaded and tongued decoration of the edge, and no.26, with similar thick, flat section; *CSE* Italia 1, I, no.26; *CSE* Vaticano 1, no.11, also thick and flat, and with beaded and tongued edge; *CSE* DDR I, no.5; *CSE* Italia 2, I, no.19, another mirror of similar type with beaded and tongued edge, flat section and obverse motif with similar elements (see *Characteristics of the decoration*).

The British Museum mirror was undeniably of fine quality, with its very distinctive frond-like motif on the obverse. This and the Berlin mirror (*CSE* BRD 4, no.26) bear what appear to be isolated forerunners of this kind of ornament. The connection of several of the parallels with Vulci may be significant (*CSE* Italia 2, I, no.19; *CSE* Vaticano 1, no.8; *CSE* Great Britain 2, no.8).

10   [figs pp.102–4]

Circular tanged mirror with extension

GR 1967.12–13.1

Provenance. Unknown. Found unregistered.

Bibliography. Unpublished.

Material and condition. The entire object has been stripped down to bare dark brown metal, generally leaving a rough, pitted surface, though extensive parts of the reverse are smooth.

Measurements. W. (if restored) 16.0cm. H. 21.8cm. H. of disc 16.2cm. W. across points 1.9cm. Wt. 565g.

Type. Circular, thick, almost flat, mirror with vertical edge, and made in one with a forked tang. The disc thickens slightly towards the rim, and has a straight-sided extension. No centre point visible.

Decoration.
EDGE. A channel is adjacent to the beading of the obverse.

OBVERSE. At the base of the disc is a motif with a nine-lobed palmette, the outlines of the lobes duplicated and with circlets at the ends. The lobes spring from a roughly triangular shape, with an internal concentric triangle, and the palmette is based upon two addorsed spirals, duplicated in outline, and bound together by a band with diamond shape decoration. Beneath the band, between the stems of the spirals, is an inverted V-shape, again with duplicate outline, with lobes to either side. To either side of the spirals extend two undulating stems, the upper one of each culminating in a lotus-type flower with two out-turned petals and a central pointed stamen topped by a circlet, the petals and the stamens all with duplicate outline. The lower stem to either side of the spirals extends further and terminates in three heart-shaped leaves. Rim beaded.

REVERSE. Plain.

Characteristics of the decoration. The lines of the decoration are now probably deeper than they were originally owing to the etching away of the surface layer together with the corrosion. The design has been carried out carefully, though the stems on the right are a little wobbly and also slightly longer than those on the left, where the lotus flower is positioned nearer to the palmette. It is unusual for the motif not to extend on to the extension.

Date. Probably about 450–400 BC. The mirror may not be Etruscan, since the obverse motif is hard to parallel, though some of the elements occur in later 5th- and 4th-century mirrors.

11

[figs pp.105–7]

Elliptical tanged mirror

GR 1814.7–4.918

Provenance. Unknown. Second Townley collection.

Bibliography. Unpublished.

Material and condition. Bronze. *Obverse.* Matt green corrosion overlaid extensively by a smooth olive-green patina, in places speckled with a dark brown waxy layer. Much of the surface has been abraded or scraped by a blade to remove the upper layer of corrosion, presumably soon after excavation. A white 'T' (for Townley) painted above the tang. *Reverse.* Smooth olive-green patina spattered with hard black corrosion, perhaps a burial deposit, in a rough arc-shape across the upper part. Considerable pitting, with traces of a whitish substance also occurring in the lines, the remains of a modern infill. The corrosion on both sides of the tang has been filed down to the metal in modern times, perhaps to accommodate a handle no longer present.

Measurements. W. 12.9cm. H. 14.2cm. H. of disc 12.5cm. H. of tang 1.7cm. W. of tang at neck 1.2cm. Wt. 216g.

Type. Small, slightly elliptical mirror. The disc tapers slightly in section towards the edge on the reverse. The raised vertical edge is irregular in thickness, being noticeably thinner at the top. The tang is perforated by a single hole, presumably made in antiquity as it is lined with corrosion, and tapers in section towards the base, perhaps as a result of filing in modern times. Centre point at centre of vortex.

Decoration.
EDGE. Repeated horizontal grooves.

OBVERSE. Plain; rim beaded, indistinctly in some areas, especially at the top.

REVERSE. The border is formed by a thick, continuous, undulating stem with heart-shaped leaves alternating to either side. In the medallion, based on the centre point, is a vortex design within a double concentric circle, in turn encircled by a row of dots.

Characteristics of the decoration. The decoration is shallowly chased, showing evidence on the whole of having been done with a fine-pointed instrument, though on the lower right the lines are broader, perhaps indicating re-cutting either in ancient or modern times. The design has been carried out carefully and symmetrically, with the compactly and neatly arranged leaves of the border and the simple centrepiece forming an attractive composition.

Date. Probably late archaic. The type of border decoration, formed by an undulating stem with heart-shaped ivy leaves, is common to a large number of mirrors dating to between about 470 and 350 BC. REBUFFAT *Miroir* p.458 suggests that the border is characteristic of a workshop perhaps in Perugia, on the basis that of the only four mirrors with this type of decoration which have a provenance, three are said to be from Perugia. The concept of giving prominence to the border decoration also occurs on a mirror in Boston, where four rows of different types, including a band of ivy, encircle a small head (*CSE* USA 2, no.4), and on a mirror in the Staatliche Museen zu Berlin, with two rows of decoration surrounding a maenad (*CSE* BRD 4, no.9). The British Museum mirror is unusual in having no figured decoration (cf. *CSE* DDR I, nos 22, 46) and the vortex design in the centre, perhaps intended to represent a shield, or possibly the sun, is unparalleled. The flat obverse coupled with the tang must put the mirror quite early, and like the Boston mirror, probably 470–450 BC. For reverses with border decoration only, see also *CSE* DDR I, no.46 and *CSE* Italia 2, I, no.19.

12

[figs pp.108–11]

Circular tanged mirror

GR 1890.9–21.17

Provenance. From Bologna. Purchased from the Reverend Greville John Chester (1830-1892), traveller in the Near East, who financed his journeys by the sale of antiquities (M. BIERBRIER *Who was Who in Egyptology*, 3rd revised edn, London 1995, pp.96-7).

Bibliography. Unpublished.

Material and condition. Bronze. The tang appears to have been broken off and crudely repaired in antiquity by melting or brazing on a piece of copper alloy, which was then roughly filed in an attempt to neaten it, and a pinning hole was made (conical, and wider on the obverse) through the repaired part of the tang, presumably for the attachment of a handle. Subsequently a roughly semicircular crack has occurred at the base of the disc, where there was a weak area adjacent to the thickest part of the repair; the crack starts from the rim of the mirror, and extends well towards the rim on the opposite side of the tang. A rivet was then inserted from the obverse as a secondary repair in antiquity, the rounded end showing on the reverse. On the reverse the cast-on metal overlaps the running wave pattern border in an irregular accretion. The patina on the reverse is blackish, the surface of the bronze generally smooth but largely overlaid with slightly rough-textured corrosion. The area within the semicircular crack at the base has been cleaned down to the brownish metal at an unknown date in recent times. The cast-on metal has a rough surface and dark green patination. On the obverse brownish gold metal is visible in places, with areas of smooth black and others of varying shades of greenish grey. There is brighter green corrosion just above the tang. The infill in the lines is a white granular material, occasionally stained green with copper salts; in some places it is mixed with a dark waxy material, charred-looking black material and corrosion deposits. In some places it overlies ancient green corrosion and spreads over the adjacent surface, suggesting that it may be a soil deposit or modern added filler.

Measurements. W. 17.1cm. H. 21.3cm. H. of disc 17.3cm. H. of tang 4.0cm. W. of tang at neck 1.3cm. Wt. 340g.

Type. Circular thin flat mirror with a small pointed tang. The disc thickens slightly towards the rim on the reverse. Slightly projecting raised edge. Centre point.

Decoration.
OBVERSE. Running wave pattern border with punched dots along the inner side of the engraving. At the base is a palmette resting on two back-to-back spirals which form the ends of the running wave border, though it is now impossible to see how this was achieved to the right of the tang in the area of the rivet and crack. The palmette has eleven lobes, the seven larger ones with a small circle at the ends, and two pointed inserts to either side of the central lobe. The rim is punched or cut to imitate beading.

REVERSE. A similar running wave pattern, with punched dots along the inner side, around the entire disc.

Characteristics of the decoration. Obverse. The decoration is engraved. The lines are very deep and firm, with the wave-crests somewhat irregular, and some of the curves are flattened. The palmette has been designed fairly carefully though it leans over to the left; the circles at the ends of the lobes are punched. There are some mis-cuts and a rough extra leaf to the left of the tang. The wave pattern is accompanied by a row of dots made by a tool of distinctive shape, punched into the metal. The shape of the tool-point, indicated by silicon rubber impressions taken of the indentations, is of a sharpened cone, slightly oval in cross-section, with one side flattened and grooved, so that the groove took a crescent-shaped 'bite' out of the metal. It was not a straightforward punch but rather resembles the tip of an engraving tool. *Reverse.* The engraving is not quite so deep and wide but the waves are rather more regular in shape and size; there are no significant differences between the tool marks on either side.

Technical comment. The alloy appears to contain a deliberate addition of lead, which is unusual for an Etruscan mirror (see Appendix). See *Material and condition* for the repair of the handle in antiquity.

Date. Late archaic. This is a very unusual mirror from the point of view of its matching decoration on both sides. For the wave pattern as a border on the obverse, see *CSE* BRD 4, no.10, of the early 5th century BC. For parallels featuring border decoration only, or where the border decoration takes precedence, see no.10 in this fascicle. The small pointed tang, assuming that its original shape was similar, and the flat disc place it no later than about 500–480 BC.

13   [figs pp.112–14, 187]

Circular tanged mirror
Inscribed with name

GR 1837.6–9.95

Provenance. Unrecorded, but presumably Vulci, since it is likely to be identical with that in the Etruscan Museum of Lucien Bonaparte; see PANDOLFINI ANGELETTI in *CIE* III, 3, no.11082, tav.XXX, who identifies it with an undecorated mirror found with an Attic red-figured kylix in the Cucumella necropolis, *Museum Bonaparte,* (c) on plate following p.4, now Museo Archeologico Bari, inv.6097, BEAZLEY *ARV*[2] p.328, no.121, 'between the Panaitios Painter and Onesimos': *CIE* III, 3, no.11079, tav.XXVIII. The Departmental register records that the mirror was bought at the sale of a portion of the Canino collection: see DE WITTE, below: 'Six miroirs ... L'un parait offrir quelques lettres étrusques'. WALTERS states erroneously: 'Campanari, 1837'. (See also nos 1, 8.)

Bibliography. BONAPARTE *Catalogo* p.4, no.581; *Museum Bonaparte,* pl. following p.4, no.581; DE WITTE *Description,* lot 298; GERHARD *ES* I p.85; *CII* no.2592; WALTERS *BMBronzes* no.725; *CIE* II, I, 2, 1923, p.141; FIESEL *Geschlecht* p.138, n.367; REBUFFAT *Miroir* p.566, n.2c; RIX *ET* Vc 2.51=OA 2.13; *CIE* III, 3, no.11082, tav.XXX; *CSE* USA 2, p.63.

Material and condition. Bronze. Disc complete but extensively pitted; the end of the tang is broken off. *Obverse.* Mainly dark brown but with patches of dark red cuprite and some green patination particularly near the areas of pitting. *Reverse.* Widely but less deeply pitted than the obverse, with some dark red cuprite, brownish green patches and areas of yellow metal; this side has probably been chemically stripped.

Measurements. W. 15.2cm. H. 15.9cm. H. of disc 14.4cm. H. of tang (broken) 1.5cm; W. of tang at neck 1.3cm. Wt. 383g.

Type. Circular mirror made in one piece with a small tang for insertion into a handle of another material. The obverse is very slightly convex, the edge vertical. No centre point visible.

Decoration. The mirror is plain apart from an inscription on the reverse. The grooves of the inscription are quite deep and have a V-shaped cross-section, resembling engraved grooves, but with other characteristics (bulged metal at the edge of lines, one groove squashed over on to another) which suggest punching or chasing. It has thirteen, or perhaps fourteen, letters, written retrograde in a curve. Pitting of the metal has obscured much of the first, second, fourth and fifth letters from the right. Enough of the inscription remains, however, to make reasonably certain the reading 'rameθas pupena', as suggested by WALTERS.

ramethas pupena

If there were a final letter, it was perhaps an 'S'. Ramtha is a well-known Etruscan female personal name, of which variations in spelling, including Rametha (J. MARTHA *La Langue Étrusque*, Paris 1913, p.42), give a genitive suffix of 'S'. Etruscan family names often end in 'na'. This mirror then was the property of a lady named 'RameΘa Pupena'.

Date. Probably early 5th century, particularly if the association with the kylix mentioned above is correct. The form of the letters 'm' and 'e' indicate an early Etruscan alphabetic form which lasted until the beginning of the 5th century BC. In addition, from the 4th century onward, Ramtha becomes the more usual form of the name (M. CRISTOFANI *Introduzione allo studio dell'etrusco*, Florence 1991, p.42). This evidence is in accordance with the date of some similar plain mirrors in Bologna, *CSE* Italia 1, II, nos 21, 22, 24. This is one of the rare instances of a possessive inscription on an Etruscan mirror; see also no.26.

PART 2:
ARCHAIC AND EARLY CLASSICAL MIRRORS WITH FIGURED DECORATION

14   [figs pp.115–17]

Circular tanged mirror with extension
Orion/Usil?

GR 1824.4–89.82

Provenance. Unknown. Bequeathed by Richard Payne Knight.

Bibliography. INGHIRAMI *MonEtr* II 2, pl.90, p.758; id. *Un specchio mistico esistente nel Museo Britannico*, Fiesole 1825, with plate; GERHARD *ES* IV pl.CCLXXXIX, fig.2, p.21; WALTERS *BMBronzes* no.545; DUCATI *RM* p.282, n.2; MANSUELLI *StEtr* 1946–7 pp.68–9; BEAZLEY *JHS* 1949 pl.1a; RICHARDSON *Etruscans* pl.29; MAYER-PROKOP pp.38, 100, 102–3, pl.46, S 41; HAYNES *EtrBr* no.49, p.263, illustrated p.152; WIMAN *Malstria-Malena* pp.59ff., 105, fig.11:3; LOCHIN in *LIMC* s.v. Orion, no.3★, pp.79–80; ZIMMER *Technik* p.22; ZIMMER *Gerhard* p.114.

Material and condition. Bronze. The metal is in good condition, covered uniformly by a smooth, hard, shiny, medium greenbrown patina. The grooves of the design are filled with modern white pigment. The lower part of the extension and the tang are missing; presumably the tang had already broken off when in modern times the existing metal was cut back to form notches either side of a short lug, which, together with the circular hole drilled into the extension, were used for the attachment of another handle, also now missing. The hole, now filled with wax, was drilled through from the reverse, where it is wider, and the drilling has pushed up the metal surrounding the hole on the obverse. There is also some blackening around the hole, which may indicate the application of heat. On the obverse a small area of patination has been deliberately scratched away down to bare metal, presumably in a crude attempt to identify it. A few random abrasions occur on both sides of the mirror. The upper part of the

motif on the obverse is well worn by rubbing of the thumb during use in antiquity, and presumably also from polishing, like the beaded rim.

Measurements. W. 15.5cm. H. 17.2cm. W. across points of extension 1.7cm. Wt. 463g.

Type. Circular, flat, disc mirror, tapering towards the rim, with an almost vertical slightly raised edge, and made in one piece with the tang. Centre point at top of figure's right thigh.

Decoration.
EDGE. Tongue decoration in relief with internal concentric arches and a channel adjacent to the beading of the obverse.

OBVERSE. At the base of the disc and on the extension, the remains of a spiral and leaf decoration. Undulating stems grow from two addorsed spirals, each ending in a leaf with a circlet at the point. Above are the remains of the bases of four lobes, but any design above this is now indecipherable. Rim beaded.

REVERSE. The border decoration consists of two deeply undulating stems with heart-shaped ivy leaves alternating to either side, the lobes of each leaf formed by two enclosed circles. The stems are entwined on the extension, and cross over and overlap at the top, terminating to either side of the central figure's head in corymbs or clusters of seven 'berries'. In the medallion is a single male figure running over the sea. He is shown in conventional archaic 'windmill' running pose, moving to the right but with his head turned round in profile to the left. He has long hair indicated in outline only, long at the back and looped up over a double fillet, and hanging in short locks in front of the ears. The sea is indicated by a wavy line below his feet, filled with six small fishes all swimming to the left, with a longer, round-nosed fish in pursuit.

Subject and interpretation. The figure has usually been identified as Orion, the mythical hunter of giant stature, and according to one tradition the son of Poseidon, who gave him the power to walk on the sea. Perhaps a more likely identification is that of the Etruscan sun-god Usil, who daily arose from the ocean and set off on his journey across the sky (cf. HAYNES *EtrBr*).

Characteristics of the decoration. The decoration is chased. The lines of the central scene are fluid and fine, of firm, moderate, even depth; they are slightly deeper and coarser for the border. There are only a few small errors of duplication, at the top of the left thigh by the waist, on both sides of the lower right shin, the right shoulder, the left elbow and in several places around the border. A small break is visible where the tool has stopped and recommenced just above the right elbow, and other similar breaks occur in the border decoration. The border decoration on the reverse is somewhat unusual in the way that the stems entwine in unruly fashion at the top and base (cf. no.23 in this fascicule and *CSE* France 1, III, no.4), in that the inner edge of the leaves is often contiguous with the outline of the stem, and that the lobes of the leaves are formed into circles. The whole is incised in a rather casual, perfunctory manner, with occasional duplication and breaks in the stem and leaf lines and the leaves being of irregular size. What survives of the motif on the obverse is similar in approach.

The sea of the reverse forms an exergue which inclines carelessly uphill to the right, with the fish drawn in naive, humorous style, the outline of the gills occasionally resembling a smiling mouth. Variety is achieved by giving them either one or two dorsal or under fins. The big fish on the right arches himself in what was perhaps intended as a slightly menacing manner.

The figure is drawn in typical archaic silhouette fashion, in the conventional 'windmill' running pose, the details of the anatomy illusory rather than realistic, with minimal internal marking. The feet are indicated like slippers with pointed toes, and the long stylised fingers have no tips on the right hand. The head is proportionately too large, and sits in the recess of the collar-bones almost like a separate portrait head in a bust; the top of the head is crammed against the border and it appears that the craftsman did not allow enough room for it. It is probably for the same reason that the torso is too short, and the arms, particularly the right, too thin. The full-frontal almond-eye, sweeping brow, 'question-mark' ear and angular forehead are all Ionic features typical of the archaic period, but the small, almost double, chin, the thick neck and indication of the projecting part of the larynx are all more individualistic touches. Despite its imperfections the decoration of the reverse is pleasing and gives the impression of spontaneity, ingenuity

and humour within the archaic conventions, the exergue constituting an almost cartoon-like image.

Date. The mirror probably dates to about 525–500 BC, being typically late archaic in type and decoration (cf. C. LOCHIN in *LIMC*, end 6th century; HAYNES *EtrBr* and MAYER-PROKOP, 525–500 BC). The swastika or windmill pose of the running figure was no doubt inspired by the tondos of archaic Greek cups, with the physique and facial features strongly influenced by East Greek types. For the distinctive type of ivy leaf of the border, see LAMBRECHTS *Mir.Mus.Royaux* no.20, pp.127–32, dated to about 470 BC on account of the similarity of the figured scene to Tarquinian tomb-painting of the period; it should perhaps be a little earlier. For other mirrors with a decoration of fish in the exergue, see *CSE* BRD 4, nos 6, 10, 15, 18, all dated prior to 450 BC. The dating of the mirror by DUCATI *RM* p.282, n.2 to the mid-5th century BC must be erroneous.

15   [figs pp.118–20]

Circular mirror
Ixion

GR 1900.6–11.3

Provenance. Unknown. Bought from Dr P. Hartwig.

Bibliography. A.B. COOK *Zeus, A Study in Ancient Religion* I, Cambridge 1914, p.204, pl.XVII; D.P. DIMITROV in *AA* 1937, p.69f., abb.3; E. SIMON in *ÖJh* XLII, 1955, p.16, n.44, p.19; PFISTER-ROESGEN *Spiegel* pp.31–2, 106–7, S 11, taf.12; LOCHIN in *LIMC* s.v. Ixion, no.16★.

Material and condition. Bronze. Part of disc broken away and missing with cracks extending from the break. Layer of rough dark green corrosion and soil especially thick on obverse but numerous tiny areas of bright metal show on both sides.

Measurements. W. 15.9cm. Original H. 16.0cm. Wt. 194g.

Type. Circular thin, flat disc with no trace of a tang or handle surviving. As the disc itself is so thin, any tang was presumably insubstantial; it would have had to be quite narrow since the left-hand edge of the break is near the centre and no sign of any protrusion is apparent, though it could have been slightly off-centre, like the tangs of nos 2 and 9. Centre point is at top of figure's penis.

Decoration.
OBVERSE. Plain.

REVERSE. The border zone has a garland of ivy, in some places obliterated by corrosion, the leaves alternating with clusters of berries. In the medallion is a bearded, nude male figure bound to a winged wheel. Around his head is a fillet, his hair at the back tucked round and behind it. He is bound to the eight spokes of a winged wheel by straps around his neck, waist, elbows, right wrist, right knee and ankle and left thigh. The legs are not aligned with the spokes but fastened in a running position, with the right knee bent up. The lower part of the left leg is missing, but from the angle of the surviving part it seems to have hung free of the adjacent spoke, like the left wrist: both the free leg and wrist were perhaps used to propel the wheel. Also missing is an object, in front of the left leg, of which only a small curved line survives; this was perhaps a broad leaf on a stem, like that to the left of the bottom spoke.

Subject and interpretation. Ixion bound to a constantly revolving wheel, his punishment by Zeus for attempting to seduce Hera. For the myth of Ixion and iconography, see LOCHIN pp.857–66, SIMON pp.5–26, and COOK pp.198–211. The object by the left leg has been described as a tree (LOCHIN p.589), in which case the implication would have to be that it is shown on a small scale viewed from high in the heavens where, according to one version of the myth, Ixion's punishment took place. This would accord with the wheel itself being winged, an unusual feature in representations of the scene (cf. an Athenian red-figured kantharos, London, British Museum GR 1865.1–3.23, C.H. SMITH, *Catalogue of the Greek and Etruscan Vases in the British Museum* III, London 1896, E 155, from Nola; BEAZLEY *ARV²* 832, 37; *CVA* BM 4 pl.33, 2; 35,2; LOCHIN in *LIMC* s.v. Ixion, p.858, no.1). There remains however the strong possibility that the vegetal motif is merely a filling ornament. The rim of the wheel is divided into sections.

Characteristics of the decoration. The composition is effective and well adapted to the disc. The grooves of the decoration are relatively shallow in cross-section, with blunt ends, general uniformity of depth and stepped curves suggesting chasing. The style of the decoration is of moderate quality, redeemed somewhat by the carefully drawn and finely hatched wings; an undulating line divides the long feathers from the top of the wing, a feature hidden on the right-hand wing by Ixion's arm. The vegetal motif at the base of the scene is crudely drawn, and the ivy garland of the border shows undistinguished and limited skill, the ivy leaves looking more like tulips; it is unusual for the berries to be indicated by stippling instead of circles. Details of the anatomy are poor, particularly the ear, breast, genitalia and right foot, though the outline of the body is firm and fluid. The artist seems to have had a good eye for overall design and composition, with less interest in minor details (i.e. no indication of the eye, finger-nails, toe-nails, etc.); the small horizontal markings on the chest may indicate scrawniness due to age, malnourishment, or stretching of the torso on the wheel.

Date. About 460–450 BC; cf. the Attic red-figured kantharos with a similar scene, mentioned above. Despite the virtual archaic 'windmill' pose and the 'frontal' eye, early Classical

features are demonstrated by the looser treatment of the hair and beard and the flowing contour of the body (cf. PFISTER-ROESGEN *Spiegel* pp.106–7). The composition was doubtless influenced by representations of Ixion on the tondos of Athenian red-figured cups of the end of the 6th century, where the wheel occupies the whole field. These offer the first depiction of the subject and, apart from the mirror, form its sole venue in the archaic and early Classical period (LOCHIN p.860).

16   [figs pp.121–3]

Circular tanged mirror
Farewell scene: woman between two men

GR 1814.7–4.915

Provenance. Unknown. Formerly Second Townley collection.

Bibliography. BYRES *Hypogaei* pt. 5, pl. 7; GERHARD *ES* IV pl.CDXIV, 2, p. 74; WALTERS *BMBronzes* no.541; DUCATI *RM* p.268; MANSUELLI *StEtr 1942* p.535n.; MANSUELLI *StEtr 1946–47* pp.10–11 (cited in error by a mistaken reference to GERHARD *ES*), 49, 74, 81; MAYER-PROKOP pp.32–3, S 40, p.94, taf.36,1–2, 54, 2; LAMBRECHTS *Mir.Mus.Royaux* p.333; SPRENGER-BARTOLONI pp.107–8, n.100; S. BRUNI, pp.392–3, fig.15 in 'Di un nuovo specchio etrusco e delle officine tarquiniesi di età tardoarcaica', *Rassegna di Archeologia* 9, 1990, pp.373–92; *CSE* USA 2, p.35; WIMAN *Malstria-Malena* pp.59ff., 113, fig.11:42.

Material and condition. Bronze. A crack penetrates from the base of the disc, splitting into two with small cracks extending from these divisions. Covered almost entirely with a smooth, relatively soft, greenish blue patina, and extensively pitted, especially on the obverse. At some time after excavation the surface was scraped to remove some of the patination, and then a dark-coloured wax was applied to fill the lines of the decoration, which also adheres to the surface elsewhere. There is also modern white paint in the lines of the decoration. Where the wax and paint could be removed, the original surface within the lines was found to be consistent with the ancient corrosion elsewhere on the mirror, confirming that the decoration is ancient. A white 'T', for Townley, is painted above the tang on the obverse. The black figures denote the WALTERS catalogue number and a reference number BM 937, of which the significance is uncertain.

Measurements. W. 12.3cm. H. 16.5cm. H. of disc 11.7cm. H. of tang 4.8cm. W. of tang at neck 2.0cm. Wt. 170g.

Type. Small, round, flat disc made in one piece with a long tapering tang and no extension. Raised, inturned edge. Possible centre point on left thigh of woman.

Decoration.
EDGE. Channel next to plain band.

OBVERSE. Plain.

REVERSE. At the junction of the disc and tang is a palmette with nine lobes, each with a double outline, on a base consisting of two parallel curved lines resting on two spirals. The spirals are linked by a downward loop, and have a semicircular band of radiating petals suspended beneath them. Extending from the palmette around the rim of the disc to either side are stems with alternating leaves and berries, meeting at the top with a final berry on each stem. In the exergue is a pastoral scene with a grape vine at the centre, its thick central stem entwined like a rope, its branches extending to either side along the top of the exergue with a few heart-shaped leaves and a number of triple-lobed bunches of grapes and tendrils growing from it. To the left, seated with his back to the vine, is a fat, naked, and somewhat wild-looking little man, perhaps a silenos, with bristling beard and hair which sticks out in an oblong shape behind him. He leans on his seat (not shown) with his left arm and with the right reaches out to a cluster of grapes. To the right, its bottom against the vine, and its nose to a bunch of grapes, is a dog or, in view of the large bushy tail, perhaps a fox, though the tail curls over more like that of a dog.

The main scene shows a woman standing between two men. The woman is shown in profile facing left, left leg behind the right, and lifts her skirt at her left hip, forming a bunch of folds which fall to her ankles. Her right arm is bent up as though she is touching or holding something at her right ear, perhaps an earring or the edge of her himation: lifting the edge of the himation to the face may be a gesture of courtesy or salutation (G. WALBERG *StEtr* 1986 p. 58). The lower hem of the garment is not indicated and neither is the upper part which would cover her torso, save for the lower part of her sleeve at the right elbow. The silhouette of her body is completely revealed, indicating a chiton of very fine cloth. Her himation is draped over her head and shoulders and falls to calf length, the edge of the part hanging down by her left breast falling in scalloped folds. Over her forehead are a series of lines, representing either her hair or the tight folds of the edge of the himation gathered up. The pointed bulge at her crown is typical of archaic profiles, indicating either the hair piled beneath the himation or a characteristic headdress or *tutulus*. In front of her ear is what appears to be a curl, and she has a large disc earring. The man on the left stands in profile facing right, right leg behind the left, with the horizontal lines on his calves indicating the tops of boots. He gesticulates with his right arm raised, the index and middle index fingers extended, and the left hand pointing down with all the fingers straight. The mantle draped around him is barely indicated save for the bunches of folds falling with scalloped edges from his arms. The crown of his head, like the woman's, is elongated. He is perhaps wearing a plain cap, from which his hair protrudes around the edges, in short wavy lines like those of his beard. The man on the right stands in profile facing left, his right arm raised with index finger pointing upwards, and his left arm out before him holding a branch, though the area where the left hand would be is pitted and the hand cannot be deciphered; the branch is of the same kind of foliage as the border. His mantle, draped around him and over his left arm, falls with scalloped edges, with a weight at the corner hanging down behind him. The silhouette of his body, like that of the woman, is revealed. He may be represented as wearing a plain cap, but unlike the other figures his crown is rounded. He is beardless, and his hair is shown in wavy lines.

Left of the group is a kind of triple-tiered bush or type of palm tree, each thick-stemmed tier having a spray of fan-shaped leaves with a pendent fruit to either side of each spray. On top of the bush is a dove or pigeon with outspread wings, that on the bird's right considerably undersized, and with no indication of a tail.

Subject and interpretation. The scene may represent a leave-taking, as depicted in the Tomb of the Baron (left wall: see *Date*, below), and specifically a leave-taking at death. The finger gestures of the two men are perhaps apotropaic, which would suit a funerary context. As with the two male figures represented in scenes in the Tomb of the Baron, there is the possibility that the pair represent the Dioscuri, especially since in the tomb each is shown leading a horse. In this case the mens' gestures could also be exhortatory, beckoning the woman (if not a mortal, then perhaps Helen) into the Underworld (cf. ROSS HOLLOWAY *AJA* 1986 pp. 447–52). The woman's gesture may be in greeting (see above). The Dioscuri appear to have had funerary connotations in both Etruscan and South Italian art, and WALBERG *StEtr* 1986 pp. 51–9 suggests that the popularity of the twins on Athenian black-figured vases about 525–500 BC may be with a view to exports to Etruria, where they corresponded with figures in Etruscan mythology.

Characteristics of the decoration. The decoration is chased, the lines consistently fine but sure, being somewhat deeper for the frame border. The shallowest lines are in the area of the exergue. The tool used was a chisel-type punch with a curved cross-section, creating round-bottomed lines. The decoration has several unusual features – for example, the apparent indecision as to whether the men wear headgear (although occasionally on archaic bronze statuettes the dome of the head is left plain while the rest of the hair is modelled, e.g. WALTERS *BMBronzes* no. 512 = M. CRISTOFANI *I Bronzi degli Etruschi,* Novara 1985, pl. 25), the incompleteness of the drapery and the 'impressionistic' treatment of the vine in the exergue, where the bunches of grapes are rendered by silhouettes filled with small curved dashes (one would perhaps expect punched dots or circles, not outlined, in the archaic period), and the contrast of the rigid archaism of the figures in the main scene with the sketchiness of those in the exergue. This contrasting treatment can, however, be paralleled on contemporary wall-painting (see below, also GERHARD *ES* I, LXXV).

Date. The style of the figured decoration much resembles that of wall-painting from Tarquinian tombs of the end of the 6th century BC (cf. LAMBRECHTS *Mir.Mus.Royaux* p.333), as does the combination of stylised and naturalistic scenes, and a Tarquinian origin for the mirror is almost certain (see BRUNI, also MAYER-PROKOP, following DUCATI, and SPRENGER-BARTOLONI). For the figures the closest parallels in another medium are those from the Tomb of the Baron (STEINGRÄBER no.44, p.285, pls.27–34), with the transparency of the woman's drapery resembling that of the girl dancer on the rear wall of the Tomb of the Lionesses (STEINGRÄBER no.77, pp.316–17, pls.97, 100); for the tree motif there are parallels from the Tomb of Hunting and Fishing (STEINGRÄBER no.50, pp.293–4, pl.50), while the myrtle branch between the figures resembles that from the Tomb of the Jugglers (STEINGRÄBER no.70, pp.310–11, pls.86–9). The subject matter of the mirror may also support a date at the end of the 6th century and its possible link with Athenian vase-painting (see *Subject and interpretation*). The attribution of the mirror to the Thesan Master by MANSUELLI *StEtr 1946–47* p.10, was erroneous, and probably due to a mistaken reference to GERHARD *ES* (cf. BRUNI p.392, n.65; error repeated by SPRENGER-BARTOLONI). The mirror is unusually small; the flat disc and simple, pointed tang also indicate an early date, probably about 510–490 BC, with the grooved decoration around the rim perhaps placing it towards the end of this span.

17   [figs pp.124–6]

Circular tanged mirror with extension
Winged goddess with two smaller male figures

GR 1884.6–14.56

Provenance. Found at Praeneste, 1872; according to HERBIG, though perhaps not reliably, in the same tomb as a Praenestine mirror of Hellenistic date, during the Frattini excavations (New York, Metropolitan Museum of Art, Inv.20.60.63: ADAM no.1, p.19). Castellani collection, and previously, with the New York mirror, Martinetti collection.

Bibliography. MICALI *Mon.Ined.* IX pl.56,1; Castellani Sale Catalogue 1884 (*Catalogue des objets d'art antiques du Moyen-Age et de la Renaissance, dependant de la succession Alessandro Castellani, Vente à Rome, 17 Mars–10 Avril 1884*), Paris 1884, no 418; KEKULÉ in *AnnInst*, 1869–73, p.126, no.1; HERBIG in *BullInst* 1873 pp.8–9; KLÜGMANN-KÖRTE *ES* pl.12, p.18; MURRAY *Greek Bronzes* pp.34–5, fig.13; WALTERS *BMBronzes* no.543; F. POULSEN, *JdI* XXI, 1906, p.212, n.237; MATTHIES *PS* pp.27f.; DUCATI *RM* p.279, abb.8, pp.281–3; DUCATI *AE* p.294, tav.318; GIGLIOLI *AE* tav.132, 4, p.27; MANSUELLI *StEtr 1942* p.551; MANSUELLI *StEtr 1946–7* p.126; MANSUELLI *StEtr 1948–49* p.69; BEAZLEY *JHS* 1949 p.2, pl.2b; HERBIG-SIMON p.9, taf.1; MAYER-PROKOP S 41, taf.37, 51,1, p.33,51; pp.94–5, taf.37; PFIFFIG *Religio* pp.261–2, abb. 115; BRENDEL *EA* p.202, fig.134; ADAM p.19, p.99, n.2; HAYNES *EtrBr* no.50, p.263; *CSE* DDR II, p.16; M. CRISTOFANI

Gli Etruschi. Una nuova immagine, Florence 1984, p.166; KRAUSKOPF in *LIMC* s.v. Eros (in Etruria), no.25★, pp. 3, 8–9; *CSE* USA 2, p.25; WIMAN *Malstria-Malena* pp.59ff.; ZIMMER *Technik* p.23.

Material and condition. Bronze. The reflecting surface is in good condition, the metal smooth and shiny with merely a tarnish of dark brown, and patches of light golden colour particularly on the left. Matt green corrosion covers a roughly crescent-shaped area on the right, the base of the extension and the entire tang, while rough brown corrosion covers most of the design on the extension, making the upper central part difficult to discern. *Edge*. Mostly covered in matt green-brown corrosion with some dark brown tarnished metal showing through. Near the centre is a small white circular label printed with a blue border with radiating lines, and the number 21 written on it in black ink. *Reverse*. The surface has been scraped and abraded in modern times and is covered by a variety of different types of corrosion of various hues, giving virtually a rainbow effect, consisting of green, dark brown, purple, reddish orange and light gold on the upper right where the metal shows through. The original surface is mostly lost, with the design being preserved in the cuprite. Two attempts have been made to drill a hole through the tang from the reverse, each about 0.2cm across, the upper one deeper, but neither penetrating through to the other side; they are both corroded over and were therefore made in antiquity, presumably to aid with the attachment of a handle. Below the lower hole is a small area of fibrous organic material, probably wood.

Measurements.   W. 13.8cm. H. 18.5cm. H. of tang 2.2cm. Wt. 372g.

Type. Circular, flat disc mirror, tapering slightly in section towards the rim, with inturned edge on both disc and extension, decorated with a row of tongues and a raised line between the tongues and the beading of the obverse. The extension shares the same contour as its decorative motif. The tang is tapered and forked at the base. No evidence of a centre point.

Decoration.
EDGE. Decorated with arches in low relief, separated from the beading of the obverse by a raised line.

OBVERSE. At the base of the disc and on the extension, a volute and palmette or fan motif. The sides of the extension are cut to the contours of the motif. Two confronting double spirals with an internal raised moulding veer apart at the top to incorporate a twin leaf design with four-lobed fans or palmettes at the outer interstices of the lower spirals, and also at the outer juncture of the upper spirals with the base of the disc. Two more spirals rise outwards above the upper pair, but the rest of the upper design is now indecipherable. Rim beaded.

REVERSE. The rim around the disc and extension is raised and flattened to form a narrow, plain border. The decoration of the border consists of a running wave pattern, within which is a single guilloche with circlets between each twist.

The figured scene comprises a robust winged goddess, left leg slightly advanced, flanked by two diminutive male attendants. The goddess, standing in profile to the left, has a pair of wings rising upwards and outwards to either side above her pelvis. An additional pair of wings (or perhaps flaring tail-feathers?) sweep down behind her from waist to knee level. The inner parts of the wings have small, scale-like coverts and two rows of longer coverts. In her right hand, two forefingers extended, she holds bunched up the plentiful folds of a skirt-like garment, bordered with a narrow plain band and circlets; it is probably the lower part of a tunic which she may be about to fasten at the shoulder. She bends up her left arm, hand over her left shoulder, to receive something that the youth on the right is passing to her. Her wavy hair hangs down her back and over her shoulder, with shorter strands parted in front hanging down in front of the ear. She wears a plain diadem, wider at the front. On her left wrist are two plain bracelets or perhaps a wide one divided into three. Her winged boots have eyelets but no laces, and decorated tongues extending up to just below her knees; the tip of the far wing of one of the boots can be seen in front of her left shin.

The two male attendants are nude apart from fillets round their heads and pointed slippers with tall backs. Both have long, wavy hair with strands spread around the shoulders. The youth on the left, standing in profile to the right, left leg forward, his arms raised, seems to be helping to gather up the folds of the goddess's garment, while the youth on the right, in antithetic pose with right leg forward, holds a sprig of leaves in his left hand, which is hidden by the goddess's lower plumage. He holds up something in his right hand which is similarly hidden by her wing, perhaps a clasp to fasten her drapery, which she is reaching back to take. Beneath the groundline, in the exergue, as it were, is the silhouette of a footstool with animal feet.

Subject and interpretation. Aphrodite (Turan) dressing, with the assistance of two small male figures, perhaps Eros and Himeros (Beazley, Brendel) or Eros and Anteros, as in Bloch in *LIMC* s.v. Aphrodite/Turan, p.176, nos.1250* and 1251*. It is hard to tell whether these two figures are intended to be boys or young adults, made diminutive in the presence of the great goddess, as for example on a Panathenaic amphora in the Bibliothèque Nationale, with two small male figures each with a branch in either hand flanking Athena (*CVA* France 474, Paris, Bibl. Nat. III He taf.88, 2) and also on two fragments from a pinax showing an Athena Promachos and a worshipper, also holding out branches (O. Benndorf (ed.), *Griechische und Sicilische Vasenbilder*, Berlin 1868, taf. 5, 5.8). Such a distinction in size between deities and mortals has a very old iconography (cf. Krauskopf), and here it serves the additional purpose of giving importance to the goddess whilst accommodating three figures in a triangular design within the available space. The deity shown on the mirror is very unlikely to be a statue, since she actively co-operates with the attendants who assist her to dress, and the object in the exergue must surely be a footstool and not a statue base, as proposed by Murray and Herbig-Simon. The scene could represent the preparations before Aphrodite's journey across the sea, with the wave pattern of the border providing an allusion, but this is only a tenuous link since the wave motif was a popular one in archaic art.

Characteristics of the decoration. The grooves of the decoration are relatively shallow-curved in cross-section, with blunt ends, general uniformity of depth and stepped curves characteristic of chasing. The outline of the extension, like certain Greek and South Italian mirrors, follows the contours of the motif on the obverse. Curiously, the design is not replicated on the reverse and the extension on this side is atypically plain. The design of the reverse is typically archaic in style, both in the border decoration and in the figured scene. The running wave pattern is somewhat irregular, but the line virtually continuous, while the guilloche is more regular and careful with only one obvious error in the centre at the top where an extra unnecessary line appears. The formal arrangement of the figures satisfactorily fills the circular space, but where the elements meet up with the border design, e.g. the tip of the left wing and the right heel of the boy on the left, the craftsman makes no attempt to fudge the issue and allows the border, which was presumably done first, to take precedence. The figures are robust in proportion with heavy thighs and buttocks; the rib-cages of the male figures have schematic patterns indicating the anatomy. The goddess's drapery falls in zigzag-edged folds, though the folds are a little looser and more realistic than is often the case in archaic art, and the cloth is shown as fine and transparent enough to reveal her contours. The small coverts of the wings are rather hastily and irregularly drawn, the longer coverts more careful. The faces of the male figures have typical archaic profiles, with diagonally receding foreheads, prominent chins and frontally drawn eyes, low on the cheeks. The goddess's profile is somewhat more unusual, with vertical forehead, short, straight nose and small, vertical line at the end of the mouth, and with bigger, more rounded eye. Apart from the eye being too far down the cheek in conventional archaic manner, the profile tends towards greater realism.

The lines are of moderate, even depth throughout, fluid and confident. There is occasional duplication where an erroneous line has been made, e.g. the forehead of Turan, the left side of the left wrist of the boy, and a wave crest on the right. There is also perhaps an error at the base of Turan's ear, where there are several short strands, below the line marking the limit of the hair and seeming to grow from immediately below the ear. The drapery, wings and hair are all patterned schematically, and the border decoration is meticulously designed and chased.

Technical comment. Unusually low tin content (see Appendix).

Date. The mirror is probably late archaic, *c.* 500–490 BC (cf. BRENDEL; *c.*500 BC, CRISTOFANI; end of the 6th century, MAYER-PROKOP; late archaic, DUCATI *RM*). Such a date best suits the style of decoration and is supported by the 'cut-out' treatment of the extension which is paralleled by a mirror in Bologna (*CSE* Italia 1, II, no.19, *c.* 500–490 BC; also, in this fascicule, nos 8, 20). The concept of reducing the scale of the attendant figures of Aphrodite is not found in late archaic Etruscan art (cf. KRAUSKOPF in *LIMC*), and representations of Aphrodite on Etruscan mirrors become fewer after about 480 BC, notably losing their diversity (see BLOCH in *LIMC* s.v. Aphrodite/Turan, p.176). The representation of Aphrodite with four wings is also an archaic or archaising feature (PFIFFIG *Religio* p.261). Erotes were not popular in Etruscan art, and single figures of Eros are not often employed before the middle of the 4th century BC (KRAUSKOPF in *LIMC* p.9; cf. also no.31 here), when he is shown full-grown. If the identification were correct, this would also be one of the earliest Etruscan representations to show an Eros wingless and nude apart from boots or sandals, which became the norm for his depiction. The fact that the mirror was reputedly found with a Praenestine one of early 4th-century date (HERBIG; MICALI; ADAM) need not make it archaising rather than archaic (again, cf. the Bologna mirror, above): compare HERBIG who suggests that no archaic mirrors were decorated with figured scenes, and that all those appearing to be archaic are actually archaising, this on the grounds that a number of mirrors of Praenestine type were found together with more ancient examples. There is, however, no reason why they should not be heirlooms. DUCATI *RM* pp. 280–2 also suggested that the British Museum mirror was archaising, largely on the grounds of the profile treatment of Aphrodite's eye (which is in fact really a frontal view though incomplete at the left corner, with the pupil also incomplete) and on the grounds of the similarity in style of the mirror decoration to that on a mirror in the Cabinet des Medailles, no.1284, REBUFFAT *Miroir* no.2, pp. 39–40 (GERHARD *ES* III pl.CXXV), accepted by REBUFFAT as being archaic, *c.*500–475 BC (ibid. pp.543, 617–18). Since DUCATI believed the date of the Paris mirror to correspond with its *corredo*, which is held by the Museo Archeologico, Florence, and belongs to the early 5th century, the controversy is not one of dating but of terminology. For the wave pattern border as a feature of archaic mirrors, see *CSE* DDR II, p.16.

18   [figs pp.127–9]

Circular tanged mirror
Woman and boy with dog

GR 1873.8–20.110

Provenance. From Chiusi. Formerly Castellani collection.

Bibliography. KLÜGMANN-KÖRTE *ES* pl.14, p.20; WALTERS *BMBronzes* no.546; DUCATI *RM* p.269; DUCATI *AE* p.330, tav.146, fig.377; LAMB *Bronzes* p.130, fig.4; MANSUELLI *StEtr* 1946–47 pp.14–15, 78; MAYER-PROKOP pp.32, 94, pl. 37, S 38, taf.34,1–2; DE GRUMMOND *Guide* p.167, fig.t, p.168; *CSE* USA 1, p.30; WIMAN *Malstria-Malena* p.109

Material and condition. Bronze. The smooth surface of the metal is generally very well preserved beneath a thin layer of hard, smooth, pale green patination. The chasing is lined evenly with the same patination. The patina appears substantially worn away around the rim, where a shiny, darker green corrosion and occasional traces of bare metal are evident. The obverse is mottled with rough, dark green corrosion, and the surface of the disc has been repeatedly scratched diagonally, presumably in relatively recent times since the scratches penetrate through the patination down into the metal. Similar scratches occur on the reverse, mostly vertical, but a few diagonal across the bust of the female figure.

Measurements. W. 14.0cm. H. 17.0cm. H. of disc 14.0cm. W. across points 2.4cm. W. of tang at neck 1.8cm, recessed to 1.4cm and tapering to 1.0cm at base. Wt. 404g.

Type. Circular, flat disc mirror, made in one with the extension and tang, which was for insertion into a handle of another material. The stout edge of the disc is raised on the reverse and is slightly inturned. The extension is almost parallel-sided, tapering only very slightly towards the base. No centre point visible.

Decoration.
OBVERSE. Plain.
REVERSE. In the medallion, a boy and a woman offering objects to one another, with a dog between them standing up against the boy's lower leg. The boy is nude, with a fillet binding his hair; he holds a hand-mirror with a large terminal in his right hand, offering perhaps a pomegranate or some other fruit or flower in his left. The woman holds in the fingers of her right hand, either to his chin, or for him to smell, a flower, while grasped in the fingers of her left hand is a flower bud. She leans forward to the boy, her weight evenly distributed on disproportionately large feet. She wears a cloak with weighted corners, the edges dotted and with two small discs, one seen in profile, above the left elbow, perhaps buttons or clasps. She wears a tunic of crinkly material, dotted at the neck and lower hem (the dots perhaps represent stitching: see no.23, this fascicule); swathed tightly around her body, it falls to her ankles from beneath the right breast in an abundance of folds, perhaps intended to be shown as grasped by her left hand, as well as the flower-bud. Her mantle hangs evenly from both shoulders and upper arms with the four corners hanging down: at the back it hangs in semicircular folds. She is bare-footed and wears a pleated snood over her bound-up hair, the ends protruding in a short pony-tail. Over the snood she may wear a plain diadem which appears to have a scroll decoration above the ear, although the 'diadem' may just be the front part of the snood, and the 'scroll decoration' a curl of

hair. She wears a disc earring decorated with four dots. Between the two figures a lean hound with his long tail up rests his front paw halfway up the boy's left shin, his head raised. In the exergue is, left, a small, crouching or leaping dog, facing left, with a band of horizontal lines presumably representing fur around the neck, and, right, a cockerel also facing left.

The border decoration is formed by two thick-stemmed, undulating ivy stems with heart-shaped leaves, growing from the ground to either side of the figures, the ends crossing at the top in roughly drawn tendrils, flanked by small bunches of berries.

For other pairs of animals or birds in exergues, see MAYER-PROKOP, S 13, taf. 12; S 24, taf.21 (= CSE Denmark 1, no.22); CSE BRD 2, no.21; CSE Italia 1, I, no.39: all occur together with a thick-stemmed vine border, and belong to the late archaic/early Classical period, though the vine stem arising from the exergue as groundline appears a particularly late archaic feature, cf. MAYER-PROKOP S 9, taf. 9; S 12, taf.11; S 27, taf.24; S 34, taf.30; S 35, taf. 31; S 36, taf. 32; S 43, taf. 38; S 42, taf.44.

Subject and interpretation. The subject may be Aphrodite and Eros or Adonis; alternatively it could be simply a genre scene of a woman with boy lover, or mother and son (MAYER-PROKOP; see DUCATI *RM* p.269, n.1 for similar groups from candelabra, which he also identifies as mortals).

Characteristics of the decoration. The mirror is chased, and the chasing is mostly of even moderate depth, generally firm and sure. The composition did not allow for the woman's greater size, so that her left heel is hidden by the ivy stem and her snood coincides with the border further up: the ivy border was obviously drawn first. The general simplicity of the overall design gives the impression that the chasing was done with some haste, as do the occasional duplicate lines where the artist has corrected errors, e.g. outlining the disc of the mirror held by the boy, and the woman's chin. Particularly poorly indicated are the quadruped left of the exergue, the boy's feet and hands, especially the left, which was barely represented, and the woman's right hand; as already remarked upon, her feet in particular are disproportionately large. The folds of her drapery are very stylised, simplified, and somewhat monotonous, as are the lines representing the hair of both figures. The boy's anatomy, particularly the lower legs, is closer to the decorative schematisation of the earlier archaic style; the right side of his rib-cage, though, is out of alignment above and below his right arm. He has no pupil to the eye, while the woman has essentially a frontally drawn eye with pupil but open-ended at the inner corner. The ivy border is rather cumbersome, with sparse leaves, but fluidly drawn. For the unusual feature of the leaves to either side of the stem pointing in opposite directions, see *CSE USA* 1, p.30.

Technical comment. The extension has had notches cut out of the lower corners to accommodate insertion of the tang into a handle. The tang itself has been rasped horizontally, most noticeably on the reverse, less so on the edges and only slightly on the obverse, presumably to give the handle a good purchase. Such rasping coupled with the notches cut into the extension probably show that the tang was broken in antiquity, and that the surviving section was roughened and lengthened by cutting into the extension to give a good purchase for the repaired or replacement handle. The base of the tang has been 'clawed' three times on both sides by a sharp tool, probably for the same purpose.

Date. This is one of the typical undistinguished works of the end of the archaic period, dating probably to about 480–460 BC (cf. DE GRUMMOND, MANSUELLI). MAYER-PROKOP would put it slightly further back on account of similarities with the work of the Andokides and Menon Painters, but the overall hastiness and simplification could argue against this. For the border also indicating a late archaic date, see above, under *Decoration*.

19   [figs pp.130–32]

Circular tanged mirror with extension
Maenad and two satyrs

GR 1853.1–10.3

Provenance. Unknown. Bought at Sotheby's sale, 18 February 1853; previously in the collection of H.O. Cureton (1785–1858), a dealer in antiquities.

Bibliography. GERHARD *ES* IV p.8, Paralip. 236a★; KLÜGMANN-KÖRTE *ES* pl.38, p.49; WALTERS *BMBronzes* no.540; MANSUELLI *StEtr* 1946–47 p.13; MAYER-PROKOP S 28, taf.25, pp.26–7, 84; LAMBRECHTS *Mir.Mus.Royaux* pp.132, 333; *CSE USA* 1, p.30; WIMAN *Malstria-Malena* pp.59ff., 105, fig.11:5

Material and condition. Bronze. Much of the surface of the obverse is extremely well preserved, and is merely tarnished. There is however a considerable amount of raised wart-like corrosion, and where lumps of this have fallen away there is deep pitting. The edge, too, is covered with this thick layer of corrosion, save for a small area where beading is preserved left of the extension. The top of the motif on the obverse is worn shallow through repeated rubbing of the thumb from use in antiquity. The reverse has been chemically stripped; the gold-brown surface of the metal is well preserved though there is substantial pitting where excesses of corrosion have fallen away or been removed, leaving a layer of cuprite, which in the area of the figures' lower legs is coated by a dark green substance. Raised warty green corrosion remains in patches around much of the edge and also at the top of the tang, which has dark tarnish like that of the obverse.

Measurements. W. 16.5cm. H. 22.8cm. W. across points 2.1cm. H. of tang 5.2cm. Wt. 580g.

Type. Circular, flat disc mirror, made in one with a small extension with tapering sides and tang. The disc tapers slightly towards the raised, inturned edge. A groove runs along either side of the beading of the edge. No centre point visible.

Decoration.

OBVERSE. At the base of the disc and on the extension, a palmette and lotus flower motif. The palmette has seven double-outlined lobes with circlets at the tips and rests on a double-curved base above lotus stems branching to either side. Beneath each lotus flower is a pair of small discs. The stems themselves spring from a pair of lobes or rounded leaves above two spirals, below which is a double V-shape, ending in a circlet.

REVERSE. The border consists of a continuous series of heart-shaped ivy leaves, the lower point of each leaf lodged between the lobes of the preceding one; to either side of each of these junctures springs a stem with a cluster of three berries. The upper border of the exergue, which forms the groundline for the figured scene, is divided into triangles, the upper, downward-pointing ones being hatched with parallel striations. In the exergue is a palmette and spiral motif, of the type often to be found on the extension of the obverse: in the centre a five-lobed palmette on a double-curved base, with an inward-curling tendril to either side, rests on a double V-shape between two addorsed spirals, belonging to two double spirals whose other coils, branching out slightly above the horizontal, are each decorated with two leaves and a tendril.

The lively figured scene consists of a maenad and satyr dancing to the music of another satyr playing the double pipes. Most of this satyr's head is now obliterated by corrosion, only some wavy locks of hair from the crown and fringe surviving, bound by a fillet, and some straighter strands at his shoulder. In gracefully curved fingers he holds the double pipes, stepping forward on his right foot which is overlapped by the maenad's right. His left leg is bent, toes pointing downwards, and a long tail with bristling hair springs from above his buttocks. The dancing satyr, shown in three-quarter view, opposes him on the right, his right arm extended in an attempt to grope the maenad's pubes, but she restrains him by clutching his wrist with her left hand. His left arm is raised above his head, apparently in a dance movement as it is matched by the maenad with her right arm; both turn their heads to face each other. The upper limit of the satyr's head is also obliterated by corrosion, but his goat's ear is clear, so, too the hair hanging down the back of his neck, bound by a fillet, and his slightly wavy beard. His penis is erect, and his tail bristles in arousal (compare with the other satyr's), resembling a horse's mane. Over his left arm and down behind his right shoulder hangs a dotted panther skin with robust paws and a tail decorated with V-shapes, the end lost to corrosion. The maenad, centre, is shown in profile to the left but turning her upper body right to face the satyr. She steps forward on her right leg, her left leg slightly bent with the ball of the foot to the ground. She wears shoes with flaps or tongues above the instep, the right one dotted round the ankle. Over a chiton of crinkly material she wears a himation bordered with a single line and a row of dots, falling in abundant folds which form a zigzag at the hem. The front of the garment has been hitched up by the satyr, revealing her legs and pubes, which is stippled. Part of her head is also marred by corrosion, including her nose and upper lip, the top and back of her head; what is visible of her hair indicates that it was partially fastened up and looped at the back of her neck, with a fillet and wavy fringe. She wears bracelets indicated by triple lines on her left and quadruple lines on her right wrist, and a choker-style necklace indicated by hatching and dots to either side of a single line.

Subject and interpretation. A genre scene of a satyr and maenad dancing to the music of another satyr's double pipes, the first satyr interrupting the choreography with an amorous approach (cf. GERHARD I, CI, also *CSE* Denmark, no.2).

Characteristics of the decoration. The grooves of the decoration are relatively shallow-curved in cross-section, with blunt ends, general uniformity of depth and stepped curves characteristic of chasing. The lines are fluid and of even, moderate depth, though the motif on the obverse is scored more deeply. The composition of the figured scene is well balanced and fills the available space well, with merely a slight indication that the whole is placed a little too far to the left, though the panther skin flying out behind the dancing satyr, and also his tail, which has more volume than the satyr's on the left, substantially fill a potential void. Symmetry is achieved by the two nude satyrs flanking the draped maenad, their matching leg patterns and the raised outer arms of the dancing couple, whose legs in their turn are posed in parallel. Variety is provided by giving the maenad shoes and jewellery, and the right-hand satyr a panther skin, and treating the satyrs' tails differently. The unusual heart-shaped leaf and berry border, whose triple berry clusters resemble the triple spots on the panther skin, coupled with the formal, typically archaic schematisation of the maenad's drapery, all impart a certain prettiness to the scene. The motif in the exergue, like the figured scene, is similarly placed too far to the left; it is not quite symmetrical, as the upper and lower parts of the central motif veer to the left and the outer spirals vary in size. The groundline is uneven, and the patterning on it irregular. The motif on the obverse with its delicately drawn lotus flowers is also somewhat unusual; the branching stems are again a little asymmetrical.

Technical comment. The tang has diagonal file marks on both sides beneath the tarnish: these were presumably intended to abrade the surface in preparation for the application of adhesive to secure the handle.

Date. Late archaic, probably early 5th century, given the typically archaic stylised drapery, frontal eyes, musculature and posing of the figures (for a date *c.* 470–460 BC see LAMBRECHTS *Mir.Mus.Royaux* pp.132, 333 on the basis of the similarity of the scene to that on a mirror in Brussels, ibid. no.20, Inv. R1270, and to the figures in the Tomba del Triclinio, and MAYER-PROKOP p.84). The groundline formed by a row of zigzag with hatched triangles, usually all hatched but here only alternate ones, is not uncommon on early 5th-century mirrors, cf. Vatican, Museo Gregoriano Etrusco Inv. 12242, PFISTER-ROESGEN *Spiegel* S 27, and *CSE* BRD 4, no.3. The unusual heart-leaf ivy border is paralleled by that on another late archaic mirror in the Museo Nazionale Romano, PFISTER-ROESGEN *Spiegel* S 17, pp.36, 116ff., taf.18,2, and *CSE* BRD 4, no.9. For continuous borders on early mirrors see *CSE* USA 1, p.30. Regarding the decoration of the exergue, for a similar use on the reverse of a motif normally found on the obverse, see *CSE* USA 2, no.5 (also early 5th century), though here confined mainly to the extension.

20   [figs pp.133–5, 187]

Circular tanged mirror extension, cast with relief decoration

Herecele (Herakles/Hercules) and Mlacuch

GR 1772. 3–4.74

Provenance. From Atri/Viterbo/Vulci? (See discussion following.) Formerly in the collection of Sir William Hamilton.

According to the French ms. catalogue of the Hamilton collection compiled under the direction of D'Hancarville (henceforward Ms. Cat.Ant.Hamilton 1779) vol. II, pp.491ff., the mirror was found at Atri in the Abruzzi together with various items of gold jewellery (listed below). Atri is in the area which was ancient southern Picenum, now covered by the Abruzzi. The provenance of 'Atri in the Abruzzi' is in the same ink and by the same hand as the body of the text, but replaces Viterbo, which has been struck out. The mirror is described in Ms. Cat.Ant.Hamilton I, p.284, and can probably be identified with the 'patera, or offering plate' showing 'Herakles subdued by Minerva' in the MS Inventory of the Hamilton Room, 1824, p.13. In the Ms Hamilton Papers compiled at some time between 1772 and 1790 p.13 (289) the jewellery is said to have been found in a sarcophagus at Viterbo in 1771, with no mention of the mirror. MICALI *Mon.Ined.* p.319, however, states that the jewellery was found at Vulci. The likelihood of a provenance of Atri is currently being studied by the author and Professor Emmanuela Fabbricotti (preliminary paper given at a colloquium on 'Sir William Hamilton: Collector and Connoisseur', held at the British Museum in April 1996): a number of scholars have recently doubted Atri as a provenance and there seems to be no existing evidence to indicate that such a group of treasure was ever found there. Atri and its port are, however, mentioned by Strabo and, since strong connections with Etruria are suggested by finds from Campovalano,

not far from Atri, it is not impossible that Etruscan objects could have been found there, especially if they came from the northeastern settlements of Etruria (in the preliminary paper cited above we discussed the origin of at least some of the jewellery in Spina). The mirror, on the other hand, was probably made at Vulci (see below), but could quite easily have reached Viterbo, and so either Vulci or Viterbo are also feasible findspots. The question of the provenance must therefore remain open, as must the association of the mirror with the jewellery: the sources are clearly confused and may include factors such as considered likely origin, a location proclaimed by a dealer, or even the origin of the dealer himself. If the group, or part of it, did not come from Atri, then the location must have been amended in error, and some other objects from the Hamilton collection should be candidates for this provenance, perhaps, for example, some of the fibulae from Picenum. The mirror is described by Edward Hawkins in his ms. *Catalogue of the Bronzes in the British Museum*, pp.224–6, but he does not discuss provenance (the date of this catalogue is unknown but some of the objects mentioned in it were acquired after 1837).

The jewellery listed by D'Hancarville comprises the following: a gold 'necklace' with eight bullae (GR 1772.3–14.28, MARSHALL *BM Jewellery* no.1460; R.A. HIGGINS *Greek and Roman Jewellery* 2nd edn, London 1980, pl.35b, p.142); two gold earrings (MARSHALL *BM Jewellery* nos 2196–7) and a finger ring (GR 1772. 3–14.131, MARSHALL *BM Finger Rings* no.216); and two agates in gold settings, each with two tubes behind (GR 1772.3–14. 129,133, the agate of the second now missing). As was shown by Swaddling and Fabbricotti's preliminary paper, the spacer beads of the 'necklace' in fact probably belonged originally with the gold settings, alternating with these and other similar settings now missing, and could have formed either a necklace or a bracelet, of which the bullae were not part. The jewellery ranges in date between about 510 and 440 BC, and together with the mirror could have formed a group of personal possessions accumulated during that period, though one spacer and one clasp of the necklace, and probably the agate, are modern; the bullae had been suspended in modern times from a Roman gold chain.

Bibliography. LANZI *Saggio* pl.II, 2, p.163; BYRES *Hypogaei* pt.5, pl.8; GERHARD *Schmückung* p.9. n.40; A. REES *The Cyclopaedia or Universal Dictionary of Arts,* 11, 1820, pl.11; MOSES *Greek Vases* pl.66; JAHN *Arch.Aufs.* p.122; VAUX *BM Handbook* p.422; GERHARD *ES* IV pl.CCCXLIV, p.88 and III p.147; *CII* no.2858; CORSSEN *Sprache* I p.339; FRIEDERICHS-WOLTERS p.198; ROSCHER II p.3074 s.v. Mlacuch; MURRAY *Greek Bronzes* p.37; WALTERS *BMBronzes* no.542; DUCATI *RM* pp.260, 282 n.2; MATTHIES *PS* pp.29, 45; BAYET *Herclé* pp.5off., 198ff., pl.VIII; DUCATI *AE* tav.144, p.328 and n.57, fig.372; GIGLIOLI *AE* tav.134,2; DELATTE *Ann.Inst.Philol.et d'Hist.Orientales* III (= *Mélanges Capart*) 1935 pp.113ff., fig.1; DE RUYT *Ann.Inst.Philol.et d'Hist.Orientales* II (= *Mélanges Cumont*) 1936 pp.665ff.; D. BURR THOMPSON *Hesperia* VIII, 1939, p.288, fig.3; MANSUELLI *StEtr 1946–47* pp.12, 49, 71, 72, 93; BEAZLEY *JHS* 1949, pp.2–3; V. POULSEN in *Etr.Culture* fig.442; S. DE MARINIS *EAA* V, 1963, p.125f. s.v. Mlacuch; HAYNES *EBU* pl.6, p.19; G. HAFNER *Athen und Rom,* 1969, p.83; DE SIMONE *Entleh.* II pp.58–9; BROMMER

Denkmälerlisten I p.121, 1; A. Hus *Les bronzes étrusques*, Latomus, Brussels 1975, p.130, pl.63; Pfiffig *Religio* pp.341–2; Sprenger-Bartoloni no.165, p.123; A. Stibbe-Twist, Herakles in Etrurien, in *Thiasos,* Amsterdam 1978, p.92; Brendel *EA* p.287, fig.202; de Grummond *Guide* no.6, pp.49, 70–1,77,87,104, 145–6, fig. 85; Haynes *EtrBr* no.71, pp.167, 272; G. Colonna *AnnFaina* 3, 1987, pp.20–22, fig.19; Macnamara *Etruscans* p.38, fig.41; S.J. Schwarz in *LIMC* s.v. Heracles/Hercle no.331★; E. Mavleev in *LIMC* s.v. Mlacuch; R. Vollkommer 'Ein verschollener etruskischer Reliefspiegel aus der Sammlung des Prinzen von Cagnino – Fälschung oder Original?', in *Der Stilbegriff in den Altertumswissenschaften*, Universität Rostock, Institut für Altertumswissenschaften 1993, pp.161–2, abb.5; *CSE Great Britain 2*, p.32; van der Meer *Interpretatio* no.5.3, pp.43–6, 247, fig.16; R. Gersht *Rivista di Archeologia* XIX, 1995, pp.92–6, fig.1; D. Emmanuel-Rebuffat *Herclé aux Enfers* in F. Gaultier and D. Briquel (eds) *Les Étrusques. Les plus religieux des hommes*, XIIes Rencontres de l'École du Louvre, Paris 1997, pp.62–5; Emmanuel-Rebuffat in *CSE France 1, III*, pp.51–2.

Material and Condition. Bronze. Good condition but the disc is very slightly warped and the rim a little damaged on the right of the reverse. *Obverse.* Dark green with lighter patches and areas of cuprite showing where the crusty layer of corrosion has broken away. Some bright yellowish metal in the region of the base-extension. *Reverse.* Dark greenish black with small areas of cuprite and bright green patches, mostly smooth but occasionally corroded into wart-like lumps.

Measurements. W. 18.2cm; H. 25.5cm; H. of disc 18.2cm; H. of tang 5.5cm; W. of extension across points 3.1cm; W. of tang at extremity 0.5cm. Wt.848.1g.

Type. Thick, flat circular mirror with trapezoidal extension and flat, tapering tang for insertion into a handle of another material. The metal is thickened towards the rim to form a band on the reverse about 2.0cm wide. No evidence of a centre point. Edge vertical, very slightly inturned.

Decoration.
EDGE. Beaded on both sides with a central channel into which is inserted a thick silver wire about half of which is now missing.

OBVERSE. The extension has a design cast in low relief of a central palmette, and inset at the ends of all but the two lowest tongues are silver globules, nine in all, indented at the centres, the three central globules being twice the size of the others. The palmette is based upon two opposed spirals which each extend in a continuous line into three further spirals set along each side of the extension with a palmette set between the last two on each side.

REVERSE. The deep border is decorated by opposing pairs of palmettes set diagonally and linked by twin-ended spirals. The outer curves of each pair of opposed spirals are linked by small rectangles of silver inlay, the colour of

which contrasts emphatically with the bronze.

In the medallion Herakles stoops forward raising Mlacuch over his left shoulder (both are named by inscriptions), having locked his left arm round her waist and gripping her chiton in his left hand; in his right hand is his club, decorated by a groove that spirals round it. He is beardless and has short tightly curled hair, carefully rendered by rows of globules, with the larger ones outside a narrow, plain fillet, indented in the centres (like those in silver around the palmette on the obverse of the extension). Wrapped round his waist is a cloth with a cross-hatched border, and the second fold down of the loop in front and the lowest horizontal fold around the waist appear to have a fringe, with a row of beads, beneath perhaps beading on the tassels. The lion's skin is tied at Herakles' throat, the head shown over his right shoulder, a paw hanging down behind him and a knot in the tail. Behind Herakles to the left his quiver hangs from the edge of the border and his bow rests by his left foot. Below him is inscribed:

꜀꜀꜀꜀꜀꜀꜀꜀꜀꜀   herecele

Mlacuch resists him as she is lifted off the ground, her left knee bent up as she struggles, thereby appropriately filling the available space within the border; her right hand stretches down towards his waist and her left hand rests upon his head. Her hair is gathered up under a diadem with beaded upper edge, with two rows of curls in front, formed of indented globules like those of Herakles. She wears a sleeved chiton of fine light material which is indicated by close wavy lines at the neck, upper arm and lower hem at the back, and a mantle falling in rich folds and pleats at the front with a dotted and cross-hatched border. Her mantle has a border of chevrons and circled dots, falling in zigzag folds, with small weights at the corners. Below her is inscribed:

꜀꜀꜀꜀꜀꜀   mlacuch

This inscription is rejected by Rebuffat (*CSE France 1, III*, p.52) as a modern addition, but having examined the lettering closely under the microscope I can confirm that it is preserved as part of the original surface, like the Herecele inscription, and has not been cut into it at a later date.

Subject and interpretation. Herakles abducting or wrestling with Mlacuch. Rebuffat *Miroir* pp.640ff. discusses the relationship between the engravings and what may have been monumental archetypes or prototypes for them. The subject of Herakles and Mlacuch is otherwise unknown, and in an attempt to explain the name Gerhard *ES* IV p.88 connects Mlacuch with Malacisch, a name associated on mirrors with scenes of bridal preparation, and which he therefore believes to be an epithet of a bride. The motif is, however, similar to that used on Greek vases for the wrestling contest between Peleus and Thetis (e.g. the cup by Douris (also from Vulci, 480–470 BC; Bibl. Nat. 539, PFISTER-ROESGEN *Spiegel* n.65), and the Peithinos cup (Berlin F2279: E. LANGLOTZ *Griechische Vasenbilder*, Heidelberg 1922, taf.11, fig.17; BEAZLEY *ARV²* 115, 2; PFISTER-ROESGEN *Spiegel* n.60). HAYNES *EtrBr* p.272 also draws attention to the close resemblance between the mirror and the Attic amphora by Phintias in the Louvre G.42, also from Vulci, representing Leto being carried off by Tityos (P. ARIAS and M. HIRMER *A History of Greek Vase-Painting*, London 1962, pl.91; *CVA* Louvre III, pl.28; BEAZLEY *ARV²* 23, 1). Suffice it to say that the Etruscans often took advantage of 'ready-made' compositions to illustrate episodes played out by characters other than those originally intended.

The scene has generally been taken to represent an exploit of Herakles unrecorded by surviving Greek mythology, and probably, given the un-Greek name Mlacuch, a new addition to his repertoire of adventures in Italy. More recently, Mlacuch has been identified with the native Italic goddess Bona Dea (G. COLONNA *AnnFaina* 3, 1987, pp.1ff.), but the linguistic links are tenuous (cf. *CSE* France 1, III, p.52). For a recent discussion of other proposed identities see now EMMANUEL-REBUFFAT 1997, pp.62–5, and for Herakles and Iole, GERSHT. I would propose a new theory, that Mlacuch is the Etruscan equivalent of the Hebrew *mlk*, signifying 'queen', and a word which may have reached them via the Phoenicians. The Etruscans had no word for queen, as the role did not exist in the Etruscan hierarchy, and they would therefore be likely to retain the word in something close to its original form rather than attempting to translate it. BAYET pp.199ff. also pondered on the possible association of the Hebrew word, without defining the identity of the woman with certainty. The only queen whom we know Herakles confronted was the Amazon queen Hippolyta, from whom he had to wrest the girdle or sash as one of his twelve labours. This mirror bears the only depiction of Herakles wearing such a sash, a garment otherwise worn only by dancers or slaves, and more usually by women. It is tempting to conjecture that here he is shown at the moment where he has seized the sash and tied it around his own waist, while Mlacuch tries to seize it back. As she reaches towards it, he lifts her on high with a move akin to a wrestler's shoulder lift. The hatched border of the sash matches that at the lower hem of Mlacuch's tunic. The thumb of her right hand may be behind the sash (otherwise it stops short at the knuckles), showing that she is grasping at it rather than repelling him. As stated above, the artist has substantially employed a stock composition in use for a variety of mythological episodes, but he has introduced minor variations to suit his theme. Supporting the proposed identification is the sculptured frieze of the Bassae temple where an Amazon often identified as Hippolyta wears a similar sash (H. ROBERTSON *A History of Greek Art*, Cambridge 1973, pl.119c: late 5th century BC).

Analogies of type. Contrary to the norm of Etruscan mirrors being hammered to shape (SWADDLING *et al.*), this type of

mirror with relief decoration must have been cast and seems to have been an Etruscan innovation. They were perhaps a speciality of Vulcian workshops, as commented upon by HAYNES *EtrBr* p.272, also noting the occurrence of the combination of linked spirals and palmette decoration (a border motif derived from late archaic Attic vases) on other Vulcian bronzes, cf. also BRENDEL *EA* pp.286–7; DE GRUMMOND *Guide* p.146. A similar conjecture regarding place of manufacture may be the reason why MICALI *Mon.Ined.* p.319 records a provenance of Vulci for the mirror. A similar border decoration on an incised mirror of far inferior quality, and of considerably later date, *c.*350–300 BC, was found at Tarquinia: F.R. SERRA RIDGWAY *I corredi del fondo Scataglini a Tarquinia* I, Milan 1996, Tomba 65₂, pp. 79–80, 287–8, II, pl.CXL; *LIMC* V s.v. Heracles/Hercle p.238, no.402. The border decoration on the Tarquinia mirror was presumably a late derivative, and place of manufacture is uncertain. For the development and distribution of this type of border decoration see NICHOLLS in *CSE* Great Britain 2, p.32. Compare for the technique of the British Museum piece the mirror from Vulci in the Vatican, Museo Gregoriano Etrusco, showing Eos and Kephalos (GERHARD *ES* II pl.CLXXX); cf. also a mirror showing Scylla, KLÜGMANN-KÖRTE *ES* pl.103, LAMBRECHTS *Mir.Mus. Royaux* pp.201–4, another showing Aplu, Tinia and Turms, Museo Archeologico, Florence, M. CRISTOFANI *The Etruscans*, New York 1979, pl.63, and a third with Minerva, Herakles and Iolaos, REBUFFAT *Miroir* no.1288 pl.6, p.64, in the Cabinet des Médailles. For mirrors of similarly high weight see R. LAMBRECHTS *Bulletin de la Classe des Lettres et des Sciences Morales et Politiques*, Académie Royale de Belge, 6, 1995, pp.35–6.

The fine pictorial composition of this mirror, so skilfully adapted to the disc, contains a number of elements common to archaic vase-painting, including the tondo-setting, palmette-spiral border, two-dimensional articulation of the figures and objects 'hung' against the background (DE GRUMMOND *Guide* p.146). Other examples of mirrors with scenes of the Herakles-Mlacuch type are perhaps all forgeries (PFISTER-ROESGEN *Spiegel* pp.18–20. See now also EMMANUEL-REBUFFAT in *CSE* France 1, III, no.15, pp.50–3, with bibliography and discussion of the series; EMMANUEL-REBUFFAT suggests that the woman in this type of scene could be identified as Alcestis, but concedes that the name Mlacuch is hard to interpret in this context).

Date. Late archaic. The mirror is dated by DE GRUMMOND *Guide* p.146 to the period 480–450 BC, 'transition (from lingering Archaism)' and more specifically by BRENDEL *EA* p.287 to the decade 480–470 BC. Similarly BEAZLEY *JHS* 1949 p.3 dates it to about 480 BC and HAYNES *EtrBr* p.272 to the beginning of the 5th century BC. BRENDEL's suggestion is probably the most accurate. The dating of the jewellery which was perhaps found with the mirror (see above) is not in conflict with this proposal.

PART 3:
CLASSICAL MIRRORS WITH FIGURED DECORATION

21   [figs pp.136–8, 187]

Circular (presumably) tanged mirror with extension

Fulnice (Polyneikes) and Evzicle (Eteokles)

GR 1847.9–9.2

Provenance. Unknown. Ms. query in Departmental Register: ? Campanari collection. Purchased from Dr Emil Braun.

Bibliography. AA 1871 p.103 n.3; KLÜGMANN-KÖRTE *ES* pl.95, p.122; WALTERS *BMBronzes* no.621; FIESEL *Geschlecht* no.34; *NRIE* no.1109; MANSUELLI *StEtr* 1942 p.543; MANSUELLI *StEtr* 1943 p.502; MANSUELLI *StEtr* 1946–47 pp.17ff., 50, 88, 116; DE SIMONE *Entleh.* I, 130 4, 55 2; KRAUSKOPF *Sagenkreis* pp.46, 86, n.302, 104 Pol 2; PFISTER-ROESGEN *Spiegel* S 34, pp.54, 145–8, 154–5; FISCHER GRAF *Vulci* V 21, p.37f.; DE GRUMMOND *Guide* p.148, n.25; S. BOUCHER in SWADDLING (ed.) *IIAA* pp.109, 116, fig.21; *CSE* BRD 2, p.51; WIMAN *Malstria-Malena* pp.59ff., 105, fig.11:13; RIX *ET* p.356 OI 5.13; *CSE* BRD 4, p.24; *CSE* Vaticano 1, p.31; *CSE* USA 3, p.62.

Material and condition. Bronze. The tang has been broken off immediately beneath the extension. *Obverse.* Shiny dark brown metal overlaid by light green/light brown corrosion; pitting and small patches of cuprite in the area of the motif at the base. Three deep gores have been slashed diagonally across the lower part of the disc down the centre, denting the disc so that it bulges out on the reverse. This damage must have been done in antiquity since the gores are lined with the same corrosion which covers much of the obverse and most of the edge. The purpose was probably to prevent further use after deposition in the grave, a not unusual practice, cf. DE GRUMMOND *Guide* p.184. *Reverse.* Smooth, matt mid-green/dark brown patina with a small amount of raised lighter green corrosion and cuprite in the area upper right of the right-hand warrior's helmet and around his left foot. A small area of the border adjacent to the foot is shiny green/brown metal. Although the original surface is no longer visible, it is preserved in the cuprite layer and the design is undoubtedly ancient. The design has been picked out on the overlying corrosion with modern white paint; this was done very carefully and must have been difficult to do accurately since the lines are very shallow.

Measurements. W. 15.8cm. H. 16.8cm. Wt. 528g.

Type. Circular disc made in one piece with a small tang for insertion into a handle of another material. Originally flat in section, tapering towards the rim of the reverse, with vertical edge. The edge of the disc curves outward to form

the sides of the extension, the base of which has been cut away as part of a modern alteration. Centre point near top of scabbard.

Decoration.

EDGE. There is a raised line between beading on the rim of the obverse and a row of raised arches with internal concentric arches.

OBVERSE. At the junction of the disc and extension is a motif consisting of a palmette with five lobes in double outline, flanked by volutes placed back to back; the lower end of each volute does not coil inwards but extends up beneath the diagonal bar of the S-shape and rises to terminate in another outward-facing spiral from around which spring five heart-shaped ivy leaves, similar to those of the border decoration on the reverse.

REVERSE. The border decoration consists of two thick-stemmed undulating ivy trails emerging at the base from addorsed spirals above a branching stem, and with two ivy leaves to either side of a spike above. There is apparently some kind of volute to either side of the branching stem, but the lower part of the design is now lost beneath corrosion. The stems at the upper ends of the trails bear bunches of berries which merge into a single mass.

The scene consists of two armed warriors, Fulnice/Polyneikes left, bearded, and presumably, though oddly spelt, Eteokles, in combat (cf. evθucle, DE SIMONE *Entleh.* I p.55, n.1; *Thes.L.E.I* p.123). They are named by inscriptions: from right to left parallel with the right shin of the right-hand figure

evzicle

and from left to right parallel with the left shin of the left-hand figure

fulnice

The first letter of Fulnice appears to have a short vertical stroke within the circle and can only be presumed to be a φ. Both warriors stretch out their left arms to grasp each other by the neck, their right arms bent up holding their swords horizontally. Evzicle's scabbard dangles from his left arm. Evzicle's left leg and Fulnice's right leg cross each other and their other legs are bent up acutely at the knee to accommodate them within the circular frame. Both wear crested Attic helmets with upturned cheek-pieces; that of Evzicle has a nose-guard. Rows of dots follow the delineation of the helmets, cheek-pieces and crest-holders. The short hair of the warriors emerges beneath their helmets. For inconsistencies in the depiction of the helmets, see *Characteristics of the decoration*, below. Both warriors' mouths are open in grimace, and Fulnice's top teeth are shown; he has a crinkled beard, while Evzicle is beardless. see *Characteristics of the decoration*, below. Both warriors' mouths are open in grimace, and Fulnice's top teeth are shown; he has a crinkled beard, while Evzicle is beardless.

Both warriors wear cuirasses of the stiffened linen or leather type, with a double row of pteryges decorated with horizontal lines. The shoulder-flaps of Fulnice, with borders filled by a row of dots, are fastened to a ring at the front. His 'bodice' section is further ornamented by a small square above the ring fastening, small chequered 'windows' to either side of the ring, and a row of dots beneath them above a crudely drawn double row of key pattern. The back of Evzicle's cuirass is decorated across the shoulders by small squares, some sitting on a horizontal band filled with a row of dots. The lower edges of the shoulder-flaps seem to show as decorative elements protruding beneath this band, whereas they should overlie the back of the cuirass. The three scallops at the top of the cuirass must be intended to represent the neck of the cuirass and the shoulder-flaps to either side though there is no reason for the rounding of the forms. Two inexplicable inverted V-shapes are shown at the centre back of the cuirass, with a dotted line extending to either side, and beneath are two rows of a castellated design separated by a band with upward and downward T-shapes, perhaps intended to represent a key or meander pattern. Both warriors have short tunics, the gathered folds of which are indicated at the shoulders and, more sketchily, beneath the pteryges. Both also wear greaves on which the musculature of the knee is indicated and the top and bottom edges are bordered by dots.

Subject and interpretation. Fulnice/Polyneikes and Evzicle/Eteokles in combat.

Characteristics of the decoration. The decoration is chased with a fine-pointed implement, and is light and of consistent firmness. The composition of the figured scene is highly schematic, symmetrical and stylised. Though it is well adapted to the circular shape, and some drama is created by the fiercely opposed antagonists, the overall impression is one of a formalised pattern of matching, antithetic figures. When traced, the figures are almost an exact template of one another, except that the arm and leg of Polyneikes nearest to the border are both skewed downwards by about half a centimetre. In addition to the errors and inconsistency in the depiction of the armour, noted above and below, the inclusion of the scabbard dangling vertically between the violently opposed pair seems highly incongruous and does not appear in comparable scenes. FISCHER GRAF *Vulci* comments on the similarity in composition between this

and the scene on the interior of a cup by the Kleophrades Painter in Athens, BEAZLEY *ARV²* 192, 105, illustrating the type of scene which may perhaps have served as a model.

There are various points of misunderstanding: the line separating the dome of Eteokles' helmet from the neck-guard, which has been extended to form the inner sweep of the crest, while the cheek-piece is not hinged as it should be, like that of Polyneikes. Eteokles' own brow extends to form the outer edge of his ear, almost as though it were the lower edge of the helmet. Two short lines emerging vertically from the crown of his helmet may be intended to represent the stem of a type of crest-holder which would hold the crest clear of the helmet, but instead the crest rests on the dome of the helmet.

Date. Late archaic/early Classical. The shape and section of the mirror itself, together with the design on its obverse, appear to belong to the period between about 475 and 425 BC. Closely related mirrors are: WALTERS *BMBronzes* no.715 = GERHARD *ES* IV pl.CCCXCII, p.40 (a later variant), Berlin, Staatliche Museen Inv. Fr. 30 (= *CSE* BRD 4, no.15), Florence, Museo Archeologico Inv. 79283, and Bologna, Museo Civico Archeologico Inv. 1821 = *CSE* Italia 1, I, no.40 (PFISTER-ROESGEN *Spiegel* nos S 35, S 33, S 36 and S 37 respectively). Although PFISTER-ROESGEN, pp.145 ff., following MANSUELLI, believed both the Berlin mirror and the London mirror to be by the same hand and attributed to the Achilles and Penthesilea Master, there are strong indications that the London mirror represents a later and inferior version of the type (cf. ZIMMER in *CSE* BRD 4, p.24, and BONFANTE in *CSE* USA 2, pp.62–3). Moreover the inscriptions seem to have been copied without total comprehension on the part of the inscriber. This could be another example of a mirror being decorated on the reverse at a date after manufacture (cf. nos 23, 28), perhaps the early 4th century. In agreement with such a dating are LAMBRECHTS in *CSE* Vaticano 1, p.31 and KRAUSKOPF *Sagenkreis* p.104. See PFISTER-ROESGEN for a discussion of the association of the armour with that on bronze statuettes of the later 5th century BC. The following mirror, no.22, is extremely close in the symmetry of the two warriors, though clearly by a more skilled hand.

22   [figs pp.139–41, 188]

Circular tanged mirror with extension
?[Z]imite (Diomedes?), Utuśe (Odysseus) and Pentasila (Penthesilea)

GR 1913.12–17.1

Provenance. Found in 1877 on land owned by Count Bucciosanti near Castiglione della Teverina, between Orte and Orvieto. Bought from Rollin and Feuardent in 1913; formerly Fitzhenry collection, Sale Lot 568 (Christies, Manson and Wood, 13.11.1913), and before that Castellani collection.

Bibliography. FIORELLI in *NS* 1877, pl.IV, p.147; *CII App.* no.650; HERBIG in *BullInst* 1880 p.9; Castellani Sale Catalogue 1884 (*Catalogue des objets d'art antiques du Moyen-Age et de la Renaissance, dependant de la succession Alessandro Castellani, Vente à Rome, 17 Mars–10 Avril 1884*), Paris 1884, p.36, no.185; KLÜGMANN-KÖRTE *ES* pp.151–2, pl.113; DUCATI *AE* p.445, tav.518; GIGLIOLI *AE* p.56, tav. 301,1 (incorrectly located in Florence); MANSUELLI *StEtr* 1943 p.503; MANSUELLI *StEtr* 1946–47 pp.19, 51, 97f., 130, 137; DE SIMONE *Entleh.* I p.68, no.4, p.96, no.2, p.125, no.7; PFISTER-ROESGEN *Spiegel* S 40 ('verschollen'), p.59, taf.45,1; FISCHER GRAF *Vulci* pp.45ff., V 28, pl.10,1; E. MAVLEEV in *LIMC*, s.v. Amazones Etruscae, p.657, no.20 (also incorrectly located in Florence); DE GRUMMOND *Guide* p.148, n.26; *CIE* 1987 no.10895, tav.L; RIX *ET* p.348, Vs S.2.

Material and condition. Obverse. Extensive raised warty corrosion of pale green/brown colour over smooth metal coated by a thin film of blue-green patination. There are some slight scratches of relatively modern origin towards the right edge of the disc, and towards the top are the remains of an old label, no longer legible, but marked with blue ink across each corner. The rough corrosion completely covers the tang and extends around most of the edge, continuing over the rim of the reverse and bespattering parts of the scene. The metal of the obverse is otherwise well preserved, and like the reverse, is mostly overlaid by a thin, lustrous blue-green patina.

Measurements. W. 16.6cm. H. 24.4cm. W. across points 2.5cm. H. of tang 6.2cm. W. of tang at neck 0.9cm. Wt. 498g.

Type. Circular, thin, flat disc mirror, in section thinning slightly and then thickening towards the rim, with a projecting edge, small extension with slightly curved sides and narrow tapering, rounded tang. Centre point below fastening of cape.

Decoration.
EDGE. The projecting edge has a band of sigma shapes along the centre.

OBVERSE. On the extension there is an extremely faint indication of a palmette design.

REVERSE. Two armed warriors supporting an Amazon who has fallen to her knees, the figures being named by the inscriptions as [Z]imite (left), Utuśe and Pentasila. The name of [Z]imite is written vertically from left to right, upwards, to the right of his helmet crest,

[z]imite

that of Utuśe, vertically below his forehead, retrograde, downwards,

utuśe

and that of Pentasila, vertically by her right side, retrograde, downwards

pentasila

The two warriors are placed antithetically, in pose each almost a mirror image of the other, the near legs straight and the far legs bent up, each supporting an arm of the fallen figure, near arms clutching her wrists and far arms bent with hands beneath her upper arms. Their heads and upper bodies incline inwards, corresponding with the curve of the mirror. Pentasila has sunk to her knees, but her upper legs are still vertical, her arms outstretched in the grasp of the warriors and her head inclining in three-quarter view to her right. All wear full armour, with crested Attic helmets with the cheek-pieces raised, though only partially in the case of Pentasila. They wear cuirasses over short tunics, cloaks dotted along the edges, and greaves, those of the men modelled with stylised, decorative musculature, part of which perhaps coincidentally resembles a long-necked animal. All are bare-footed and have armlets composed of a row of small discs. The principal differences between the armour of Pentasila and that of the two male warriors is that she has a muscled cuirass, such as was made of bronze, while the others have the type made of leather or stiffened linen, and that her helmet has no nose-guard, but instead a dotted band above the brow, ending in a scroll; Pentasila's cheek-pieces are not entirely raised. Other minor differences are that she has no dots along the crest-holder, as do the other two, and that she has a row of dots around the neck, perhaps a necklet. Pentasila's elaborately sculpted cuirass includes an intricate series of scrolls and shapes rather like those of a tortoiseshell. Both men have short, slightly wavy hair emerging from beneath their helmets; Utuśe is bearded, [Z]imite not. There are slight differences in the decoration of their cuirasses: [Z]imite has a castellated design above a meander motif, and dots on the end of the shoulder-flap, while Utuśe's shoulder-flap is plain, and beneath it a row of dots over a shallow castellated pattern, below that a deeper one, and then a row of short vertical strokes around the waist. Bumpy ground is indicated beneath the figures. At the base of the design is a seven-lobed palmette, placed over a pair of shell-like scrolls, beneath which, over a hatched design, are spirals branching upwards and each dividing into two scrolls, beyond which the ivy border begins. The border is formed of undulating ivy stems with closely packed leaves alternating regularly to either side, each terminating at the top in a large cluster of berries arranged in circular fashion.

Subject and interpretation. The Greek heroes [Z]imite (Diomedes) and Utuśe (Odysseus) supporting the wounded Pentasila (Penthesilea), queen of the Amazons, who had led her troops to fight against the Greeks in defence of Troy.

The names are somewhat dubious, particularly the first, which is the most difficult to decipher. The combination of the figures here is surprising, since in Greek art one would expect Achilles to be shown supporting the dying Amazon

– according to tradition he fell in love with her the instant that he dealt her a fatal blow. There seems to be some contamination here from the story of the murder of Dolon, the Trojan spy, by Diomedes and Odysseus (cf. KLÜGMANN-KÖRTE *ES* p.152), and possibly also from their theft of the Palladion. At least one Greek vase-painter used an antithetic composition of an Amazon attacked by two male warriors (VON BOTHMER *Amazons* p.11, no.59, pl.26, 2, a lip cup in Canterbury University College, Christchurch, New Zealand); this however may relate to the battle against Herakles at Themiskyra or against the Athenians on the Areopagus. Also on a mirror in Madrid, it is Zimite (here Zimaite) who catches at Pentasila as she falls (Mus. Arqu. Nac. 9283: MAVLEEV in *LIMC* s.v. Amazones Etruscae, p.657, no. 19; PFISTER-ROESGEN *Spiegel* S 38, taf.41). As often in Etruscan art, the artists appear to have known representations of myths rather than the myths themselves and to have added names which merely seemed appropriate. The Etruscan archaic gems showing one or more warriors with fallen opponents (for which see PFISTER-ROESGEN) are uninscribed and so cannot tell us whether the Etruscan artists were mindful of the Achilles-Penthesilea episode.

Characteristics of the decoration. The grooves of the decoration are relatively shallow-curved in cross-section, with blunt ends, general uniformity of depth and stepped curves characteristic of chasing. This is a fine piece of work, the lines being of even, moderate depth throughout, and the drawing confident and masterly. The composition has been carefully worked out and is well balanced, the border meticulous. Only a certain sameness in the details – that of the men's armour, the helmet crests of all three figures, the drapery folds – and the repetition of decorative details such as the discs of the armlets, dotted garment borders, simple patterns on the cuirasses and the leaves and berries of the border, make the representation somewhat mechanical. For the anatomy, the internal indications are minimal but effective, and the foreshortening of Pentasila's lower legs is convincingly done. The three-quarter view of her helmet and face is also successful (and quite like that of Menerva in no.27, as too is the general treatment of the hair on the two mirrors), that of her torso less so. Although her left hip is given more prominence, and more of the decoration is shown on the left side of her cuirass than on the right, the scrolls at the base look merely askew and the drapery seems flat. All the eyes, even the men's which are intended in profile, are simple almond shapes, punched with a dot. Pentasila's mouth, however, is sensitively drawn: though there is no upper line, the middle line and more lightly indicated lower lip are expressively done, and also effective is her faraway gaze as she loses consciousness. Overall, this seems an artist of considerable ability, perhaps constrained in creativity because he was copying from another work, which may have had to be adapted for the circular frame and antithetic composition required for the mirror; he is nonetheless a master of patternwork and economical representation.

Date. Classical period. Although this mirror has been given a date of *c.* 400–350 BC (MAVLEEV; MANSUELLI *StEtr 1946–47* pp.19, 51 ('Maestro di Pentesilea caduta'), 97; GIGLIOLI), the general style and quality of the piece, akin in general terms to the Peleus and Atalanta mirror in the Vatican (GERHARD *ES* II pl.CCXXIV; DE GRUMMOND *Guide* fig.88) pull it back into the 5th century, probably *c.* 425–400 BC. The schematisation of the figures and of the border are nearer to the archaic, and so too, perhaps, is the unusual sigma decoration of the edge, of which there is a roughly similar example of the archaic period in the Villa Giulia, Inv. 24900, FISCHER GRAF *Vulci* S 21. The expressiveness and comparative realism of the figured scene, however, show a firm advance into the Classical period. It is very close in style, though clearly superior to, the preceding mirror, no.21, and may have originated in the same workshop, or have been influenced by the same prototype. Similarities include the symmetry of the warriors, the dotted borders on the clothes and armour, the design of the helmets (though with crests of different lengths), decorated cuirasses and tunics, and proliferation of berries (more naturalistic on no.21) at the top of the border; also more advanced on no.21 is the profile treatment of the eyes. The general type and shape of the mirror and extension accord well with 5th-century examples, cf. PFISTER-ROESGEN *Spiegel* S 7, 26, 42, 49, 57. The stylistic comparisons with red-figured vase-painting of around the middle of the 5th century, as listed by PFISTER-ROESGEN (for example, the Amazon krater from Ruvo, Naples 2421, BEAZLEY *ARV²*, 600,13; the New York Amazon krater, Inv. 07.286.86, *ARV²*, 613,1 and the Niobid krater in the Louvre, G 341, BEAZLEY *ARV²* 601,22) are certainly valid, but more compelling, perhaps especially since they are devised to fill a similarly shaped frame, is the mirror's association with Etruscan middle archaic gems, notably WALTERS *BMGems* no.634 (ZAZOFF *Skarabäen* p.46, no.48, p.15) which also shows a warrior grasping at the dying Pentasila.

23   [figs pp.142–4, 188]

Circular tanged mirror with extension
Usil (Helios) and Uprius̀ (Hyperion)

GR 1847.9–9.3

Provenance. Provenance uncertain; perhaps Vulci. Purchased from Dr Emil Braun.

Bibliography. MOMMSEN in *BullInst.* 1847 pp.117ff.; *CII* no.2142; GERHARD *ES* IV pl.CCCLXIV, p.116; KLÜGMANN-KÖRTE *ES* p.64, n.1; WALTERS *BMBronzes* no.707; C. KOCH *Gestirnverehrung im alten Italien*, Frankfurt 1933, p.48; *NRIE* no.717; ENKING in *RE* IX, 1961, A1, p.930, s.v. Uprium; DE SIMONE *Entleh.* I p.122; M. TIRELLI *StEtr* 1981 S.7, pp.43, 50, tav.16c; DE GRUMMOND *Guide* p.126, n.145; *CSE* BRD 1, p.34; *CSE* BRD 2, p.56; KOSSATZ-DEISSMANN in *LIMC* s.v.

Hyperion, no.2; KRAUSKOPF in *LIMC* Addendum V 1 s.v.
Helios/Usil no.20 and pp.1045–6; WIMAN *Malstria-Malena*
pp.59ff., 109 ; RIX *ET* Vc S.21; *CIE* 1994 no.11190, tav. LI.

Material and condition. Bronze. In generally good condition.
Obverse. Mostly covered by rough-textured corrosion in various
shades of green, with occasional small patches of bare metal
showing through; in modern times the rough corrosion has been
removed from the area of the design at the base and from the
tang, to reveal a smooth dark green surface overlaid by cuprite
extending over most of the design. *Reverse.* Mottled smooth
green corrosion which has blistered off in a number of places,
particularly in the lower part of the figured zone, leaving purplish
patches. *Edge.* Rough green corrosion.

Measurements. W. 16.3cm. H. 23.4cm. H. of tang 4.8cm. W. across
points 1.7cm. W. at neck 1.0cm. Wt. 455g.

Type. Circular, flat disc mirror, made in one piece with the
extension and tang. The disc is very slightly convex on the
obverse, tapering in section towards the rim, with a channelled, almost vertical, edge. Centre point beside Usil's left
hip.

Decoration.
EDGE. A groove runs between the two rows of beading.
OBVERSE. At the base of the disc and on the extension, an
elaborate palmette motif: a nine-lobed palmette with dotted circlets at the tips is based on two addorsed spirals,
above another inverted addorsed spiral motif, the band
joining these two lower spirals being decorated with a diamond pattern. Between the pairs of spirals is a four-lobed
palmette, the central lobe replaced by a downward-pointing spike emerging from between the two upper spirals. To
either side of the upper spirals emerges another long-
stemmed spiral embellished with a five-lobed palmette,
again with circlets at the tips, and beyond each of these spirals is yet one more, with two ivy leaves rising from it, each
with three punched dots at the tip. The lines of the upper
spirals and palmette are accompanied by rows of dots. The
rim is raised and shallowly beaded, slightly more distinctly
at the base of the disc and along the sides of the extension
(see *Technical comment*).

REVERSE. The border consists of two thick undulating ivy
stems, crossed over each other on the extension, with
heart-shaped leaves alternating to either side, decorated
with a punched dot in each lobe of the heart shape. The
stems meet at the top, each terminating in a spherical cluster of buds or corymbs. The rim is raised and beaded.

The figured scene consists of the personification of the
sun, whose name is inscribed right to left at the tip of his
right wing:

usil

He holds a crown to Upriuś (Hyperion), whose name is
inscribed left to right above his left shoulder:

upriuś

Usil stands frontally with his weight on his left leg, his
head in profile looking upwards to the right, as though
about to crown his companion. He wears a long, flowing
chiton of fine cloth, the breasts and nipples showing
through as one might expect with a woman's drapery. The
arrangement of the chiton is difficult to follow: the 'sleeves'
do not match, for on Usil's right is a short sleeve with dotted borders, while on his left arm is a longer sleeve fastened
along the top in three or four places; in addition, a long
piece of cloth hangs down from his left arm, which is probably part of the cloak wrapped around his waist, the upper
edge decorated with a row of dots like his right sleeve,
while the bottom edge has a border partially at least filled
with a row of short vertical strokes. On Usil's right there is
a similar design from shoulder to waist. Both these strokes
and the dots on the other borders may be intended to indicate stitched seams, as later on Romano-Egyptian painted
mummy portraits (see for examples K. PARLASCA, *Ritratti
di Mummie, Repertorio d'Arte dell' Egitto greco-romano,* Serie
B, vol. III, ed. A. Adriani, Rome 1980, numerous examples).
There also seems to be an extra tier of cloth beneath the
cloak. The numerous random folds in the chiton give Usil
a somewhat crumpled look. He appears to be bare-footed,
but his right foot looks strange, the toes being marked horizontally and emerging from the foot rather like bird's
claws, perhaps meant to be indicative of advanced age.
Along the top inner edge of his outspread wings are zigzag
rays, joined in a double row above his head, perhaps intended as a halo of light. Suspended from his right hand is a
particularly elaborate garland, with inner and outer rays,
various circlets, spines and an ornate central embellishment, perhaps his own crown or necklace. The simpler
radiate crown which he holds up to Upriuś has an internal
line and is punched with dots. Upriuś also stands in frontal
pose, his head in profile to the left, looking at Usil; his
weight is on his left leg and his left shoulder is slightly
down, and since little of his neck is shown he is perhaps
lowering his head for Usil to place the crown. He is nude
save for an ample cloak slung over his left shoulder, covering his left arm and falling behind his back, with a simple
border along the lower edge hatched with short vertical
strokes. In his right hand he holds what appears to be a
small sprig of leaves.

Subject and interpretation. Usil (Helios) about to crown
Upriuś (Hyperion) right. The reason that Usil is not wearing his own crown is perhaps that the craftsman found it
difficult to portray on Usil's head in such close proximity
to his radiate 'halo' and wings. The problem with this scene
is that though in Greek mythology Hyperion is usually
considered the father of Helios, here he looks an altogether

younger person; later Hyperion became an epithet for Helios himself. It is doubtful that the Etruscan craftsman perceived Upriuś as Usil's father. As KRAUSKOPF has suggested, were it not for the inscribed names, one could conceive of the scene as a meeting between a god and a mortal (*LIMC* s.v. Helios/Usil p.1046); KOCH suggested that Usil in his long charioteer's robe is here to be identified as the god of athletes and the circus, since the Latin sources state that the early circus games were held in honour of Sol, the first being held under the patronage of Tarquinius Priscus, and that the Etruscans were fond of athletic games; in that case Usil would then be crowning a victorious athlete. Upriuś' muscular, thick-set body certainly looks athletic and is reminiscent of depictions of Herakles, and one almost expects to see him holding a club in his right hand rather than grasping a sprig of leaves. Alternative explanations are that in Etruscan mythology Usil and Upriuś had a relationship other than father and son, or that the craftsman made an error in the use of the names.

Characteristics of the decoration. Light to moderate depth engraving, the lines reasonably sure, though the depiction of the hair is rather scrappy and unkempt. The composition is fairly satisfactory, though a little cramped on the right. The figures' heads are too small, perhaps because the craftsman did not allow enough space for them, or perhaps because anatomy was not his strong point. He seems to know roughly the positions of the contours and muscles but does not combine them with total success. The feet of both figures are noticeably sketchy, the hands more careful. The diadems and Usil's left wing are drawn with a certain amount of care, but the artist does not have time for meticulous ornament, as is shown by the contrasting roughly drawn right wing and by the hatched zigzag border of the exergue, which tails off in quality to the right. In fact all the decoration consists of short strokes and punched dots. The folds of Usil's drapery at first sight appear a little unkempt, perhaps because the artist was trying to convey the impression of old age (cf. the treatment of his feet, above), as he might also have been attempting in his depiction of the head and in the rather awkward pose and stature. He may in addition have been hoping to indicate the movement of the drapery as the figure moves to the right.

For the border, the crossing of the ivy stems to fill the exergue is a novel idea, but the stems themselves are thick and clumsy compared to the daintily drawn and decorated leaves, and the schematised clusters of buds or embryonic berries at the top are of little merit.

Technical comment. The design on the obverse is well worn, probably from polishing and by rubbing of the thumb from repeated use in antiquity. Continued polishing may also be responsible for the indistinctness of the beading on this side.

Date. Early Classical/Classical. The mirror has generally been dated to the late 4th century (e.g. KRAUSKOPF in

LIMC, TIRELLI, DE SIMONE; early 4th century: PANDOLFINI ANGELETTI in *CIE*), but the flat, thickish section of the disc and the straight sides of the extension seem more likely to indicate an earlier date, as does the almost full-frontal eye intended for the profile view. The motif on the obverse is particularly distinctive, and has three fairly close parallels: *CSE* Italia 1, I, no.39, dated *c.* 450–425 BC, *CSE* Denmark 1, no.22, *c.* 470–450, and *CSE* BRD 1, no.13, *c.* 330–320 BC; all three mirrors are of similar type, and the last should perhaps be dated somewhat earlier. The British Museum mirror could provide another instance of the design on the reverse being applied at a later date than the manufacture of the mirror (cf. nos 21, 28), but stylistic features indicate that it is unlikely to go far beyond the end of the 5th century BC.

24   [figs pp.145-7, 188]

Circular tanged mirror with extension
Thanr, Tinia, Menerva, Ethauśva (birth of Menerva)

GR 1873.8–20.103

Provenance. Praeneste. Acquired from Sig. A. Castellani. Formerly in the collection of Count Tyskiewicz.

Bibliography. MonInst VIII pl.56, no.3; R. KEKULÉ *AnnInst* XLV, 1874, p.129; CORSSEN *Sprache* I pp.372, 1007; *CII Suppl.* III, 1878, no.394; SCHNEIDER p.15, no.5; DEECKE in ROSCHER I p.1390 s.v. *Ethausva*; KLÜGMANN-KÖRTE *ES* pl.6, p.12; WALTERS *BMBronzes* no.617; COOK *Zeus* III pp.676, 678, fig.487; MANSUELLI *StEtr 1943* p.506n.; MANSUELLI *StEtr 1946–7* pp.22, 83, 98, 132; MANSUELLI *StEtr 1948–49* p.62; F. BROMMER *JbZMusMainz* 8, 1961, pp.79–80, nr.5; HERBIG-SIMON p.38, no.14, tav.3; L. BONFANTE *StEtr* 1977 p.161; DE GRUMMOND *Guide* pp.92, 93, n.21; 103, n.14; G. BONFANTE and L. BONFANTE *The Etruscan Language,* Manchester 1983, p.124, fig.27; G. COLONNA *LIMC* p.1068 s.v. Athena/Menerva, Nascita di Menerva a) 217; BONFANTE *EtrLife* p.224, fig.VII–15; A.R. COHN and L.A. LEACH (eds) *Generations,* Smithsonian Institution 1987, no.2, p.260 (exhibited); C. WEBER-LEHMANN in *LIMC* p.38, s.v. Ethausva, no.1; WIMAN *Malstria-Malena* pp.59ff.; H. SALSKOV ROBERTS *Acta Hyperborea* 5, 1993, pp.287–317; RIX *ET* p.345, La S.3; LAMBRECHTS in *LIMC* p.908 s.v. Thanr, no.3; VAN DER MEER *Interpretatio* 12.2, pp.122, 251, fig.53; EMMANUEL-REBUFFAT in *CSE* France 1, III, p.47.

Material and condition. Bronze. *Obverse.* Mottled, green and brown matt patina with some raised green corrosion, small patches of which have flaked off to reveal the metal, thinly covered with a layer of cuprite. A fine crack about 6.0cm long penetrates inward from the left edge of the disc, from just below half way. Edge as obverse. *Reverse.* A thin layer of dark green patination has been partially removed revealing extensive areas of cuprite, with gold/brown metal occasionally showing through. Much modern white powder infill remains in the engraved lines and gives a patchy appearance where it has adhered to the corrosion, particularly around the seated figure's left arm. Rough green corrosion on the tang.

Measurements. W. 17.9cm. Total H. 23.6cm. W. of extension across points 1.6cm. H. of tang 4.0cm. W. at neck 0.9cm. Wt. 390g.

Type. Large, thin, flat, circular disc thickening towards the rim on the obverse, with a vertical channelled edge. Centre point at the middle of Tinia's chest.

Decoration.
EDGE. Groove separating beaded edges of obverse and reverse.

OBVERSE. Plain, with beaded rim continuing down to the points of the extension.

REVERSE. Beaded rim as on the obverse. The border is formed by a band of opposed double spirals with random alternating points and curves in the interstices and random dividing lines between the spirals. It is squeezed in between the figures.

The four figures of the scene are each inscribed with their names. To the right of the seated figure's head, left to right:

TINIA

tinia

To the right of the head of the small winged figure:

MENEDCA

menerva

To the right of the head of the figure on the left, left to right:

OAND

θanr

Below the left hand of the figure on the right, right to left:

AJMVAOƷ

eθauśva

Tinia, in the process of giving birth to Menerva, is seated centre on his throne, in three-quarter view, head to the right in profile, his right arm raised and holding the thunderbolt which points downward. His left arm is lowered, fingers extended. The overall pose gives the impression that he is about to take aim with the thunderbolt, moving both arms to the horizontal like a javelin-thrower. His long hair and beard are depicted by undulating, roughly parallel lines, and his head is being bound by Thanr, perhaps to ease the birth pains or to help suture the aperture from which Menerva has emerged. His drapery encircles his legs, passes behind his back and over his left arm, its pointed end hanging down beside his left foot. Tinia has a youthful face, but the long wrinkles across his stomach are indicative of maturity. The thunderbolt is of delicate construction, its elements resembling the incised decoration on mirror

extensions: volutes back to back, the point emerging like a bud between two leaves and the flights a little like rudimentary curled acanthus leaves. Tinia's stool or throne has slender legs, the dowels of the seat socketed into the tops. It is uncertain whether the converging lines above his right upper arm indicate the top of the back of the throne or ill-matched drapery folds falling from the arm of Thanr. Tinia rests his feet on a footstool with short bole-like legs with lion's feet.

Menerva, emerging from Tinia's head, is seen from the thigh upwards in three-quarter view, her snake-fringed aegis belted round the waist over a chiton with a circular button or brooch at the shoulder. She wears an Attic-type helmet without cheek-pieces, with a curious tall tuft emerging vertically from the front of the crest; strands of her hair emerge from beneath the helmet. Her shield is of conventional hoplite type with arm-band and handgrip, but unaccountably the spear has three horizontal struts on the lower part of the shaft (cf. here no.34, WALTERS *BMBronzes* no.544). She is winged, as often in Etruscan mythology (for this feature see R. DE PUMA in DE GRUMMOND *Guide* p.93).

To the left stands Thanr, on what appears to be a small rock. She is also winged, right knee bent up to accommodate her leg within the frame and head slightly bent forwards, as she attends to the bandaging. In her right hand is one end of the strip, while her left, with thumb and forefinger extended upwards, secures the part already bound round Tinia's head. Her long tunic is fastened by a disc with two circular pendants and she is wrapped in a himation with dotted border. Above her elbow and round her neck are rows of beads or discs and also round her neck is a bulla on a cord or thong. Her hair is arranged in a small, ragged pony-tail with a diadem decorated with a row of small circles and with points along the upper edge.

To the right stands Ethauśva winged and in profile facing Tinia, her right hand holding the crown of his head while Thanr binds it, her left hand steadying his left shoulder. She inclines her head towards him, standing like Thanr with her left knee bent up to fit her within the frame, her right foot poised on the edge of Tinia's footstool. Also like Thanr she wears an armlet and necklet of beads or discs and round her neck a bulla, and long tunic with himation with dotted border. Her hair is tucked up round the back of her diadem with the ends hanging loose, the side hair looped down over her ears. She wears a similar diadem to that of Thanr, but deeper, and decorated with larger circles. Tinia, Thanr and Ethauśva all wear sandals of similar design.

Subject and interpretation. The birth of Menerva (Athena), fully armed, from the head of Tinia (Zeus). He is aided by Thanr, left, and Ethauśva, right. The subject is depicted on four other Etruscan bronze mirrors: Bologna, Museo Civico IT 1073, the so-called 'Patera Cospiana', *CSE* Italia I, I, no.13; GERHARD *ES* I pl.LXVI; COLONNA *LIMC* s.v. Athena/Minerva p.1068, no.218 (illustrated); Paris, Louvre Br. 1738 (= *CSE* France I, III, no.13: COLONNA *LIMC* p.1069, no.219; *ES* IV pl.CCLXXXV, 1); Berlin, Staatliche Museen, now lost (GERHARD *ES* IV pl. CCLXXXIV, 1; COLONNA *LIMC* p.1069, no.220a (illustrated), and p.503 no.24a; F.H. MASSA PAIRAULT in CRISTOFANI *Civiltà* p.363), and British Museum, GR 1856.12–13.4 (WALTERS *BMBronzes* no.696; GERHARD *ES* IV pl. CCLXXXIV, 2; COLONNA *LIMC* p.1069, no.220b; BONFANTE *Etruscan* fig.19, p.36). See SALSKOV ROBERTS for a discussion of the religious connotations of these mirrors. The subject also occurs as a modern copy of the Bologna scene on an ancient mirror (DE GRUMMOND *Guide* fig.73, Princeton University, The Art Museum). Another mirror apparently representing the birth scene was seen by Corssen in 1870 in the collection of the Marzi brothers at Tarquinia, and by Gerhard in 1885 in Milan, then in the possession of Alfonso Garovaglio of Loveno, Lake Como; even then the engraving was almost completely obliterated, however, and no drawing survives (KLÜGMANN-KÖRTE *ES* p.12, GERHARD *ES* IV p.82, n.2; SCHNEIDER p.15 no.6; CORSSEN *Sprache* I p.378). BONFANTE (*StEtr* 1977 p.161) suggested that the composition was adapted from a scene representing the grooming of Malavisch, or Helen, where the two attendants adjust her hair and diadem, with their gestures needing to be only slightly changed to perform their current midwifery duties. But the similarity in the gestures of the female attendants shown in the birth scene on archaic Greek vases (e.g. Louvre E 861, BROMMER p.68, no.9, taf. 28) indicates that the engraver must have seen such a representation, or something based on it. DE GRUMMOND *Guide* p.103 notes the strong difference between Etruscan and some Greek portrayals, with Sethlans (Hephaistos) in the former taking a relatively minor role, standing back for the female attendants to take over. In Greece, where the scene was most popular in the 6th century BC, he is a chief protagonist, having struck the head of Zeus with his axe to relieve a headache. For a discussion of the scene in Greek art, see F. BROMMER 'Die Geburt der Athena', *JbZMus-Mainz* 8, 1961, pp.66–83. In the Etruscan scenes other attendants depicted are Thalna, and the male figures Maris, Laran (Ares) and Preale. This mirror represents the only instance of the attendant named Ethauśva. The theme is also discussed by E. BRAUN, *AnnInst* 1851, pp.141–53, tav. G–M, and briefly by E.H. RICHARDSON, *ArchNews* 5, 1976, pp.126–7; BEAZLEY *JHS* 1949 pp.9–10 and M. DEL CHIARO, *Archaeology* 27, 1974, p.125.

Of the mirrors with scenes representing the birth of Athena, the subject of this catalogue entry is the only one to show Athena winged. One cannot help but notice a certain resemblance to the small Nike figure held by the Athena Parthenos, and wonder whether there is some conflation of ideas here. The mirror also shows both attendants winged, a feature echoed only by the Paris mirror, on which only the female attendant on the left (unnamed) is winged. The other mirror with the same subject in the British Museum (WALTERS *BMBronzes* no.696) and the Berlin mirror now lost, both of the *Kranzspiegelgruppe*, show a very similar composition and treatment of the subject,

which in both occurs in front of a temple(?) façade. All the figures stand or sit by in relaxed pose, even Tinia, who could be taken as being completely unaware of the event. The female figures lean on the back of Tinia's throne, and both they and the male figures look notably unmoved. Perhaps the craftsman of WALTERS *BMBronzes* no.696 and the Berlin mirror was simply re-using a standard conversation group for the birth scene. In support of this there is another mirror with a similar composition of figures, though unnamed, with similar attitudes and before an architectural façade, but without Menerva (GERHARD *ES* IV pl.CCLXXXV, 1, on the Paris market in 1845; *LIMC* p.503, no.24b). Both GERHARD and SCHNEIDER (p.16, no.7) viewed the mirror on the Paris market and another in the Collegio Romano, Museum Kirkerianum (GERHARD *ES* IV pl.CCLXXXV, 2) as scenes depicting the moment before the birth of Athena: the two female figures on both were speciously identified as Juno and Diana on the former, and as Eileithyia and Juno on the latter; Turms (Mercury) appears on both mirrors, and the remaining male figure was identified as Sethlans (Hephaistos), or Aplu (Apollo), as he wears a laurel wreath on the Rome mirror. There seems no firm reason, however, for accepting either of these mirrors as depicting the imminent birth of Athena.

The mirror concerned in this entry, the Bologna mirror and the Louvre mirror are more in sympathy with the subject and show attendants either helping Athena forth or tending Tinia. Another peculiarity of the mirror of this entry is that Tinia appears about to hurl his thunderbolt. On the Bologna mirror his right hand holds the thunderbolt simply by his side, whilst it is not shown at all on the Paris mirror where, though his right hand is raised, the pose is predominantly passive.

Characteristics of the decoration. The decoration on the reverse is engraved, as revealed by the deep grooves, V-shaped in cross-section with longitudinal striations, and the fact that in many cases the lines end in an increasingly shallow, narrowing point, with occasional 'off-shoot' strokes. The engraving is of even, moderate depth, firm and sure, much of the drapery lines fluid and effective. The dots of the himatia and Thanr's diadem are shallowly hollowed out in the bronze and these features, together with the generally fine detailing of the hair, provide some differentiation in texture.

The composition is well adapted to the frame, the two antithetic figures of Thanr and Ethauśva pleasingly arranged and the outline of their wings gracefully curved to follow the rim of the disc. Tinia, seen in three-quarter view in a twisting movement, gives action to the centre of the scene, with the small figure of Menerva in contrast somewhat static, though echoing the three-quarter view of her father. The border design is attractive but to some extent vies for attention with the main scene.

The artist has effectively drawn the swirls and folds of falling drapery, though he seems rather to have lost interest with the monotonous parallel folds of Ethauśva's himation. The feathers and pinions of the wings are realistically indicated, and the anatomy confidently delineated, with a good, three-dimensional depiction of Tinia, though there is no indication of his left shoulder. While the hair of Tinia and Ethauśva is carefully drawn, that of Thanr is comparatively careless, although it could be interpreted that her disarray, including her bulla sent askew, and her perhaps tired expression, are indicative of the tussle of Athena's birth. The artist is somewhat lacking in imagination regarding variety in decoration of garments and diadems, types of jewellery and sandals, but otherwise competent.

Date. A late Classical dating is most likely. The mirror has been dated to the first half of the 4th century BC by COLONNA, mid-4th century by WEBER-LEHMANN (in *LIMC*), and second half of the 4th century by LAMBRECHTS (in *LIMC*). The flatness of the disc, coupled with its circular shape and tang, and the treatment of the hair in roughly parallel striations, hark back to the 5th century BC (cf. SALSKOV ROBERTS p.293 for a stylistic parallel for Ethauśva in a funerary statue from Città della Pieve, Ny Carlsberg Glyptothek no.H.214). The size of the disc, however, is more in accordance with later 4th-century dating. Indirect influence may well have come from the east pediment of the Parthenon, which inspired Greek vase-painting for the decades after its construction (cf. B. SHEFTON, 'The krater from Baksy', in D. KURTZ and B. SPARKES (eds) *The Eye of Greece: Studies in the Art of Athens*, Cambridge 1982, pp.149–81, pls.41–8). The depiction of temple façades becomes common on Etruscan mirrors: though in the instance of this early mirror there is no indication in the drawing of such a façade, one wonders whether there may be some allusion to the Parthenon (cf. SALSKOV ROBERTS pp.311–12, our conclusions reached independently). This is the earliest surviving representation of the birth of Athena on an Etruscan mirror, with the depiction of the scene being preceded in Etruria only by that on a Caeretan krater, Paris, Louvre D 151, of the early 6th century BC, perhaps locally made by a Corinthian.

25   [figs pp.148-51, 189]

Circular tanged mirror
Aivas (Ajax), Ectur (Hektor)

GR 1847.9–9.5

Provenance. From Vulci, 1847. Purchased from Dr Emil Braun, by whom it was previously exhibited (*BullInst* 1847, p.139). Manuscript note in the Departmental register: (Campanari ?). See p.6.

Bibliography. CAVEDONI in *BullInst* 1847 p.139; GERHARD in *AZ* VI 1848 p.332; GERHARD *ES* IV p.40, pl.CCCXCII; *CII* no.2148 bis; WALTERS *BMBronzes* no.715; MANSUELLI *StEtr*

1942 p.543; MANSUELLI *StEtr* 1946–47 pp.18f., 50, no.3, 89, 90; COMOTTI in *EAA* III, 1960, p.209; DE SIMONE *Entleh.* I p.12, no.8, p.54, no.2; PFISTER-ROESGEN *Spiegel* p.55, S 35, p.148, pl.38; FISCHER GRAF *Vulci* pp.38ff.,V 22, pl. 8,3; O. TOUCHEFEU-MEYNIER in *LIMC* s.v. Aias I, pp.319ff., no.39; ibid. s.v. Hektor p.486 (E 1, Hektor et Ajax); WIMAN *Malstria-Malena* pp.59ff., 105, fig.11:14; RIX *ET*,Vc S.7; *CIE* 1994 no.11184, tav. XLVIII.

Material and condition. Bronze. *Obverse.* Matt grey-green patina overlaid by brighter green areas, particularly lower left. *Reverse.* Shiny black-green patina spattered with raised nodules of green corrosion, most densely over central figured zone. A double blow to the obverse of the mirror has dented, bent and cracked it. This damage must have occurred in antiquity since corrosion covers the struck area and the broken surfaces. The crack extending from the upper rim inwards appears to have been filled with plaster in modern times, and the lines of the decoration have been picked out with modern white paint. There are mineralised organic remains (wood or plant) on three sides of the tang. An ancient hole in the centre of the tang does not appear to penetrate through to the other side.

Measurements. W. 15.5cm. H. 19.9cm. H. of disc 16.3cm. H. of tang 3.7cm. W. of tang at neck 1.1cm. Wt. 375g.

Type. Circular disc made in one piece with a small tang for insertion into a handle of another material. Originally flat in section, thickening towards the rim on the reverse. Projecting channelled edge. No centre point visible.

Decoration.
OBVERSE. Originally flat, with beaded rim and groove encircling edge. Running wave pattern border. At the base above the tang are the remains of a motif now difficult to decipher due to wear which was presumably caused by repeated use in antiquity, the user's thumb rubbing against this part of the disc. The motif seems to have consisted principally of two spirals back to back with a double wavy line extending from each outwards along the edge of the disc. A vertical decoration between them is now almost completely lost.

REVERSE. The border decoration consists of two thick-stemmed undulating ivy trails, the two stems emerging from just above the tang and meeting at the top, each ending in a cluster of three large berries. The scene consists of two warriors in combat. They are named by inscriptions. To the left of the right forearm of the left figure, vertically, from right to left:

)Λ∃'Ⴈ   aivas

To the right of the right fist of the right figure, vertically, from right to left:

ⴘ√↑)Ⴏ   ectur

Both men have beards and their faces are shown in

profile. They wear crested Attic helmets with upturned cheek-guards, the crest-holder of Ajax decorated with cross-hatching and that of Hector with a zigzag. Both wear cuirasses of leather or stiffened linen; on Ajax this can be seen to be tied at the side while his shoulder-flaps are tied down at the chest. Both have a tunic beneath, which is shown around the upper arms and beneath the double row of pteryges, and bordered at the lower edge by a double line which may indicate a hem. Both wear greaves on which the musculature of the leg is indicated in stylised, decorative fashion. Ajax raises a round hoplite shield on his left arm, the arm-band and handgrip indicated, and clutches a large stone in his right hand. Three more large stones are in the field. Hector holds a sword in his right hand; part of the sword can also be seen beneath his left armpit. His round hoplite shield, shown in profile, covers his left arm and is decorated by the head of the Gorgon surrounded by small snakes framing the head. The warriors' legs are posed symmetrically, left legs outstretched before them and right legs bent up behind.

Subject and interpretation. Ajax (Aivas) and Hector (Ectur) in combat.

Characteristics of the decoration. The decoration on both sides of the mirror is chased. The lines are of moderate depth, for the most part firm and controlled. Although the composition of the figures might have suited the circular field well, with variation achieved by showing Ajax in front view and Hector in back view, it is here mishandled: Hector's upper right arm is too short, while his right leg is misshapen and squashed up against the border. His right foot overlaps the leaves of the ivy border, as does his helmet-crest, which the artist has had to reduce in height in order to make it fit the available space. It appears that the border was incised first and the figured scene then added without proper calculation of the size and placing of the figures. The musculature is shown in a rudimentary manner, and the gathers and movement of the tunic folds summarily and unconvincingly indicated. The construction of the Attic helmet seems not to be fully understood, as the cheek-flaps are positioned partially over the ears rather than in front of them. Ajax's helmet seems to have no neck-guard, the straight lines of hair emerging from immediately below the vertical section beneath the dome, whereas the corresponding vertical section on Hector's helmet is reduced to a narrow band. The horse-hair of the crest is indicated quite carefully on Ajax's helmet, more roughly on Hector's. Short diagonal strokes on the cuirass at Hector's right shoulderblade seem confused with the zigzag folds of drapery shown in error emerging beneath the shoulder-guard on the left. Both faces are shown in profile; the eyes are in profile but elongated and without pupils. There is a slight attempt to differentiate between the faces, Hector having a slightly hooked nose, and a longer beard, with the individual hairs indicated by a number of short, close strokes in rows while those of Ajax's beard are longer and fewer.

Likewise, Ajax has fewer strands of hair showing beneath his helmet whereas those of Hector are closer and more even. The anatomy is haphazardly indicated, the whole scene giving the impression of being a hasty and rather careless sketch.

Date. Classical, probably 400–350 BC (cf. TOUCHEFEU-MEYNIER in *LIMC)*. A late, debased variant of a Vulcian type showing two warriors confronted (cf. PFISTER-ROESGEN *Spiegel* S 33 and S 34) and affiliated by MANSUELLI to the Achilles and Penthesilea Master (*StEtr 1946–47* pp.18, 50, no.3).

26   [figs pp.152–4, 189]

Circular tanged mirror

?Utuśe (Odysseus), ?Kirke/Antikleia; inscribed with name of owner

GR 1868.5–20.55

Provenance. Unknown. Previously Fejérváry-Pulszky collection, Hungary, having been bought from the collection of Baron v. Palm in Augsburg, though it was not mentioned in the *Katalog des Palm'schen Antiken Sammlung*, Karlsruhe 1843 (SZILAGYI p.538); prior to this it was in the collection of the dealer and collector Francesco Ficoroni (1664–1747) in Rome.

Bibliography. Liber Antiquitatis, Fejérváry's Sammlung gezeichnet von Jos. Bucher und Wolfg. Bohm, Eperjes(?) 1842, cat.1853, no.113, taf.49; GERHARD *ES* IV pl.CDXVII, p.77; *Catalogue des Antiquités Grecques, Romaines, du Moyen Age et de la Renaissance composant la collection de MM. de Fegervary-de Pulsky,* Hotel Drouot, 18–23 Mai 1868, Paris, no.48; *CII Suppl.* I, 1872, no.469, p.81; C. JUSTI *Winckelmann und seine Zeitgenossen,* Leipzig 1923, II, 137, 265; III, 39; *NRIE* no.1083; E. LESSING *The Voyages of Ulysses,* London/Melbourne 1966, fig.75; *TLE* 749; REBUFFAT *Miroir* p.565, n.2; BONFANTE *Etruscan* p.30, fig.11; WIMAN *Malstria-Malena* pp.59ff., 109; SZILAGYI no.51, pp.538–9, fig.32; RIX *ET* OA 2,63, p.338; F. CANCIANI in *LIMC* s.v. Kirke, no.71, p.57; VAN DER MEER *Interpretatio* p.13; *Pulszky Memorial Exhibition* 1997, drawing, cat.no. 59.14 p.106 and p.187.

Material and condition. Bronze. Smooth patination of light to medium green: the upper fragile layer has broken away over much of the mirror to reveal a granular, light green surface. *Obverse.* Some pitting, especially just above the centre and in the vicinity of the left edge. On top of the green patination there is a spattering of rough-textured dark brown corrosion, which occurs on both sides of the disc, around the edge, and on the sides of the tang. The beading is slightly less visible on the obverse, perhaps due to repeated polishing, which is probably also responsible for the wear at the top of the palmette decoration. The lines are filled with modern white paint over burial debris.

Measurements. W. 15.3cm. H. 20.2cm. H. of disc 15.6cm. H. of tang 4.4cm. W. at neck 1.3cm. Wt. 506g.

Type. Circular, flat, disc mirror of thick section tapering slightly towards the rim made in one piece with a tang. Vertical channelled edge. Centre point part way along inscription.

Decoration.

EDGE. A channel runs between the 'beading' of both sides.

RIM. Either beaded and well worn in antiquity, or serrated in imitation of beading.

OBVERSE. The motif at the base of the disc consists of a nine-lobed palmette above a double arc over a short band beneath which is a single lobe with point downward. The band links the inner coils of two double spirals, whose outer coils extend along the rim of the disc, each terminating in another single lobe.

REVERSE. The border decoration consists of a double ivy stem, intertwined, apparently growing up from either side of the exergue as the leaves on both sides point upwards, but nevertheless forming one continuous trail. In most cases where the stems cross a leaf grows to one side and a group of three berries on the other, both on longish stems, but there are interruptions to the pattern and at the top the stems are bare to either side. The exergue is formed by the groundline, with four groups of four berries beneath it. The central scene is formed by two confronted figures, a man standing on the left leaning his weight on his staff, which divides the scene by running vertically down the centre, and a woman seated right extending her right hand up to him and holding out a cup(?) in her left. The man is naked save for drapery hung over his left upper arm and falling down behind him, visible to both sides behind his right leg; his right hand, which he rests on his hip, is intended to be wrapped in the drapery, for the horizontally curved lines on it are presumably drapery folds, being too gross to represent fingers. He is mainly in three-quarter view, inclining his upper body towards the woman, his hand at the top of the staff, his head in profile to the right, with the corner of his mouth downturned possibly in a grimace, if indeed an expression were intended. His hair is short, of even length all over, the locks curved but straight at the back. His right leg is frontal and the left in profile to the right. The woman gestures toward him in a beseeching attitude, holding what seems to be a cup in her left hand, with her face set in a grim expression looking up at him in profile to the left, her upper body in three-quarter view. Her head is swathed in what appears to be a close-fitting headdress, with no hair showing, and she wears a long garment whose details are difficult to follow, save that it is sleeved and the edges at her left side fall very approximately in zigzag folds. She is seated on a stool with both her legs in profile, the heel of the right one drawn back but overlapping the front legs of the stool, so that she appears to be sitting over the near edge of it. The legs of the stool are shaped like those of a hoofed animal, and the joint where they meet the seat is covered

by a disc enclosing another disc. The spaces around the figures are loosely filled with circles, a row of three to the left of the man and another row of seven between his legs. Above the woman's head are two groups of four berries, like those in the exergue.

To the left of the central staff is an inscription naming the owner of the mirror (fig. 17), written vertically from right to left, top to bottom:

mi than( )cvilus fulnial

I (belong) to Thancvil Fulni

WALTERS read Thamsvil, which was indeed exactly how the inscription appeared to read before modern white paint was cleaned off. BONFANTE read Thancvilus, as was also assumed by REBUFFAT *Miroir* p.565, n.2 (cf. also *Thes. L.E.I.* p.184; though GERHARD *ES* IV p.77 = Thancfiuls). There is a slightly larger gap between the 'n' and 'c' than between the other letters, but probably not enough room for another letter, and 'a' (for Than*a*cvil) would not be expected after the first quarter of the 5th century. The next letter is not readily recognisable, but was probably intended as a 'c' with some difficulty in carrying out a single long curved stroke (cf. also *CIE* III, 3, no.11299; cf. *Thes.L.E.I.* p.184 and RIX *ET* pp.119–20 for variations on the name of Tanaquil). The full genitive form IAL of Fulnial suggests a 4th-century date.

Subject and interpretation. WALTERS' suggestion that the scene represents Circe and Odysseus was condemned by CANCIANI. The possibility should not altogether be discounted, however, since the representation of the pair on a late 5th-century skyphos from the Kabeirion in Thebes bears a certain resemblance – shown as grotesques, Circe is seated by a loom, holding out a small unidentifiable object, while Odysseus stands leaning on his staff, facing her (Harvard 1925, 30, 127: TOUCHEFEU-MEYNIER no. 194, p.99, pl.XVI,1). Another scene on a skyphos in the British Museum and of the same date and style is comparable, with Circe, here identified by an inscription and a pig beside the loom, advancing holding a skyphos towards Odysseus, who is again leaning on his staff (TOUCHEFEU-MEYNIER no.192, pl.XVIII). Yet a further interpretation could be Odysseus and his nurse.

Another possibility is that the woman is Antikleia, Odysseus' mother, whom he met in Hades, where like the other spirits she implored him for blood from the sacrificed sheep (*Odyssey* XI 85), though he should perhaps in that case be equipped with a sword, as when confronting the other spirits. Though there is no other surviving identified representation of this scene, it was featured in the painting by Polygnotos in the Lesche of the Cnidians at Delphi, dating to the mid-5th century BC (Pausanias 10, 28–31; *LIMC* I, 1, p.329, s.v. Antikleia, no.3), and also on the lost stylopinakion built by Attalus II and Eumenes in the first half of the 2nd century BC in memory of their mother Apollonis and decorated with scenes of filial piety (*LIMC* ibid. no.4). As this is one of the unusual mirrors with an inscription denoting ownership, it was perhaps specially commissioned.

Characteristics of the decoration. The decoration on both sides is chased. The lines are of even, moderate depth throughout, and have been chased freely and firmly. Those of the palmette on the obverse, however, are fainter, perhaps due to repeated polishing in antiquity. The curves show extremely pronounced 'fanning' marks made as the heel of the tool turned and the metal surface on each side of the lines is pushed up in a bulge where the metal has been displaced. The profile of the channels and the length of the shorter strokes indicate that the tool used was a very narrow chisel type with a sharp V-shaped profile, the cutting edge about 0.15cm long. The inscription appears to have been made in the same way as the design. The figured scene fits the available space fairly well, though the craftsman has relied heavily on filling ornament to fill the voids. The circles appear to have been made with a curved punch, which probably formed the curved segment of a circle, so that four strokes were needed to complete the circle. There are many tentative hits and mis-hits and few of the circles join up completely – most have a small bridge of metal at one point. The standing figure is rather too tall to fit in neatly, with the result that the border stem has been left bare and pushed upwards out of shape to avoid him becoming tangled with the leaves and berries. The border itself is quite sloppily done, with a number of overlapping lines and misshapen leaves, particularly on the right where the decoration has been compressed between the woman's head and the edge of the disc. The evidence is that, contrary to the norm, the figured scene was done before the border. The individual stems of the leaves and berries are too thick and there is no logic in the way the main stems seem to grow back into the ground. The groundline slopes noticeably up to the right. The drapery is portrayed very summarily, that of the man apparently crossing his left upper arm as an afterthought, since the lower outline of his upper arm was already drawn; it is unclear what happens at his left shoulder. The craftsman has avoided showing the lower edge of this drapery, and he clearly has no interest in the woman's, which has no edge to the left sleeve and very little indication of how it was arranged. The headdress has avoided any need to show her hair. The man's hair has the short locks which become typical of the late Classical period in Etruscan art. The anatomy is schematic; though the man's outline is fair, the internal indications are merely a formula of patterns which make little sense. The concave-sided boxes round the waist, the vertical almond-shape at the navel, the 'string of sausages' below the breast, double knee joints and illusory genitals point to a vague awareness of what should be there, but no skill or care in reproducing it. He has obviously seen works by better craftsmen, who were by then using series of short strokes to indicate shading, but he merely throws them in here and there for good measure. The man's profile is again fair, but the woman's is a caricature, with thick neck, short, flattened nose and hefty

jaw. Hands are another weak point, looking crude and glove-like, and the man's right conveniently shrouded in drapery. His right, frontal, foot is effective, but the ankle is excessively tapered.

Date. The mirror probably belongs to the Classical period, early 4th century BC, and the border could indicate a Vulcian origin; hatching for details of the anatomy seems to have begun at the end of the 5th century. The mirror has been dated to 325–300 BC by SZILAGYI and to the end of the 4th century by CANCIANI, but the inscription could tally with an earlier date. The inscription appears to be contemporary with the figured scene, but not to have been worked out prior to incising since the letters had to be reduced in size to fit between the man's left knee and the staff. This is one of the rare mirrors to be inscribed with the name of the owner (for other examples see REBUFFAT *Miroir* pp.565–7 and n.2).

---

27   [figs pp.155–7, 189]

Circular mirror with modified tang and extension, and bone handle

Ferśe (Perseus), Menerva (Athena), Turms (Hermes)

GR 1888.11–10.1

Provenance. Found near Perugia, 1888. Purchased from Professor Helbig, who found it on the Roman art market.

Bibliography. MURRAY *Handbook* p.129; KLÜGMANN-KÖRTE *ES* p.221 n.18; WALTERS *BMBronzes* no.620; E. KUHNERT in ROSCHER 1902–9 s.v. Perseus 2042; MANSUELLI *StEtr 1946–47* pp.96, 103, 130, 137, 221; *NRIE* no.409; K. SCHEFOLD and F. JUNG *Die Urkönige, Perseus, Bellerophon, Herakles und Theseus in der klassischen und hellenistischen Kunst,* Munich 1988, p.112, fig.134; DE SIMONE *Entleh.* I p.128, n.4; FISCHER GRAF *Vulci* V 39, p.61, pl.17; U. LEIPMANN in *CSE* BRD 2, p.65; RALLO *Donne* pp.163, 259, pl. LXXIX; BALENSIEFEN p.227, K23, pl.16,2; BONFANTE *Etruscan* p.31, fig.14; WIMAN *Malstria-Malena* pp.59ff., 109; RIX *ET* p.353, Pe S.3; ROCCOS in *LIMC* s.v. Perseus, no.75★, pp.337, 346 (= Gorgones [in Etruria] 113); VAN DER MEER *Interpretatio* p.253, no.6.

Material and condition. Bronze disc with bone handle. *Obverse.* The metal is in good condition with only a little pitting to the lower right of the centre. A matt green patina covers much of the surface, though golden coloured metal can be seen near the pitting, and a smooth, shiny, dark green-brown patina covers part of the right of the disc. In the area of the motif and on the extension there is smooth, dark brown metal, probably where the corrosion has been cleaned away in an attempt to reveal the design, most of which was obliterated when the tang was repaired in antiquity (see *Technical comment*). Edge. Also has a smooth, dark, shiny patina with some matt green corrosion. *Reverse.* Thin lustrous, green-brown corrosion, slightly rough on the left half. *Handle.* Greenish in the top half, perhaps through staining from the bronze. Some vertical cracks with a long, narrow section missing near the top and slots to either side of the rim. These may have been cut to accommodate the extension, and it is possible that, since the edges of the slots are patinated over, they were cut at the time of the ancient repair as being necessary modifications. The moulding at the top has a large chip missing and wear beneath the right-hand slot when seen from the obverse, perhaps from rubbing of the thumb where the handle was gripped in antiquity when the mirror was picked up, in addition to wear when it was in use when the thumb rubbed against the base of the disc, as is indicated by smoothing over the extension motif and perhaps polishing after the ancient repair. The base of the handle is now restored (the area beneath the line on the drawing) though a section of the turned decoration underneath remains.

Measurements. W. 16.0cm. H. 23.6cm. H. of tang 7.4cm. W. across points 1.6cm. Wt. with handle, 446g; handle only, 38g.

Type. Circular, flat, disc mirror with tang which, including a rudimentary extension, has been cast on to the disc in antiquity; it is perhaps the original tang rejoined or a replacement after breakage. It veers a little to the left when seen from the obverse. The disc tapers slightly towards the offset vertical edge. The handle is of turned bone, and now fits only loosely onto the tang. It was presumably originally packed with some kind of filler and glued on to the tang with adhesive. Centre point on central panel of overfold of tunic.

Decoration.
EDGE. A row of tongues with internal arches in very shallow relief, adjacent to a narrow rib and then the beading of the obverse.

OBVERSE. Little remains of the motif at the base of the disc and on the extension, due to the repair to the tang. The decoration continuing on to the disc consisted of spirals or tendrils, perhaps ending on either side in clusters of three berries.

REVERSE. The border consists of two mildly undulating ivy stems, with closely placed leaves alternating regularly to either side, meeting at the top in a large cluster of berries or umbels. Any additional motif at the base has been obliterated by the repair to the tang.

The figured scene consists of Menerva in the centre holding up in her right hand the head of the Gorgon Medusa, viewed in a reflection on the ground by Ferśe, seated left, and Turms, seated right. The names are inscribed. Below Ferśe's face, from left to right:

ferśe

To the right of Menerva's head, from left to right:

menerva

Below this inscription, to the left of Turms' head, from right to left:

turms

Menerva stands frontally with her weight on her right leg, the left slightly bent to the side, her left arm at her side, holding her spear erect beside her. Her head is shown in three-quarter view to the right, inclined towards Ferśe, at whom she gazes. Her long hair, crinkly below the plain fillet which binds it, hangs down at her back, drawn to either side at the front, with shorter strands in front of the ears. Her sleeved peplos, pinned at the shoulder with a circular brooch or button, has an overfold with a broad, plain border, and at her right the two edges hang in zigzag folds. The aegis, fringed with snakes, goes over the left shoulder and under the right and, together with the overfold, is girdled round the waist. On her left forearm are two plain bracelets, and above the elbow are armlets, with what are probably bullae hanging down. The Medusa head has short bristling hair and a broad jaw, with an uncharacteristically benign face, though it is less so in the reflection. Ferśe, left knee bent and right leg stretched out, holds out his right hand in front of him, perhaps trying partially to block out the image. His left hand rests on his left knee, holding the sickle, whose handle ends in a sphere or disc. He wears a short tunic which is belted and has a wide, plain border at the lower edge, and a cloak also with a plain border fastened at the throat with a disc; a similar disc appears on his right upper arm, perhaps fastening the sleeve of the tunic, but the folds of the garment are here somewhat confused. A conical cap decorated with a leafy stem hangs on a cord at the back of his neck. He has short hair, wavy at the back and with a fringe. To the left of his right shin is a small plant, probably intended to be growing from a crevice in the rock on which he sits. Turms is nude apart from a cloak with plain border and weights or tassels at the corners, and fastened at his throat, and has his right knee bent up, his left slightly bent and inclined out towards the spectator. His right hand rests on his right knee, while in his left he holds the top of his caduceus, which stands in front of him. Above his left elbow is an armlet with a bulla. His hair is short, wavy in front of the ears and over the forehead, and his broad-brimmed hat hangs on a strap at the back of his head, the crown decorated with spirals or tendrils. The Medusa head at the base seems to be reflected in a raised pool or puddle in rocky ground, with Ferśe's and Turms' feet resting on rocks beside it, while Menerva's feet are hidden behind the far rim.

Subject and interpretation. Ferśe (Perseus) and Turms (Hermes) observing the severed head of Medusa in a reflection, presumably in a pool, while Menerva holds it aloft. The theme is unknown from archaic and Classical Greek art (apart from a black-figured lekythos where Ferśe holds up the severed head, K. SCHAUENBERG *Perseus in der Kunst des altertums*, Bonn 1960, p.25), but appears in Italy from the 4th century BC (*LIMC*). The mirrors with the Ferśe and Medusa theme, of which this is the best and earliest of six surviving from the 4th and early 3rd centuries BC, were probably influenced by South Italian Greek vase-painting. There are several vases which show her head reflected in water, the most relevant being a calyx-krater in Gotha, Schlossmuseum Ahv. 72 (Tarporley Painter: ROCCOS in *LIMC* s.v. Perseus, no.66*, p.336; *CVA* Gotha 2, pl.79,1; TRENDALL *RVA* I pp.39, 51; id. *RFSIS* fig.106). The curious border around the pool on the vase is presumably an edging of thickly outlined rocks – a later variant on a cameo of the 1st century BC shows Perseus holding up the Medusa head for Andromeda to see in a rock-pool (Leningrad AB I,19, SCHEFOLD-JUNG p.113, fig.135). Although the documented version of the myth refers to the head being reflected in a shield (ROCCOS in *LIMC* s.v. Perseus p.332: Apollodoros, *Bibliotheke*, 2 iv, 2; Ovid *Metamorphoses* IV, 782–3; see also Scholiast n.41515 on *Argonautika*, *Frag. Hist.Graec.* vol.1, Pherekydes no.75, fr.26; in Athena's shield, BALENSIEFEN pp.113–20), the water version was obviously quite well known. The designer of the mirror scene clearly adapted the composition into a symmetrical configuration to suit the circular space, and it resembles that of Ajax, Athena and Achilles on FISCHER GRAF *Vulci* V 48.

Characteristics of the decoration. The lines are of firm, moderate, even depth throughout, save on the obverse where they have been obliterated by the repair to the tang and perhaps also by ancient wear and polishing. The only noticeable error is that Turms' caduceus is drawn over his feet and substantially over his right wrist. The largely symmetrical composition fills the circular space well, with the figures projecting into the border area, which shows that they were drawn first; the impression that the figures are in front of the border makes them stand out. The two male figures have been differentiated by making Turms almost nude, varying the poses slightly, giving slightly different hair, differently decorated hats, and, of course, different attributes. The ivy garland of the border decoration is meticulously done, but very two-dimensional in contrast to the figured scene, the one concession to naturalism being the slightly irregular bunch of berries at the top, with the single stray berry to the left. The contrasting treatment of the border and the figures may be a last link of the Classical period to archaic schematisation. Perhaps the main incongruity is the relaxed, nonchalant pose of Menerva while she holds up the head of the monster, but then the pose of the other two figures is very much at ease. The three-quarter view of Turms is particularly successful, as is that of the face of Menerva, who gracefully inclines her head to look down at the reflection. The faces are idealised but nonetheless realistic, and their elegance contrasts well with the short, broad, wiry head of Medusa, cf. Pentasila, no.22. The hair is done for the most part in parallel lines, again reminiscent of the archaic period, but given a looser, more naturalistic treatment, as is the pubic hair of Turms. The silhouettes of the figures are of high quality, the inner anatomical markings less so; they are few, but are largely pattern-like indications

of what the artist thought should be there. The toes are too large, but the hands are well done, merely lacking fingernails: the one fundamental mistake is that the right hand is shown as though it were the left. The drapery is convincing and realistic, while economically indicated. The main problem is that the artist has not made the nature of the reflecting object on the ground absolutely clear – the most likely explanation is that he intended a rock-pool with Ferśe's foot on a rock beside it and Menerva's feet below a rock on the other side of it.

Technical comment. The tang has been repaired in antiquity and is either the original tang rejoined or a replacement. In all probability it broke because the extension and/or tang were not strong enough to support the weight of the disc. It was a skilled repair, achieved presumably by heating the base of the disc and the tang, securing them in a partial mould and pouring in molten metal. On the obverse the join has been polished so that it is flush with the reflecting surface; on the reverse, the craftsman has achieved the minimum disruption to the decoration, whilst managing to thicken the extension in order to strengthen it. During the process the extension must have been reshaped, because slots had to be cut into the moulding of the bone handle to accommodate it. An alternative explanation is that the handle has been re-used from another mirror.

Date. Classical. The mirror has previously been dated to about 300 BC (BONFANTE); 375–350 (LIEPMANN *CSE* BRD 2, p.65); *c.*350 BC (SCHEFOLD-JUNG); 350–325 BC (FISCHER GRAF; *LIMC)*. The stylistic arguments of FISCHER GRAF concerning the anatomy and drapery hold good, but the flat, fairly thick section of the mirror, and the archaic links mentioned above in *Characteristics of the decoration,* would seem to push it back more into the first half of the 4th century. Unfortunately the ancient repair to the extension seems to have altered its shape so that this cannot be used to help with dating.

28   [figs pp.158–60, 190]

Circular tanged mirror with extension
Hamfiare (Amphiaraos), Lasa, Aivas (Ajax)

GR 1847.9–9.4

Provenance. Bought from Dr Emil Braun. Perhaps from Vulci.

Bibliography. G. RATHGEBER *BullInst* 1846 p.106; *AZ* 1846 p.293; 1848 p.331; GERHARD *ES* IV pl.CCCLIX, p.112; *CII* no.2514; WALTERS *BMBronzes* no.622; R. ENKING 'Lasa' in *RM* 57, 1942, pl.1, p.2; MANSUELLI *StEtr* 1946-47 p.96; MANSUELLI *StEtr* 1948–49 p.92; S.DE MARINIS *EAA* IV, 1961, s.v. Lasa, pp.488–9; HERBIG-SIMON pp.28, 37, fig.10; DE SIMONE *Entleh.* I p.12, no.14; p.16, no.5; KRAUSKOPF *Sagenkreis* pp.46, 86 n.304, 97–8

Amph 4; RALLO *Lasa* p.18, tav.1; PFISTER-ROESGEN *Spiegel* S 53, pp.170–2, pl.57; M. SCHMIDT, A.D. TRENDALL, and A. CAMBITOGLOU *Eine Gruppe Apulischer Grabvasen in Basel,* Basle 1976, p.61, n.186; FISCHER GRAF *Vulci* p.97, n.894; I. KRAUSKOPF in *LIMC* 1981 s.v. Aias, no. 103★, pp.328, 333–4; s.v. Amphiaraos no.48★, pp.700, 709; DE GRUMMOND *Guide* no.34, pp.77, 114–15, fig.93; G. BONFANTE and L. BONFANTE *The Etruscan Language,* Manchester 1983, no.34, p.125, fig.28; I. KRAUSKOPF in CRISTOFANI *Dizionario* p.148, s.v. Lasa; R. DE PUMA in *Muse* 19, 1985, pp.47, 52; L.B. VAN DER MEER *BABesch* 60, 1985, p.79, fig.5; RIX *ET* p.356, OI S.6; LAMBRECHTS in *LIMC* 1992 s.v. Lasa, no.1, p.217; ; VAN DER MEER *Interpretatio* 23.1, pp.222–4, 255, fig.105; *CSE* Vaticano 1, pp.30–1.

Material and condition. Bronze. The mirror suffers on both sides and on the edge from extensive, warty green corrosion. Elsewhere the dark brown metal has a thin layer of green patination and traces of cuprite. Modern white infill in the decoration. A chip almost 2.0cm long is missing from the edge, where corrosion has lifted off the surface of the metal.

The centres of the spirals of the motif on the obverse have brown crystalline deposits and traces of a white metallic layer which appears to be the remains of ancient solder, indicating that some decorative element, possibly globules of silver, was applied in these areas (cf. no.7).

Measurements. W. 16.3cm. H. 22.7cm. H. of tang 4.9cm. W. of tang at neck 1.5cm. Wt. 538g.

Type. Circular, flat, disc mirror with vertical edge, made in one piece with an extension and tang forked at the base. Centre point below centre of overfold of Lasa's tunic.

Decoration.
EDGE. A row of narrow tongues with internal concentric arches based on a raised line adjacent to the beading of the obverse.

OBVERSE. Rim of disc and sides of extension beaded. On the extension and the base of the disc, an elaborate spiral and palmette motif drawn for the most part in double outline. In the centre are two addorsed double spirals, the upper and lower spirals bound by bands. Above the top pair of spirals is a seven-lobed palmette, and in the enclosed space above the lower pair a five-lobed palmette with internal strokes on the lobes, which rise from a small spiral. At the centres of the spirals and at the base of the upper palmette are slight remains of solder, perhaps for the attachment of siver globules (cf. *CSE* BRD 4, nos 8, 18, 34). At the base of the motif is a downward-pointing double V-shape. Two more spirals curve outward to either side from the upper pair, with a leaf shape at the interstices, and heartshaped ivy leaves on long stems spring from their coils, three to the left and four to the right.

REVERSE. The border is formed by two mildly undulating ivy stems, meeting at the top in two small clusters of

berries, the lower ends coiled and linked to a pendent bell-shaped flower with two layers of petals and a single stamen. The central scene comprises three figures, a winged Lasa in the centre with two seated warriors on rocks to either side facing inwards. The Lasa stands on uneven ground; her wings are partially furled, and the scale-like coverts have three rows of longer coverts and primaries beneath. She looks down at a partially unrolled scroll which she holds out before her to her left. Her body is frontal but her head is shown in profile to her left, and her left foot points left while the right foot is almost frontal. Her peplos, over a long-sleeved chiton, has a long overfold fastened with what look like bow fibulae above each breast, and also a girdle round the waist, tied in a reef knot, with one split end threaded through the loop. Her hair is short, of uneven length and she wears a diadem decorated with vertical lines and a narrow plain border.

Inside the scroll, written retrograde, are the names of the figures:

lasa

aivas

hamfiare

On the left, seated in profile to the right and inscribed downwards to the right of his clasped hands:

   hamfiare

Hamfiare (Amphiaraos) grasps his right knee which is bent up, the heel resting against his round hoplite shield which leans against the rock on which he is seated. He has short, slightly wavy hair, and wears a muscled bell-type cuirass over a short tunic which protrudes at the arm-holes and below the pteryges. To the right, seated in profile to the left and in sorrowful pose, inscribed diagonally, retrograde and downwards above his head:

   aivas

With his right foot up on the rock on which he is seated, Aivas (Ajax) rests his left hand on the rim of the round hoplite shield at his side. His head, with short, unkempt hair, rests heavily on his right hand, placed on the pommel of his sheathed sword which he balances vertically on the rock, his right elbow resting on his thigh. He wears a cuirass made up of rows of rectangular scales, with shoulder-flaps tied down over each breast, and a short tunic showing at the arm-holes and beneath the pteryges.

Subject and interpretation. A winged Lasa holding a scroll on which is written her own name, Lasa, and that of the heroes to either side of her, Amphiaraos and Ajax. It is uncertain whether this is Ajax, son of Telamon, or Ajax, son of Oileus, neither of whom are linked with Amphiaraos in known mythology, and were separated from him by generations. It has been suggested that the association between the two heroes was that they were both killed by treachery, but though this concept may be applied to Amphiaraos, who was killed fighting at his wife's insistence in the war against Thebes (she herself having been bribed by Polyneikes with the fatal necklace of Harmonia), it is not strictly true of either Ajax. Ajax son of Telamon committed suicide after being denied the arms of Achilles and being driven mad by Athena to prevent him from seeking retribution, while Ajax son of Oileus was shipwrecked at the will of the gods on the way home from Troy, and was then killed by Poseidon, after boasting of his escape from divine wrath. This Ajax was, incidentally, also known for his small stature, as shown on the mirror, but this may be a quirk of the craftsman (see *Characteristics of the decoration*). Perhaps a stronger link between the heroes is their association with a daimon, and if this is the case, then it strengthens the identification of this Ajax as the son of Telamon, for according to Aischylos it was a daimon who indicated to him his only vulnerable spot, beneath the arm, when he was thwarted in trying to commit suicide (cf. BEAZLEY *EVP* pp.42,140). Although it is more commonly Athena herself who performs this function, as on a mirror in Boston (*CSE USA 2*, no.9, Inv. 99.494; cf. also *CSE Vaticano 1*, no.11, with Athena consoling two unnamed heroes), another Etruscan representation, on a late red-figured stamnos in Palermo (KRAUSKOPF in s.v. *LIMC* Aias I, p.329, no.107; BEAZLEY *EVP* p.139), shows the same subject but with a male daimon standing behind Ajax with his arms outstretched towards him. Amphiaraos was himself a seer, had an oracle at Oropos, and foresaw his death fighting in the war against Thebes. The two heroes are perhaps here being foretold their destinies. SCHMIDT *et al.* considered the link between the two not to be the similarity of their fates, but the contrast: whereas Ajax met his death in suicide, Amphiaraos continued his existence as an honoured hero in Hades; further, their contrasting fates are emphasised by the differences in their expressions, Ajax downcast and slumped upon the sword that was to end his life, but Amphiaraos looking steadfastly ahead towards the scroll. The mirror in the Vatican, mentioned above, is similar in composition, subject and mood, showing Athena consoling two unidentified, cuirassed, downcast heroes, both with swords; she herself looks equally grief-stricken. LAMBRECHTS *CSE Vaticano 1*, pp.30–1 suggests possible identifications of the heroes as Achilles and Ajax, Theseus and Pirithoos, or Ajax and Amphiaraos, as here. Also similar in theme is a mirror from Vulci in the Fitzwilliam Museum (*CSE Great Britain 2*, no.8, of Classical date) showing Adrastus and Amphiaraos seated, the latter in a state of consternation, with Tydeus standing centre addressing the alert and keen-looking Adrastus, left.

The representation of Lasa with the scroll, as a divinity of fate or destiny, like Vanth, is unique. VAN DER MEER draws the comparison of Athrpa foretelling the death of Meleager. There are thirteen named representations of her – twelve on mirrors and one on a ring – where she is frequently associated with the circle of Turan, but occasionally with other deities and heroes (cf. KRAUSKOPF in CRISTOFANI; LAMBRECHTS in *LIMC* s.v. Lasa p.223; DE PUMA). There are, however, several other instances of her uniquely being represented with other objects, and she clearly performed a variety of functions, no doubt also being represented by some of the numerous unnamed winged female figures in Etruscan art. On a mirror in Boston (*c.*325–300 BC, *CSE USA 2*, no.7) an unnamed seated, winged, predominantly nude female figure comforts a standing, nude male with a spear, perhaps Achilles, and she, too, is perhaps identifiable as Lasa. It is unclear why Lasa on this mirror should have her own name on the scroll.

Characteristics of the decoration. The decoration is chased. The lines of the motif on the obverse are of moderate depth, firm and meticulously worked out, while those of the reverse are light, even and fluid throughout. The border decoration is reasonably well drawn but somewhat free-hand in appearance and uneven in that the leaves are mainly, but not always, in pairs to either side of the stems and are more densely packed on the right stem; there are more breaks in the left-hand stem, where the leaves spring out, than on the right. The right-hand stem begins from a spiral and the left from a loop. Both stems terminate in unimposing small clusters of berries. The bell-flower at the base is more imaginative and unusual. In contrast the motif on the obverse is conventional, formal, neat and complex, the only irregularity being the tightly clustered four leaves on the right contrasting with the loosely branching three leaves on the left. The motif is almost certainly by a different hand.

The border appears too wide for the figured scene, with the result that Amphiaraos is rather cramped between the border and the Lasa, his head overlapping a leaf of the border, and showing that the figures were probably drawn first. There is in contrast a slightly awkward gap behind Ajax's head. The three-quarter pose of Amphiaraos is very successful, unlike that of Ajax, whose upper body looks flat; while the posture of his head is not totally convincing and, further, there is an awkwardness in the perspective of the right arm. The craftsman has a fair degree of skill but seems to find right-facing poses more difficult, and was a little too ambitious for his ability with the pose of Ajax. The warriors perhaps look a little too young and boyish, especially if this Ajax is intended as the son of Telamon, noted by Homer for his magnitude and usually represented in both Greek and Etruscan art as mature and bearded (cf. KRAUSKOPF in *LIMC* s.v. Ajax I, pp.333–4, who also comments that there are a number of unique illustrations representing him that are either personal inventions or relate to now unknown stories). It may be, however, that the craftsman had in mind Ajax, son of Oileus, who was known for his small stature, rather than Ajax, son of Telamon (see *Subject and interpretation*), or perhaps he merely confused the two. The craftsman appears to have a good knowledge of anatomy, with the feet especially well drawn in frontal, three-quarter and profile, the limbs competently muscled and articulated, and Amphiaraos' profile neck with larynx well observed. He seems to have been less happy about faces, all three shown in somewhat monotonous profile, Amphiaraos' and the Lasa's very similar. He has achieved a suitably gloomy atmosphere with the poses and resigned expressions with downturned mouths. Variation is achieved by giving Amphiaraos a muscled cuirass (unrealistically shown without the join between front and back) and Ajax a scale-cuirass, this latter rather sketchily portrayed. A curious and perhaps deliberately 'ancient' feature are Lasa's fibulae, which appear to be bow-types of the orientalising period. Alternatively they could be open rings attached to the shoulder folds of the back and employed to gather up the folds of the front section.

Technical comment. The motif on the obverse was probably ornamented with silver globules (see *Material and condition*); cf. nos 7, 20.

Date. Classical/late Classical. The mirror has usually been dated to the 4th century BC (*c.* 350 BC, DE GRUMMOND, LAMBRECHTS in *LIMC* s.v. Lasa, p.217; 4th–3rd century, BONFANTE; 400–350 BC, KRAUSKOPF *Sagenkreis* p.98 and *LIMC* s.v. Amphiaraos, p.700). FISCHER GRAF notes the popularity of the three-figured composition with one figure standing and two seated to either side in the 4th century BC, and LAMBRECHTS s.v Lasa comments on the date span of all representations of Lasa between 350 and 200 BC. The flat, thick, even section of this mirror would normally indicate a date right at the beginning of this span, though the pendent bell-flower of the extension on the reverse indicates that it must be heralding the Hellenistic era. Of particular interest is the motif on the obverse, with its addorsed, double-outlined spirals and distinctive, delicate, upward springing ivy leaves to either side, and which is paralleled by several mirrors: *CSE* DDR I, no.22, has a similar motif, though of poorer quality, with a bird to either side, and is dated to about 400 BC. Also similar is the obverse motif of *CSE* Denmark 1, no.22, an archaic mirror decorated with a scene of Eos and Memnon, dated 470–450 BC, but with a thinner, slightly convex section, probably indicating that it should be put a little later. Ironically, in the same volume mirror no.26, with an obverse extension motif not too dissimilar, has a thick, flat section but is dated 330–320 BC. It seems a strong possibility that the reverse of this mirror was decorated at a later date. Considerably closer is the obverse motif on *CSE* BRD 1, no.13, dated 330–320 BC, on the basis of the naturalistic three-quarter-view head which fills the reverse, but again in view of the mirror type and the obverse motif one wonders whether the reverse decoration could be a later addition. *CSE* BRD 2, no.34 has a similar but poorer quality, simpler obverse motif, and is an early 5th-century mirror of which the reverse has been incised in modern times. These last three mirrors then have a reverse decoration perhaps or certainly added at a later date, while the reverse of *CSE* DDR I, no.22, above, has merely a border decoration and no figured scene. It seems not uncommon, then, for this

type of mirror with such an obverse motif to have been made with little or no reverse decoration (or for the reverse to have been decorated contemporarily but by another hand?). Closest of all to the British Museum mirror, however, in a number of ways, is *CSE* Italia 1, I, no.39: it has a very similar extension motif, a similarly thick, flat disc, and close parallels in the details of the figured scene, which represents Herkle and Athena at a fountain. The musculature, particularly of the legs, is close, as is the treatment of the hair, though the drapery is less naturalistic. It is dated 450–425 BC, the name-piece of MANSUELLI's 'Maestro di Ercole alla fonte' (MANSUELLI *StEtr 1946-47* pp.21, 50), and put by PFISTER-ROESGEN soon after 450 BC (pp.126–7). None of these mirrors have provenances, but they presumably originate from Vulci. All, incidentally, have a forked tang, except *CSE* Denmark 1, no.22, and the Bologna example, where the tang is broken. It is difficult to date the British Museum mirror in view of the diversity of dating for parallels. Again, in view of the differences in technique between the decoration of the obverse and the reverse (see *Characteristics of the decoration*), it is possible that the reverse was decorated at a later date, say mid-4th century, the mirror having been made in the mid to late 5th century (cf. nos 21, 23). One would then have to put forward a similar argument for the dating of the Bologna mirror, but again, given the diversity of style between the obverse and reverse – particularly noticeable between the casually done border and the meticulous obverse motif – this is readily supportable. The increase in popularity of figured decoration on the backs of mirrors in the 4th century could account for these additions. Alternatively one could hypothesise that the workshops where the backs were decorated were producing the mirrors with traditional motifs already cut in the obverse (see p.14). A mid-4th century date is also given to the Vatican mirror mentioned above (*CSE* Vaticano 1, no.11), which is similar in type, section, composition, mood, treatment of the hair and the general appearance of the ivy-wreath, but which differs in having bunches of berries alternating with the leaves and clusters of berries at the top; the extension motif of the obverse of this is not so formal and meticulous as that of the mirrors mentioned above, and could be contemporary with the reverse decoration.

29   [figs pp.161–3]

Circular tanged mirror with extension
Satyr, maenad

GR 1814.7–4.967

Provenance. Unknown. Second Townley collection.

Bibliography. GERHARD *ES* I pl.XCIV, 2; III p.100; HAWKINS III p.222; VAUX *BM Handbook* p.421; WALTERS *BMBronzes* no.631; MANSUELLI *StEtr 1946-47* pp.18, 50, 116, 130; PFISTER-

ROESGEN *Spiegel* S 43, p.62, 157, pl.47; FISCHER GRAF *Vulci* pp.47–8, pl.12; WIMAN *Malstria-Malena* pp.59ff., fig.11:8.

Material and condition. Obverse. For the most part badly corroded and pitted; there is very extensive cuprite overlaid by thick, rough, green corrosion. At the top of the tang is a white-painted 'T' referring to the Townley collection to which the mirror previously belonged. The edge bears the same corrosion products but the surface is better preserved, while the reverse has only a thin layer of green corrosion over the dark brown metal, which has a number of tiny warty eruptions.

Measurements. W. 15.5cm. H. 22.0cm. W. across points 1.7cm. Wt. 366g.

Type. Disc mirror, flat in section and with a very slight taper towards the rim and a deep, slightly inturned, edge, made in one piece with the extension which has slightly tapering sides and a pointed tang. No centre point visible (central depression marked on drawing appears too large and irregular for a centre point)

Decoration.
EDGE. Indistinct design is adjacent to the beading of the obverse. There is perhaps a row of tongues with internal concentric arches.

OBVERSE. At the base of the disc and on the extension is a palmette and spiral motif. The seven-lobed palmette rests on a double-curved base with a spiral and leaf decoration to either side; the upper ends of the spirals perhaps extended to form further decorative elements, but these are now obliterated by corrosion. Beneath the spirals there appears to have been an inverted palmette, but this, too, is no longer decipherable. Rim beaded.

REVERSE. The border consists of two undulating stems of ivy which originate from a palmette and scroll design located at the base of the disc and on the extension. Leaves alternate to either side of the ivy stems with clusters of three berries growing beneath each leaf, and each stem also ends in three berries where they meet above. The seven-lobed, elongated palmette rises from two out-turned leaves resting on the lower coils of two double spirals, beneath which are two downward-turned leaves with a downward V-shape between. The upper curves of the double spirals divide into two at the ends and from the upper curves spring the ivy stems of the border.

The figured scene consists of a satyr and maenad seated on rocks leaning towards each other and engaged in intimate conversation, their heads and legs in profile, torsos in three-quarter view. Both have the leg further from the spectator bent back, the other almost straight with the maenad's left foot overlapping the satyr's right. The naked satyr, with his left arm crooked up holding what is presumably a thyrsos, his right arm lifted from his lap with palm uppermost as though amplifying a point of conversation, looks intently at the maenad. He has a typical satyr's tail, goat's ears, wavy beard, prominent high forehead, flat crown and shoulder-length hair. The maenad, her face close to the satyr's, returns his gaze attentively, resting her right elbow on her thigh, the right hand relaxed and limp. In her left arm she holds a thyrsos(?) with the head downwards. A cloth is draped over her left shoulder, the end hanging down in front to the waist, the rest hanging down behind her back with part wound round her right thigh, another end hanging down between her legs and the rest tucked beneath her seat. She wears soled shoes with apron fronts, a wavy strap or tag emerging from behind the aprons over the instep. Her slightly wavy hair is parted in front with strands hanging before her ears, and the rest, bound by a fillet, is loosely tucked up behind, the ends of the top hair escaping.

Subject and interpretation. A satyr and maenad conversing, apparently a popular genre scene attested by several other examples.

Characteristics of the decoration. Obverse. The decoration appears to be chased (the grooves are relatively shallow-curved in cross-section, with blunt ends, general uniformity of depth and stepped curves characteristic of chasing). What remains of the extension motif appears carefully cut and symmetrical. *Reverse.* The lines are made by a fine tool and are light but firm, even and sure. The composition is well balanced, symmetrical and well adapted to the circular space. The poses of the figures are similar but the craftsman has avoided monotony by seating the right-hand figure slightly higher, varying the positions of the legs and making the outer ones overlap, adopting different positions for the thyrsoi and draping the right-hand figure. Only the thyrsoi give the impression of being unfinished for they are drawn in silhouette with no internal detail, but this may be part of the craftsman's general desire for simplification. The border and extension motif are careful and regular and an attractive enhancement to the central scene. The craftsman is of high calibre, capable of first-class representation with simplicity and economy of line.

Date. Late Classical. Probably around the middle of the 4th century BC. This type of seated, two-figured conversation group was popular on late Classical Etruscan mirrors: cf. *CSE* Great Britain 2, no.25; *CSE* USA 2, no.3; *CSE* BRD 2, no.6 and 3, no.5; *CSE* Hongrie/Tchecoslovaquie no.12; REBUFFAT *Miroir* nos 1285 (pl.3), 1325 (pl.74). Some of these mirrors have a similar extension motif, as do *CSE* Great Britain 2, no.8; *CSE* BRD 1, no.31; 2, nos 2 and 25 (which has an altogether much freer treatment); REBUFFAT *Miroir* pls.39, 46, and both the Cambridge mirrors have a similar border. All these mirrors are dated *c.*350–300 BC. The genre was no less popular for the relief decoration of South Italian Greek lidded mirrors of the late 4th and early 3rd centuries BC. In type and section, however, the British Museum mirror is unlikely to be much later than about 350 BC, the disc being flat and fairly thick with no concavity on the sides of the extension, while the figures too are still Classical in appearance; see as general parallels the Ajax and Achilles mirror in Basle (FISCHER GRAF *Vulci* V 27, taf.11) and the Peleus and Thetis mirror in the Vatican id. V 19, taf.6), where Peleus, like the satyr, has vertical hatching defining the genital area.

30 [figs pp.164–7, 190, 192]

Circular tanged mirror with extension

Thethis (Thetis), Pele (Peleus)

GR 1966.3–28.13

Provenance. Perugia. Seen in London in 1844 by J. de Witte. Formerly collection of Capt. Spencer-Churchill MC (purchased from the Executors), who acquired it in February 1927 through Messrs Spink from Mr Weightman.

Bibliography. G.B. VERMIGLIOLI 'La favola di Peleo e Tetide', *Giornale scientifico letterario di Perugia*, Perugia 1845, 12, p.8; E. BRAUN in *AZ* IV, 1846, p.260; E. CONESTABILE *Dei monumenti di Perugia etrusca e romana*, 1855–70, pp.467ff., pl.78; GERHARD *ES* IV pl.CCCLXXXVI (reversed), p.35; *CII* no.1068; MANSUELLI *StEtr* 1946-7 p.19; R.A. HIGGINS in *JHS Archaeological Reports* 87, 1966–7, p.49, 11d, fig.14; HAYNES *BMQ* 32, 1967–8, pp.114–16, pl. 36; HAYNES in *Art and Technology* pp.180–2, fig. 7; FISCHER GRAF *Vulci* pp.83–6, pl. 22, 4; HAYNES *EtrBr* no.177, p.313, pl. on p.111; *CSE* BRD 1, p.68; *CSE* BRD 2, p.20; *CSE* BRD 3, p.41; RIX *ET* p.354, Pe S.6; R. VOLLKOMMER in *LIMC* s.v. Peleus, no.73*, also listing modern copies; MACNAMARA *Etruscans* pp.48, 50, fig.61.

Material and condition. Bronze disc with bone handle. The metal is in good condition, except where a sharp instrument has dented it from the obverse, upper right of the centre, making a vertical gash about 1.0cm long and pushing up the surface of the reverse: this was the result of a slanting blow from the right. The bright metal in the gash suggests that the damage occurred in modern times. There is also on the obverse a small diagonal wavy cut, about 1.0cm long, above the first blow and slightly left, but this is patinated over and may have happened in ancient times. *Obverse.* Smooth, hard, shiny green patina of various shades with a spattering of rough corrosion lower left of the disc and to the top and right of the rim, extending on to the edge. The extension motif, particularly the upper part, is worn faint from repeated rubbing of the thumb and from polishing in antiquity. The beading of the rim is also fairly worn from polishing, and is almost completely missing for a stretch of about 5.0cm lower left, perhaps indicating that the user in antiquity repeatedly held the disc with his or her right thumb gripping here. *Edge.* Patination mainly as obverse, with some rough brown corrosion to the left of the obverse. *Reverse.* Patination as obverse, with isolated small warts of corrosion and small patches of rough grey-brown corrosion to the left and right near the rim. The design in the centre of the figured scene appears to be worn from polishing in antiquity.

Handle. The turned bone handle is made in one piece and stained green in the upper half by contamination from the bronze. The bone is shiny and polished, with some vertical cracks but is otherwise in good condition, except where it is gripped by the bronze fitting at the base, where it is roughened and whitish. The X-ray photograph shows the handle to have a drilled vertical hole of perfectly even diameter. Two horizontal holes have been drilled through the bone, each about 4.0 mm in diameter, one through the moulding at the top and one through the deep base. The holes run diagonally to the disc, and are not quite aligned with one another. Both holes have modern dark infill, but the bottom one contains the remains of a presumably ancient bone pin: probably the handle has been attached or reattached in modern times. Inside the handle is a modern soft, brown, waxy filling. There is in fact no evidence to show that it belonged to this particular mirror: to the contrary, the X-ray photograph shows that there is no hole in the tang to match that in the bone handle. At the top of the handle is a thin bronze disc or washer with a vertical slot to accommodate the tang; it is tarnished dark brown in colour with very slight green corrosion and is probably modern. The disc at the base of the handle, with a serrated edge bent up to grip the handle, has similar tarnish to that of the washer at the top and is probably also modern. The bronze finial cone is covered with thick green patination and some cuprite, making it difficult to identify all the decoration. Protruding from a hole at the base of the cone is a small steel or iron rod extending about 8.0 mm and then bent back on itself, with raised, reddish corrosion to either side, again probably modern. The X-ray shows that it penetrates about 2.0cm into the handle (fig.34, p.192).

The handle was excluded from VERMIGLIOLI's drawing but included in GERHARD, perhaps because it was detached at the time of the former and later added; HAYNES commented that the green of the mirror patination matched the stain on the handle so well that it was likely to belong, but any bronze mirror, or whatever bronze object it belonged to, would be likely to create the same coloration over a prolonged period of contact. The staining could have occurred in modern times, since the modern paraffin wax in the horizontal holes of the handle is similarly stained green. Although most ancient mirror tangs do not have holes for the attachment of a handle, which must in these instances have been bonded on with a resinous filler, the existence of the hole at the top of the bone handle still has to be explained. The handle may have belonged to another object and been re-used for this mirror in antiquity, but there remain the dubious washers at either end, and the dubious modern wire attaching the finial. In addition, the roughened surface of the bone handle at the base may indicate that even if it did belong to a mirror in antiquity, it has perhaps been inverted for re-use, as the top end would have been likely to receive most wear. This may also explain why a differently aligned hole was then made.

Measurements. W. 17.0cm. H. 23.5cm. H. from base of extension 18.0cm. H. of tang 5.2cm. H. of bone handle 10.4cm. H. of bronze conical finial 2.0cm. Total H. 30.3cm. Wt. 618g.

Type. Circular, flat, disc mirror, thick and fairly even in section with offset, projecting edge with a very slight extension, the sides of which are a continuation of the curve of the disc. Centre point to right of Thethis' left buttock.

Decoration.

OBVERSE. On the rim, a row of beading is adjacent to the relief decoration of the edge, which consists of a rib and then a row of tongues, the tips of which are missing where the rim has been smoothed or worn down, with internal concentric arches. The motif at the base of the disc consists of a five-lobed palmette with a small circlet to either side of the central lobe, over a double arc above a downward loop enclosing a single leaf on a stem pointing downward and held at the neck by a band, decorated, it seems, with three rows of punched dots with horizontal lines between. To either side the ends of the loop rise above the band and curl outward, with an isolated leaf below each. Flanking the palmette are two upward-curving leaves with scalloped outer edges, and beyond them single stems each with a small bell-shaped flower.

REVERSE. The border decoration consists of two mildly undulating ivy stems with leaves alternating to either side and berries alternating with leaves near the bases of the stems. The stems meet at the top, terminating in a single leaf, one pointing up and the other down. At the base the stems grow from a spiral and double palmette motif; the upper palmette has seven lobes and the lower one nine, with an additional inverted lobe to either side, above which sit two addorsed spirals, whose stems extend outwards into thick tendrils with pointed lobes extending downward from them.

The figured scene consists of a winged female figure running off to the left but caught by a young man who pursues her, grasping her left arm with both hands. The figures are inscribed as follows.

Above Thethis' head, left to right:

θeθis

In front of Pele' right shoulder, right to left:

pele

Thethis, turning towards her pursuer with body in three-quarter view to the left and head in three-quarter view to the right, has large wings outstretched, with small scale-like coverts above and rows of longer ones beneath. She is of short, hefty build and stretches her right arm forward, hand outstretched, in the direction that she is trying to go. Her translucent chiton or peplos has an overfold belted at the waist, the drapery of the 'skirt' swirling around her legs. The garment is fastened at the shoulders with circular clasps or buttons and has an additional overfold with a narrow border decorated with vertical strokes. Her short, wavy hair flies out to either side from a central parting, and

she wears a wide crown or diadem, the two curved ends meeting above the forehead. She wears sandals with slender thongs and hooked backs. Pele, in three-quarter view to the left with head in profile to the left, is nude apart from a short cloak fastened at the throat with a circular brooch. It flares behind him, emphasising the swift motion of the pair, his right leg bent up well behind him as he runs. He wears a conical cap, his wavy hair hanging down the back of his neck with a fringe and shorter strands in front of the ears. A running wave pattern, evened out into a simple curving line between the figures' feet, follows the outline of Thethis' right leg up to the waist, and curves round behind Pele up to his shoulder, forming an additional border decoration and also a filling ornament. It also signifies the environment of the episode, Thethis being a sea-nymph.

Subject and interpretation. Pele (Peleus) seizing Thethis (Thetis). The gods had declared that the Nereid should marry the mortal Peleus, but in her attempts to escape, the unwilling Thetis transformed herself into fire, water, and various wild beasts (cf. ROSCHER s.v. Peleus; *RE* s.v. Peleus). The fact that Thethis is winged may indicate her divine nature, and the abundance of wave decoration is perhaps intended to suggest her natural element. The struggle between Peleus and Thetis was a popular theme in Greek vase-painting, and no doubt inspired Etruscan representations. This depiction was probably more directly influenced by South Italian Greek vase-painting, where youths are more frequently depicted with a pilos and cloak fastened at the throat, than Attic vase-painting. The representation of Thetis is, however, decidedly more Etruscan in character, with the addition of wings and her over-sized hands. The subject appears on three other Etruscan mirrors, all of the archaic period, on which as commonly on the Greek vases with this theme, Peleus is seizing Thetis round the hips or merely pursuing her (Florence, Museo Archeologico, Inv. 79022 (though modern decoration?); Vienna, Kunsthistorisches Museum, Inv. VI 2627; Rome, Museo di Villa Giulia, Inv. 6303 = MAYER-PROKOP S 9–11, pp. 16–18, 57–9, and see FISCHER GRAF *Vulci* pp. 85–6).

Characteristics of the decoration. Obverse. The motif was presumably originally of moderate depth, carefully done but tilted slightly to the left, with a variety of elements: bell-flowers, acanthus leaves and a palmette. Like the decoration of the reverse, it was chased and not engraved, but on the obverse with a slightly broader tool.

Reverse. Chased. Border decoration deep and carefully done, with small irregularities, e.g. the overlaps on the stem, lower right, and a missing leaf-stem just above the middle on the left, and another lower down. The depiction of the berries only on the lower part of the stems is unusual, as is the lack of a cluster of berries where the stems meet at the top, instead terminating simply in a leaf, one pointing up and one down. The motif at the base is asymmetrical in that the stem on the left is a continuation of the tendril whereas the one on the right grows separately from it. The lobes of the palmettes are somewhat uneven and the overall impression of the decoration is rather free-hand, particularly the running wave pattern used as a filler around the figures.

The figured decoration is slightly less deeply cut, but wear in the centre probably makes this more noticeable than originally. The anatomy is effective in silhouette, though Thethis is rather brawny and high-breasted, and Pele too short in the torso, while his right foot is incomplete. The internal markings are few, though the craftsman has taken pains to show the inside of Thethis' hand, with the palm, finger-joints and wrist lines indicated as are those of the inside of the elbows and of her neck, though the last is imprecisely done, as is the inside of her right ankle. Her anatomy is somewhat masculine, and there even seems to be an attempt to make her look rather mature (sagging jaw-line, lines at neck, wrist and inner elbows, angular calves). Thethis' transparent, swirling drapery is very effective, though the extra overfold is rather incongruous; less successful is the cloak of Pele, which blows back realistically though the folds behind his waist are broken and shaky. The wings of Thethis have all the requisite details but are of uneven quality – her right one is better, with more differentiation between the types of feathers. The hair is treated in parallel lines but is naturalistic, while the three-quarter view of Thethis' face is successful, if the expression is somewhat blank. The whole composition is well designed and adapted to the available space, with Thethis appearing to be brought up short as she is seized by Pele.

Handle. The moulding at the top has four pairs of ribs with three curved bands between, while the grip swells out and then tapers down to an outward-flaring, offset collar at the bottom, set on a deep curved base which tapers in a little at the end. The bronze disc at the top of the handle is decorated with a herring-bone pattern around the rim and in six rays from the centre to the obverse and reverse. The disc at the base of the handle has a serrated edge, the points bent up to grip the bone. It is difficult to identify all the bands of decoration on the bronze conical finial, but there are at least two rows of beading and one of tongues with internal concentric arches.

Technical comment. No remarkable features. See X-ray photograph, *Characteristics of the decoration* and *Material and condition* regarding the handle and its attachment.

Date. Late Classical. Although the mirror was found at Perugia, it is likely to have been made at Vulci (see FISCHER GRAF *Vulci* and HAYNES *EtrBr*). It probably dates to *c.*350–325 BC (cf. HAYNES *EtrBr*) on the grounds of its style of figured decoration, though the border decoration is rather like that of no.22: the type seems to have had a long life (cf. also no.27). Thethis' swirling drapery has been likened to that on the Faliscan 'Aurora' krater (*c.*340 BC; FISCHER GRAF *Vulci* p.85) and for the subject, see the pelike with Thetis from Kertsch (C.H. SMITH, *Catalogue of the Greek and Etruscan Vases in the British Museum* III, London 1896, E 424, *c.*340–330 BC; FISCHER GRAF *Vulci* p.86;

BEAZLEY *EVP* p.83; BEAZLEY *ARV²* pp.1475, 1695; BROMMER *Vasenlisten* 328.33). The palmette decoration with profile acanthus leaves on the obverse can be paralleled by an inferior and later example on a mirror from Bologna, dated by its *corredo* to the end of the 4th or beginning of the 3rd century BC (*CSE* Italia 1, II, no.4; for another variation see also *CSE* USA 2, no.14, made probably at some time in the 4th century BC but difficult to pinpoint). Mirrors with this type of border decoration are dated by LIEPMANN from the last third of the 4th century to the early 3rd (*CSE* BRD 2, p.20). The bell-flowers of the obverse motif are elements from floral decoration on South Italian vase-painting which were widely adopted in Etruria.

It is interesting that already in the 4th century we see the type of face which remained the popular ideal for female beauty for the next two centuries. The representation of Seianti Hanunia Tlesnasa on her painted terracotta sarcophagus from Chiusi, belonging to the mid-2nd century BC, is remarkably similar, with its brachycephalic head, full lips, prominent, straight nose, arched brows and deep-set eyes, even the somewhat absorbed expression, which is not really appropriate to the seizure of Thetis on the mirror (H.B. WALTERS, *Catalogue of the Terracottas in the Department of Greek and Roman Antiquities, British Museum*, London 1903, D 786 = H.D. GENTILI, *I Sarcofagi Etruschi in Terracotta di Età Recente*, Archaeologia 108, Rome 1994, A 69 tav.XXXI). Similar, too, is the stature, with heavy, thick-set limbs. The internal markings on Thethis' arms and neck seem to give her a maturity of physique and ruggedness which was perhaps thought appropriate for her wrestling exploits with Pele: she has essentially a male physique with the awkward addition of the right breast. The silver strigil and aryballos found in the Chiusine sarcophagus may indicate that some form of sport or exercise was not unusual for Etruscan women, and that this made the theme of the match between Peleus and Thetis all the more appropriate for the mirror decoration. Frequently, though, strigils seem to have been used simply for cleansing purposes (for strigils in female burials, see F.R. SERRA RIDGWAY *I Corredi del Fondo Scataglini a Tarquinia*, Milan 1996, p.295 with references).

The popularity of this mirror among modern forgers resulted in its reproduction in ten copies, at least some of which seem to have stemmed from Perugia, where the mirror was found. The following list of copies, occasionally considered in past publications as ancient, is compiled from FISCHER GRAF and VOLLKOMER in *LIMC*, updated: Vatican, Mus.Greg. 12276, 12278; Edinburgh, Royal Museum of Scotland 1136; Philadelphia, Pennsylvania University Museum; Frankfurt, Mus. für Vor- und Frühgeschich. 1984,7 (= *ES* IV pl.CCCLXXXVII, 1, then Perugia Museum, = *CSE* BRD 1, no.42); Rome, Astorri collection; Boston, MFA 1919.314 (= *CSE* USA 2, no.31); Geneva Museum; St Petersburg; Nijmegen, Rijksmus. XXI.f/App.I,3 (= *CSE* The Netherlands, no.33). The copies and their complexities are discussed by FISCHER GRAF, VAN DER MEER (*CSE* The Netherlands) and HÖCKMANN (*CSE* BRD 1, p.68).

PART 4:
PROBLEM MIRRORS

Circular mirror of South Italian origin
Winged youth

GR 1814.7–4.966

Provenance. Unknown. Second Townley collection; previously in the collection of P.A. Rolando Magnini. It is illustrated by a drawing and an engraving made for Townley (Townley Drawings and Prints nos 25, 26, in the Department of Greek and Roman Antiquities, British Museum)

Bibliography. DE LA CHAUSSE pl.19, p.84; GERHARD *ES* I pl.CXX, fig.2; III p.120; FRIEDERICHS p.20; A. DUMONT *BCH* I, 1877, p.109; *DA* I s.v. Cupido, p.1598, fig.2147; ROSCHER p.1351 s.v. Eros; GERHARD *Schriften* p.63, pl.52, fig.3; C. SITTL, *Die Gebärden der Griechen u. Römer*, Leipzig 1890, pp.268–9, fig.24; MURRAY *Greek Bronzes* pp.32–3, fig.12; WALTERS *BMBronzes* no.244; J.D. BEAZLEY, *The Lewes House Collection of Ancient Gems*, Oxford 1920, p.28; BEAZLEY *JHS* 1949 p.2, pl.1b; REBUFFAT *Miroir* pp.350–1, n.3; DE GRUMMOND *Guide* fig.4 (bottom left), p.2; KRAUSKOPF in *LIMC* p.2, no.8, s.v. Eros; *CSE* BRD 2, p.50.

Material and condition. Bronze. Over the entire surface there has been added over the original hard, slightly rough, dark green patina a blackish varnish, perhaps applied as long ago as the 18th century; this both diminishes the imperfections and partially fills the incised lines. The layer was found to contain, among other substances, traces of malachite, and no corrosion products which might be expected on an ancient bronze. The modern white infill accurately follows the engraving but occasionally seeps into small surface anomalies to either side. Where a presumably alien handle had been attached, post-antiquity and prior to 1690 (the date of the earliest surviving illustration of the mirror, which shows it with the handle, DE LA CHAUSSE II, no.19, reproduced here, fig. 35, p.192) modern solder remained, and for the purpose of this study this was cleaned away to reveal any traces of an original handle. The edge of the disc had however been filed away in this area to facilitate the 'new' soldering, obliterating all but a very small patch of what appears to be ancient soft solder, which merely serves to indicate that there was, as was to be expected, an original handle of some kind. At the top of the disc around the edge, however, there remains an area of ancient soft solder, about 5.5cm in length, indicating an original attachment of some kind, presumably a suspension ring or decorative attachment. REBUFFAT, unaware of the traces of ancient solder, believed this mirror to have been of the lidded type, but the section of the disc is not consistent with a lid.

Measurements. W. 14.1cm. H. 14.3cm. H. of edge 0.8cm. Wt. 345g.

Type. Circular disc of even thickness, slightly convex, with deep, vertical, channelled edge. Only a small area of soft solder may indicate the attachment of a handle in antiquity (see *Material and condition*). A handle seen attached to the disc in the Townley drawing, in the form of a miniature Ionic column, is now missing (see *Provenance*). Centre point in front of left hip; another perhaps on obverse.

Decoration. EDGE. The beaded rim of the obverse is separated from a smooth vertical band by a deep groove.

OBVERSE. Within the beaded rim is a border decorated with a row of tongues with two internal concentric arches; this is very slightly recessed from the main part of the disc, which is decorated around its circumference with a double cable pattern, having between the twists of rope a punched decoration consisting of a circlet enclosing a dot.

REVERSE. Within a single cable border, which is a simplified version of the double cable pattern on the obverse, a winged youth running to the left, holding a flower and a tortoiseshell lyre. The figure is naked apart from high ankle boots which are winged, the wings being striated and bound, as it were, to the ankles by a band of stippling. The figure's slightly wavy hair, long at the back, is bound by a fillet of beads or discs. He holds the flower up to his face perhaps to smell it (cf. *CSE* BRD 2, p.50, where a satyr holds out a similar flower for a maenad to smell) while in his left hand the tortoiseshell lyre is held horizontally by the outer bar. His robust wings are outstretched, the upper parts covered in scale pattern to represent small feathers, and with two rows of graduated flight feathers beneath.

Subject and interpretation. As will be discussed below, it is uncertain whether the decoration of this mirror is of Etruscan, Greek or modern origin. The most obvious identity for the figure is Eros, but he could alternatively be either Hyakinthos or Adonis; Hyakinthos occasionally carried a lyre, and both he and Adonis appeared winged in Etruscan art (KRAUSKOPF in *LIMC* p.8; also *LIMC* s.v. Hyakinthos p.549, no.47, and s.v. Adonis, p.225, no.16 (= s.v. Eros, p.2, no.5)). GERHARD (*ES* and *Schriften*) identified the figure as Eros in his capacity of deity of lovers fighting together in war, associating both the flower and the lyre with lovers' activities in the palaistra, and cites a cult of Eros as such which was located at Thebes. This leads us to the question of whether this mirror can actually be classed as Etruscan. As to the subject matter, Eros was not usually given single billing in Etruscan art, whereas in Greece he frequently appears on his own in both red-figure vase-painting and on gems (cf. BEAZLEY and *DA*). What makes him particularly Etruscan here is the double set of wings, at his shoulder-blades and ankles. The mirror itself, however, is definitely not of Etruscan type, but is identical with certain Greek mirrors produced in southern Italy, both in section and decoration, and particularly in the disc being cast as a separate entity (see CAMERON *Hand-mirrors*, Group C, pp.29ff., esp. no.16, pls.44–5). The flower in fact resembles the rose on the reverse of Rhodian coins (cf. G.K. JENKINS *Ancient Greek Coins*, Fribourg 1972, fig.685). There was never any extension or tang on this mirror, and the decoration and beading around the rim run without interruption; a decorative handle with curved edge would presumably have been soldered contiguously on to the rim. The early publications almost all identified the mirror as Greek (e.g. WALTERS *BMBronzes*, MURRAY *Greek Bronzes*, *DA*, FRIEDERICHS), and the earliest surviving illustration of the mirror (DE LA CHAUSSE, published in 1707, reproduced here fig. 35, p.192) shows the mirror mounted on a stand which was perhaps not ancient but constructed to imitate a Greek mirror support rather than an Etruscan mirror handle. Furthermore the cable decoration, which features in single form on the reverse and in double form on the obverse, is most closely paralleled by the South Italian mirrors, particularly in its more complex form. Where the double form occurs on Etruscan mirrors it usually has a kind of central division, making it virtually into two cables or plaits, and generally the dots in the interstices are not present; the exception, strangely, is the painted decoration on the Boccanera plaques (R.P. HINKS, *Catalogue of the Greek, Etruscan and Roman Mosaics and Paintings in the British Museum*, London 1933, no.5). On Etruscan mirrors it occurs almost always on the reverse and is common on archaic mirrors of about 520–480 BC – see MAYER-PROKOP pp.107–8, nos 29, 33, 41, 42, 46, 55, and a discussion in REBUFFAT *Miroir* pp.436–7 on the motif ('*tresses*'; the complex form disappears from Etruscan mirrors after the archaic phase); an isolated example of its occurrence on the front of a mirror is *CSE* Italia 1, I, 2, no.19, dated to 475–450 BC. The British Museum mirror almost undoubtedly originated in southern Italy, though mirrors from that area are traditionally not decorated with figured scenes; possibly the only exceptions are the next entry (no.32) and a mirror from an excavated context from the Pantanello necropolis at Metaponto, found in 1983 (Metaponto Museo Nazionale, inv.305283: J.C. CARTER *The Pantanello Necropolis, 1982-1989. An Interim Report* (The University of Texas at Austin), Austin 1990, pp.93–5, with detail photograph and reconstruction; M. PROHASZKA *Reflections from the Dead. The Metal Finds from the Pantanello Necropolis at Metaponto. Studies in Mediterranean Archaeology* CX, 1995 pp.28, 37, 45, 47 cat.no.M15, Inv.T350–30, fig.6, pl.5; G. PUGLIESE CARRATELLI (ed.) *The Western Greeks*, Exhibition Catalogue, Palazzo Grassi, Venice 1996, no.163, p.700, pl. on p.367). On the back is a scene of Aktaeon attacked by his dogs; the disc has a suspension loop at the top, spool attachments to either side, and a curious, separately made handle in the form of a caryatid, made in bronze from the waist

up, with a tang beneath fitted into a skirt modelled from wood. Coincidentally another mirror from this site and of the same type, but without the incised decoration, was fitted with a handle in the form of a bronze Ionic column, like that once attached to the British Museum mirror, but now lost (PROHASZKA, op.cit. p.31, cat.no.M22, Inv.T292–2, pl.9b, described tentatively (p.46) as a Greek import of the late 6th century BC). This type of handle is rare in southern Italy and is generally considered to be a Greek type (CAMERON *Hand-Mirrors* p.57). PROHASZKA suggests that mirrors from southern Italy with incised scenes on the back are of Italiote manufacture, inspired by Etruscan prototypes; she does not, however, list any other instances, and the only other example known to me is no. 32 in this volume, the decoration of which is under some suspicion. The Aktaeon mirror is dated about 440 BC (PROHASZKA op.cit. p.45). Various possibilities therefore exist for the British Museum mirror: it may have been embellished with the figure either by a Greek craftsman working in the Etruscan style or by an Etruscan craftsman working for a client in southern Italy, or it may have been brought from southern Italy to Etruria and the figured decoration added then. The Greeks of southern Italy undoubtedly had a proclivity toward imitation of Etruscan metalwork (e.g. incense-burners, vessels), and so this could be an Etruscanising embellishment, but it would have to be archaising, since in general the mirror's closest South Italian parallel belongs to a group with openwork handles generally dated no earlier than 450-400 BC (CAMERON, ibid.).

Characteristics of the decoration. Chased. Generally deep, firm, confident lines, save for an error where a double line delineates the back of the left calf. The top of the figure's left boot is bordered with a double line and that of the right by a triple line. The figure's full, rounded chin is reminiscent of archaic Greek vase-painting prototypes rather than Etruscan mirror engraving. From the waist downward his anatomy is more slender than one would expect for the archaic period. For the execution of the cable motif, see *Technical comment*, below.

Technical comment. The figural decoration and the cable motifs on both sides of the mirror appear to be chased rather than engraved: the tools used to chase and punch the cable decoration are evident from occasional 'repeat' marks, where the tool was moved slightly while still in the same place; there are changes in depth of line, without changes of width, and also surface bulges alongside lines where metal has been displaced (engraving removes metal rather than displaces it). The figure seems to have been created at the same time as the surrounding cable motif since there is no detectable difference in the nature of the incised lines; additionally the line indicating the underside of the right big toe is integral with an outer curve of the cable motif. The chasing on the reverse is deeper than that on the obverse, perhaps due to wear from continued polishing of the reflecting surface in antiquity. The punched dots of the cable pattern on the obverse, however, are smaller, as are the circlets, being roughly approximately 0.15cm rather than 0.2cm across. This could be explained by the use of different tools for different types of cable motif, but the curved lines of the cable tend to be less regular than those of the obverse, noticeably so in the areas of greater corrosion, and in these rougher-textured areas the circlets are also larger, particularly adjacent to the lower part of the figure's right wing, as though trying to negotiate difficult patches (figs. pp.169, 171). Such corrosion would presumably not have existed in ancient times, and the possibility that this side of the mirror was decorated post-antiquity cannot be ruled out.

Date. This Greek mirror is included here on account of its various recent publications as an Etruscan object. On the basis of the South Italian Greek parallels for the mirror type, it should belong to the period 450–400 BC, but this is a little hard to reconcile with the archaic style of the figure, despite the lingering on of that style in Etruria. There is no doubt that the mirror itself is ancient: the figured decoration could be ancient but deliberately archaising, although another possibility is that it constitutes a recent addition of no later than the 17th century, in view of the technical points made above. The Metaponto mirror, however, which CARTER suggests to be one of a class of mirrors made locally by a rather unskilled workshop, perhaps strengthens the possibility that the figure on the British Museum mirror is of ancient and of South Italian origin. In the present circumstances it is impossible to be absolutely sure.

32   [figs pp.172–4]

Circular mirror of South Italian origin
? Mean/Meanpe (Nike), Eros, Turan (Aphrodite)

GR 1840.2–12.8

Provenance. Unknown. Bought at the sale of the collection of Samuel Butler, Bishop of Lichfield, 1840, lot 126.3. Butler (1774–1839) published on Classical texts and ancient geography. The sources of his collection are unknown. Biographical details: *Dictionary of National Biography* VIII, 1886, pp.76–7. See also no.36.

Bibliography. MS Acquisitions: Greek and Roman Antiquities 1840–1845, p.4

Material and condition. Bronze. Virtually all the patina has been removed from the reverse, and only two small areas of the original surface remain, on the 'skirt' of the woman's drapery. The whole object has been soaked in acid which has etched the surface and eaten particularly into the chased lines so that some are now much deeper than they were originally, and at least some re-cutting has been carried out. Only a little green corrosion now remains in some of the pitted areas, and the entire surface has

been waxed over. There is some modern white infill, particularly in the area of the Nike. On the obverse and most of the edge a thick, hard, rough corrosion of mottled green remains, occasionally revealing a smooth layer of reddish orange cuprite. There are, however, on the obverse about six places where the original surface remains, two preserving remains of the border decoration. Originally there may have been a separate handle and ornament opposite, as there are two areas bearing what appear to be traces of original soft solder at the top and bottom of the mirror. The soldering cannot have been very secure, since the milled edge was not filed smooth. In more recent times, however, two other areas on the rim, each about 11.0cm long and on opposite sides of the disc, have been filed down and solder has been applied, perhaps for new attachments or for re-attachment of the original fittings. When the disc is placed with the figured scene upright, these areas occur on the top left and bottom right edges of the disc and are thus out of alignment with the scene, and it is hard to conjecture why the attachments should have been located in this way. The darkening of these areas of the edge continues on to the adjacent parts of the obverse, and was perhaps caused by heating for modern soldering. Two pin-holes are pierced into each of these stretches along the rim, those top left being 3.7cm apart and those bottom right, which are slightly larger, 4.1cm apart.

Measurements. W. 15.5cm. H. 16.0cm. H. of rim varies between 1.0 and 1.3cm. Wt. 554g.

Type. Circular mirror, slightly convex and thickening towards the rim, with a tall vertical milled edge. Originally there was perhaps a separate handle and a separate ornament opposite it (see *Material and condition*). Possible centre point between figures.

Decoration.
EDGE. Milled, with the milling pointed at the top.

OBVERSE. The border, marked off from the reflecting surface by a single incised line, consists of a double-outlined tongue pattern, adjacent to the beaded rim, and within it a row of herring-bone, the outer row of lines being finer than the inner ones, and then a guilloche motif with punched dots in the enclosed spaces.

REVERSE. Within the beaded rim are three figures, presumably Eros and Turan/Aphrodite with a small figure of Mean/Nike flying towards the goddess's head with a garland to place upon it. Eros, on the left, in profile facing right, offers a leafy stem which he holds vertically in his right hand, and raises his left hand apparently gesticulating towards the Nike. He is nude, save for a plain fillet, perhaps with a vertical ornament at the front, which binds his straight hair, hanging just below ear level at the side and longer at the back. His wings spring from high on his back, the small feathers represented by scale pattern above the long flight feathers. Aphrodite, right, stands in profile facing Eros with forearms extended, holding a lotus flower upward in the fingers of her right hand, with a dove nestling in or about to take flight from her left hand – the whole scene is generally so poorly drawn that it is difficult to be precise about the details, and here the goddess's fingers are confused with the bird's feathers. She is bare-footed, standing with her right foot advanced, and wears a long chiton, the overfold indicated at the back in the region of the waist; perhaps the line at the base of her neck is intended to represent a necklace. Her long, slightly wavy hair is looped up at the back under a fillet, and she wears an earring with two pendants. The Nike, flying or hovering almost horizontally between the pair, holds a garland of leaves already touching Aphrodite's head, and in her right hand a long fillet. She wears a long tunic and her wings consist of long flight feathers beneath smaller ones indicated by scale pattern, or perhaps by punched dots. Her hair is bound up at the back and she may wear a diadem.

Subject and interpretation. There is some question as to whether the figured scene on this mirror should be termed Etruscan or Greek, as discussed below. The identification of the figures is likely to be Eros and Turan/Aphrodite presenting each other with gifts, with Aphrodite about to be crowned with a garland by Nike. In Etruscan art Mean or Meanpe can often be equated with Nike, and like her she is shown in a number of scenes crowning someone (see DE GRUMMOND *Guide* pp.117–18, with bibliography in the notes). In 80 per cent of the cases where Mean appears on Etruscan mirrors, she is shown holding a garland of leaves, as here. On one she appears with a garland seated next to Aphrodite, while on two more she appears as an attendant of Aphrodite (LAMBRECHTS in *LIMC* s.v. Mean, p.384, nos 8, 1 and 9 respectively). In Greek art Nike is also often shown with a garland or fillet, and on at least one occasion crowns Aphrodite, at the judgement of Paris, GOULAKI-VOUTIRA in *LIMC* s.v. Nike, p.900; it is there suggested that Nike is rarely shown with Eros because of their similarity as winged and, one could add, small-scale, figures. On this mirror there is no question of confusion between Eros and the minuscule winged figure, and one could tenuously argue that this indicates a Greek artist, since the Etruscans had no qualms about a proliferation of winged persons of similar stature (cf. Leningrad, Hermitage, DE GRUMMOND *Guide* fig.98 = GERHARD *ES* IV pl.CCCXXII). There is at least one Praenestine mirror which shows a small winged Nike flying down to crown Paris (British Museum GR 1814.7–4.787: GERHARD *ES* III pl.XCI; MATTHIES *PS* no.11, pp.63, 70–1; ADAM no.5, p.23). Otherwise the subject matter gives no means of determining Greek or Etruscan origin.

Characteristics of the decoration. For the effect of modern etching on the appearance of the decoration, see *Material and condition*. The composition has been thought out with some care and has attained a fair degree of balance, but the craftsman appears to have changed his mind about Aphrodite's original height and position. He seems originally to have intended her to be on a much smaller scale,

with the otherwise inexplicable bulge at the back of her leg at first construed as her buttocks. He also decided to move her further to the right, making her unnaturally deep in profile and with the silhouette of her back view below the waist, which he had presumably already drawn – and in triplicate – now awkwardly placed too far forward. It should perhaps be noted that the wavy lines of this 'triplicate' back view may not in fact have originally been part of the silhouette but perhaps some form of decoration on the drapery, later distorted by the etching and re-cutting: this would still leave Aphrodite unnaturally deep in profile, though not unlike certain archaic korai. The general poorness of the drawing has already been observed, and the anatomy is very summary. Aphrodite's feet are disproportionately small, and her right one, incorrectly, appears to be in front of her left. Her left elbow is distorted. The fingers of the hands are indicated merely by roughly parallel lines, save for Aphrodite's right, which is considerably more careful; Eros's left hand is too big and drawn as though it were his right. Eros is also particularly badly drawn, his legs too long and thin, torso too deep and head too small. There are very few inner markings for the anatomy; that on his left forearm may be another corrected error for the outline. The hair of both is sketchy and the faces are also poor, the eyes too low on the cheeks and Aphrodite's shown as full frontal. The craftsman has made some effort to indicate the patterns of the different types of feathers on Eros's wings, but the lines are hasty and irregular. The chasing is now of uneven depth, some of the lines appearing almost carved out, such as a few of the lines of Aphrodite's drapery and that of Eros's back, but this is largely due to acid etching in modern times (see above). The decoration of the obverse is poorly preserved beneath the thick corrosion layer, but the bands of decoration seem to have been rather imprecise and irregular.

Technical comment. The figured scene is so badly drawn that it is hard to see it as ancient, but poor quality of drawing cannot be the criterion of authenticity. There is no doubt that the mirror itself is genuine, and in the two places where the original surface of the bronze is preserved on the reverse, there is a possibility that the chasing does not cut into the corrosion but is preserved within it. There is some uncertainty about this since the areas concerned are so small, but it could be argued that if this is the case, then the figured decoration, too, must be ancient. If these vestigial lines are ancient, then they indicate that the original drawing may have been done with a fine instrument like that used on the obverse, whose relatively carefully chased border is in some contrast to the now, at least, shabby scene on the reverse. Even the tongue decoration of the obverse, it should be noted, is unusually uneven and irregular.

Date. Like no.31, this mirror is of South Italian type but is included here on the grounds of its similarity to that mirror, in having figured decoration on the reverse which is common to Etruscan mirrors but an extremely rare feature of South Italian ones. It is for this reason that no.31, which is decorated by a far more competent artist, has occasionally been published as an Etruscan object. For the one other example of this type known to me, see the Metaponto mirror, discussed in the entry for no.31. The nature of the drawing of the present mirror makes it difficult to date – like no.31, the mirror itself probably belongs to the period 450–400 BC and, if ancient, the drawing must be contemporary or at least not much later, but is for some reason of more archaic appearance. The subject matter gives barely any indication of whether the figured scene might be Greek or Etruscan (see above), and one can only conjecture as to whether the figured scene might have been done by an Etruscan emigré or by a craftsman in southern Italy influenced by earlier Etruscan mirrors: perhaps the latter would be more likely in view of the fact that the craftsman might be unaccustomed to figure-work.

33   [figs pp.175–7, 192]

Circular mirror with extension and handle in the form of a female figure
Turan/Aphrodite, Eros

GR 1814.7–4.704

Provenance. ?Praeneste (see discussion below). Purchased in 1814 from Peregrine-Edward Townley, Charles Townley's cousin, together with other bronze objects, including Townley's so-called *cista mistica*, said to have been found together by Cesare Petrini in 1786 (HAWKINS I pp.188–90). In that same year the group had been purchased by James Byres, who sold them on to Townley. The group is, however, miscellaneous, and includes pieces dating between the 9th century BC and the 2nd century AD: see further discussion on **Townley's *'cista mystica'* group** at the end of this entry. GERHARD (*ES* III p.118, n.243) appears not to be convinced that the group was found together. A findspot of Bomarzo is given to the mirror by KRAUSKOPF, who attributes it to Gerhard's collection, presumably in error. GERHARD himself states that the mirror was previously in the Borgia collection, but notes by HAWKINS in his MS Catalogue (vol. I, opp. p.190) state that the Townley cista was one of the four cistae found in the neighbourhood, and that of the other three, one went to the Borgia collection, one to Casali and one to the Museo Kirkeriano in Rome (the Museo Kirkeriano formed the basis of the Pigorini collection, part of which was incorporated in the Villa Giulia Museum, part in the Palazzo Massimo). Perhaps GERHARD was under the misapprehension that the mirror was found with the Borgia cista rather than the Townley one; the error was reiterated by BEAZLEY *EVP* p.46.

Bibliography. GUATTANI *Mon.ant.ined.*, 1787, p.29; RAOUL-ROCHETTE *Mon.Ined.* p.263, n.9, p.264, pl.76,3; HAWKINS III, p.224; GERHARD *ES* I pl.CXVII; III p.118; VAUX *BM Handbook* p. 422, ill.; D.M. BAILEY in SWADDLING (ed.) *IIAA* no.VIII, pp.135–6, figs 2, VIII, 3 & 4 in 'Charles Townley's *cista mystica*',

pp.131–41; KRAUSKOPF in *LIMC* s.v. Eros (in Etruria) no.26⋆, pp.3, 9.

An engraving by William Skelton of the mirror together with a group of bronzes with which Townley acquired it is bound along with engravings of Townley's Etruscan mirrors in a volume belonging to the British Library, pressmark 140 h. 4 (BAILEY, pp.133, 137, fig.2). Another copy of the engraving and also the original line and wash drawing for it – presumably by Skelton but unsigned – are in the Department of Greek and Roman Antiquities of the British Museum, bound in a volume of drawings and engravings entitled *Drawings and Prints made for C.Townley: Bronzes and Sculpture*. The mirror, however, does not seem to have been drawn at the same time, being done in a grey wash rather than the green of the main group. It is, though, depicted in an engraving entitled 'Patera Aenea', also in the Department (BAILEY, fig.3; M. CLARKE and N. PENNY (eds) *The Arrogant Connoisseur: Richard Payne Knight*, Manchester 1982, no. 78). It has been suggested that this collection of engravings is also by William Skelton, but none is signed.

Material and condition. The metal is of generally sound condition, for the most part covered by a hard, fairly even layer of green corrosion, save on the handle where the front of the figure has been worn down to dark brown metal, presumably by repeated handling. The figure's nose and the central bulla on the necklet are flattened, apparently from repeated placing of the object on a flat surface; the back of the figure is similarly worn, on the fillet round the hair and slightly less so the mound of the shoulder-blades. The feet are broken off at the ankles and missing, with some green patination, similar to that on the rest of the object, over the broken surfaces, indicating that the feet have been missing for some considerable time. A muddy deposit remains between the strands of hair at the back of the head. There is a filler section of metal between the top of the head and the extension, about 0.5cm in height, the result of the handle having been brazed on to the mirror. The same fine corrosion layer occurs over the entire object, including the lines of the decoration, and is missing only where modern repairs have been carried out. There is a small overflow of metal on to the hair at the back, and a horizontal oblong recess, about 0.4cm in length, where the extension joins the filler section on the obverse. The mirror does not rise vertically from the figure but skews over at an angle, veering to the right when viewed from the reverse. At some time the upper part of the disc has broken away from the base in a rough arc-shape which cuts across the lower part of the figured scene on the reverse (a small section of metal about 1.4cm long is missing where the crack traverses the border), and another crack continues upward from the break to the garland held by Eros; on the obverse this same crack can be seen to continue upward to the rim of the disc. On the obverse two small cracks penetrating inward from the edge of the disc can be seen to the left of the top and midway down on the left, and a lesser one occurs on the right about two-thirds of the way down the disc. On the reverse another deep crack (now consolidated) traverses the extension diagonally up to the right, with a further split branching out to follow the curve of the right-hand spiral of the extension motif. All the cracks on the lower part of the disc have been repaired in modern times with a filler which has been coloured with green pigment similar to the patination, and it is hard to tell whether they are of ancient or modern origin: the filler is obvious from rough-textured areas on the obverse, but the diagonal crack on the extension does not penetrate to the obverse and may be a flaw which survives from the time of the object's manufacture. The incised scene has modern white infill.

Measurements. W. 16.2cm. H. 30.5cm. H. of disc from base of extension 19.1cm. W. across points 2.8cm. Preserved H. of figure to top of fillet 11.5cm. Wt. 561g.

Type. Circular flat disc of almost even thickness throughout, with vertical, rounded, slightly offset edge, and an extension with very slightly concave sides. The figured handle has been attached by casting it onto the extension. Possible centre point by left elbow of Turan, but very small.

Decoration.

REVERSE. The border is formed by a garland with a continuous stem, with pairs of leaves alternating with pairs of long-stemmed berries, growing upwards to either side. In the centre at the top is a cluster of berries, and at the base rising from the stem is a linear design which could represent a sprig of fir, or perhaps a palm branch. The motif on the extension was largely obliterated when the handle was joined on but the remains of an inverted palmette are visible below, beneath an inverted triple arc, between two thick addorsed spirals with a curved extension spreading to either side, and on the right it is linked to the lower leaf of the first pair to the right.

The figured design consists of a female figure seated on a throne holding out at arm's length a winged boy, the two gazing at each other. The female figure sits in profile to the left on the near edge of the throne, her left leg resting over the side with the foot slightly back, poised on the toe. She holds out the winged boy in an awkward, improbable manner, her right arm at his back and left hand around his right leg. She wears a long chiton buttoned down the sleeves, the lower folds draped across her legs with a short expanse of the underskirt visible above the ankles. Her slightly wavy hair hangs down her neck at the back with shorter locks in front of the ear, and round it she has a diadem with a leaf design at the front. She wears an earring apparently of the *a grappolo* type, the large top section covering the ear with poorly drawn triple discs below. The boy, short-haired, in a sitting position facing right, holds his left hand out and down towards the woman, and in his right hand behind him he dangles a garland with discs, inside and out, some incomplete and some missing. His wings seem to spring not from his shoulder-blades as usual for Etruscan winged figures but from his outer shoulders and upper arms. Each wing is composed of three sections: an inner curved shape decorated with roughly drawn circles, a plain band, and then a row of coverts increasing in length from the outer to the inner edge. The throne is elaborate, with a curious back

which bends over and down instead of rising vertically, with a dove-like bird standing on the top facing right. Only the two nearside legs of the throne are shown, both turned and swelling in the middle, the rear one socketed on to a dowel at seat level. A band of lattice pattern stretches between the legs below the seat (see *Characteristics of the decoration*).

HANDLE. This takes the form of a female figure, broken off just above the ankles, nude apart from a necklace with five bullae and at the back, a piece hanging down, perhaps a fastening, and an armlet on each upper arm each with three bullae. The bullae on her right arm have realistically slipped round beneath her arm as she raises it. She lifts her right hand to adjust the plain fillet round her thick short hair; the fillet is rounded at the front but angular at the sides and flattened at the back where it rests on the surface when laid down. Her right hand has been pierced, perhaps at the wax stage, possibly for some small attachment, circular in section, to be inserted between the thumb and forefinger; alternatively perhaps a small rod or drill was used to make the hole simply to convey the idea of articulation of the hand, which is rather crudely modelled with only three fingers visible from the back and the fingers differently aligned when seen from the front. A similar ineptitude is shown by the fingers of the bronze warrior also associated with the group, which has, too, a certain similarity in the pose and modelling of the legs. The warrior, disconcertingly, may well prove to be modern (see discussion under **Townley's** *'cista mystica'* **group**). If the warrior is of modern manufacture, it could be conceived as casting doubt on the mirror handle, or a modern addition to the group assuming stylistic traits of the mirror figure-handle in order to give the warrior credibility and to increase the interest of the group. The female figure holds her left arm down at her side with an indeterminate object in her hand; it forms a thick bulging loop through which she inserts her fingers. It is perhaps a sponge, as held together with an aryballos by a seated figure on an Attic red-figured vase, *CVA* Palermo, Museo Nazionale I, p.6, tav.8 (Inv. V658): a fake scene incised apparently before 1859 on a mirror in Perugia, *CSE* Italia 2, I, no.32, seems to copy this.

Subject and interpretation. Probably Turan/Aphrodite and Eros; Adonis is unlikely, given the small scale of the figure, and its wings, though a mirror in Berlin, FR 53 (Misc. 3312) (=*CSE* BRD 4, no.34) has a scene of Adonis/Atunis winged and youthful, and Aphrodite/Turan named as *ati*, mother.

Characteristics of the decoration. The decoration of the reverse is engraved and is of even, moderate depth, save where damaged or obliterated by modern repairs. The entire background of both the scene and the border is stippled. The decoration of the reverse has several unusual features, most noticeably the continuous stem of the border where one would expect to find two antithetically placed trails, and the fact that it traverses the cluster of berries at the top. The wings of Eros are unusual in that the primary feathers on Etruscan winged figures normally point downwards and the upper part of the wings are composed of scale-like coverts (see nos 23, 28, 30). The throne also presents oddities: its droop-back may be based on throne-backs terminating in dipped swans' heads familiar from archaic Greek vase-painting (cf. G.M.A. RICHTER *The Furniture of the Greeks, Etruscans and Romans*, London 1966, figs 40–51). An Etruscan version of it exists from archaic down to Hellenistic times but the feature is much less pronounced (S. STEINGRÄBER *Etruskische Möbel*, Rome 1979, Throntyp 1c, pp.25–6). Only two legs of the throne are shown as if in profile view, despite a reasonable attempt to show Aphrodite in three-quarter view, with left thigh overlapping the side of the throne. Aphrodite's drapery is very sketchy and illusory; her diadem, with its leaf-like frontpiece, is again hard to parallel. The rows of circles round Eros's garland seem never to have been completed, and were made with the use of a punch, unlike the berries of the border. His anatomy is fairly successful in outline, but the internal markings are only roughly placed; the ear is unrealistic and the hands have only three fat fingers (notably cf. the figured handle), while his face, like Aphrodite's, has no demarcation between the outline of forehead and nose, and the nostril is exaggerated. The depiction of Aphrodite's anatomy also leaves much to be desired, the toes banana-like, the fingers of her left hand seemingly added as an afterthought as parallel lines on Eros's right leg, her forearm misaligned, her right forearm and hand conveniently omitted, and too large to have been concealed behind Eros's torso; her eye is in profile but too long. Her *a grappolo* earring, if it is such, is very roughly drawn; this type of earring was introduced into Etruria in the 4th century BC (cf. M. CRISTOFANI in M. CRISTOFANI and M. MARTELLI (eds) *L'Oro degli Etruschi*, Novara 1983, no.239, p.311), and if correctly identified would present a *terminus post quem* for the engraving on the mirror. The bird on the back of the throne is done moderately well, though it has no feet. Overall the drawing is somewhat hasty and summary, though the composition is well suited to the circular space, apart from the toes of Aphrodite's right foot missing behind the border. The leaves of the border are also irregular, some having short stems, some none; the berries at the top float randomly instead of growing organically and the fir sprig or palm at the bottom is an incongruous filler; it resembles an element on the obverse motif of a mirror in the Louvre, decorated in modern times, but prior to 1858 (*CSE* France 1, III, no.5). The design is also found as maker's mark on Roman lamps (I am grateful to my colleague Dr Donald Bailey for this information).

Technical comment. The handle was brazed on to the disc and not made in one with it (see Appendix). The patination appears to be ancient though this cannot be proved entirely beyond doubt, and there is a deposit of cassiterite on the obverse which may indicate tinning. It could be a natural corrosion product, but this does not explain why it does not occur elsewhere on the mirror. This practice, though widely known from Roman mirrors and lidded Greek mirrors, does not seem otherwise to be paralleled on an Etruscan mirror, though it seems that some mirrors of the 5th century BC from southern Italy may have been tinned (M. PROHASZKA *Reflections from the Dead. The Metal Finds from the Pantanello Necropolis at Metaponto*, Studies in Mediterranean Archaeology CX, 1995, pp.28 (M15), 38–41). The disc and the handle were made of different alloys, the principal difference being that the disc contains about 1 per cent lead and the figure 13 per cent (see Appendix). This does not necessarily mean that the two parts did not originally belong, as the divergence could well have been deliberate – a greater proportion of lead in the disc would have marred its reflecting properties, while its high content in the figure aided the metal's penetration into the extremities of the mould. (Reports by the British Museum's Department of Scientific Research: BMRL 19797X, RL File No.4895, 18 January 1983 and 6 March 1996, by Susan La Niece.) Recent research by the author and colleagues at the British Museum indicates that in any case the disc would not normally be cast but hammered to shape (SWADDLING *et al.*). See Appendix, p.64.

Date. This mirror presents a variety of problems. If it is ancient, as the scientific evidence suggests, then it is difficult to date. A Hellenistic date would suit the style of the figured handle, but not the type of mirror, which is thick, flat, and of even depth throughout, a type more common for late archaic and early Classical mirrors. Both the scene and the border have a number of curious features, noted above in *Characteristics of the decoration*, which would not be at home in combination in either the archaic, Classical or Hellenistic periods. They have not been incised at a later date, since the patina traverses the incisions. There appears to be only one convincing parallel for the figured scene, and this is on an early red-figured stamnos on the Rome market at the time of *ES* I (1841), of which the only illustration survives in E. GERHARD *Trinkschalen und Gefässe des Königlichen Museum*, Berlin 1848–50, p.30, pl.C,1, depicting a rather top-heavy Aphrodite apparently running, nude from the waist up save for a piece of drapery over her left shoulder, and with a small winged Eros alighting(?) to the left of her torso, his hands obscured by her right shoulder (BEAZLEY *EVP* p.46, no.1). The general style of the figures on the vase is somewhat bizarre, but similar to that on another Etruscan red-figured stamnos, H.B. WALTERS *Catalogue of the Greek and Etruscan Vases in the British Museum*, London 1896, F 484 (Painter of London F 484, see BEAZLEY ibid.) The Berlin mirror showing Aphrodite, inscribed *turan ati* = mother Aphrodite, and Adonis, youthful and winged (see *Subject and interpretation*), apparently the first representation of the pair (*c.* 400 BC), offers an alternative identification of the figures on the British Museum mirror.

The mirror is one of the very few examples to have a figured bronze handle: a mirror in the Walters Art Gallery, Baltimore, inv. 54.105, has a handle in the form of a nude Lasa, but this may be alien (cf. DE GRUMMOND *Guide* p.11, n.13); an example from the Collection Dutuit has a standing support in the form of a female figure with drapery swathed around the legs, whose association with the mirror is also somewhat suspicious, though REBUFFAT-EMMANUEL decided nonetheless that it must belong (D. REBUFFAT-EMMANUEL in *MonPiot* 60, 1976, pp.65–6). The handle of the British Museum mirror, which resembles Etruscan paterae handles of female form, cf. WALTERS *BMBronzes* no.755 (= HAYNES *EtrBr* no.179), appears to have been brazed on; if it was an addition in antiquity, as the uniform patina indicates, then the original tang must have been cut off, but it is a little odd that such an elaborate handle should have been added to a mirror of such inferior quality. There are also certain features shared with the warrior figure, of which the authenticity is in doubt (see discussions below). One wonders, too, why the disc suffered so many breaks, being of such stoutness: deliberate disfigurement for the tomb normally involved blows with a chisel-like object, not dropping on a hard surface, as was the possible cause of the damage to this mirror. In addition, the feet of the figure seem to have been broken off before they became patinated (I understand from Dr Susan La Niece in the British Museum's Department of Scientific Research that the corrosion is likely to have been produced over centuries of burial rather than during two hundred years or so above ground, but as yet there is no scientific means of proving this). Another curious feature is the high level of cassiterite on the reflecting surface of the disc, which could indicate that the mirror was tinned, again a feature not paralleled by any other Etruscan mirror, at least not by any published examples (as discussed above, the cassiterite could be a natural corrosion product, but this does not explain why it has been found only on the obverse).

The authenticity of the mirror is therefore in serious doubt, like some of the other objects in the so-called *cista mistica* group. Perhaps it is worth noting that it was a silversmith who originally brought the group to the attention of James Byres (BAILEY p.131). The miscellany of objects, belonging to such widely differing dates and origins, some having undoubtedly been 'improved upon', certainly did not form a true tomb-group.

Townley's '*cista mystica*' group (fig.36, p.192).
The group of objects with which the mirror is associated were said to have been found together by Cesare Petrini (BAILEY p.131 and n.7), but although Petrini found the Casali cista, it is uncertain whether he also found the other cistae. His brother says these were found in two 'caverns' in Palestrina, but does not name the finder (P.A. PETRINI *Memorie Prenestine disposte in Forma di Annali*, Rome 1795, p.27). The *cista mistica* group was acquired by James Byres in 1786, and sold by him to Townley: in 1793 Byres wrote a letter to Townley giving information about the group, but it is uncertain whether the bronzes were already in the latter's possession. The letter is in the Department of Greek and Roman Antiquities, and is quoted in full by BAILEY (p.131). A folder of Townley's also in the Department,

containing documents regarding the *cista mistica*, has on the outside a heading written by Townley stating that the objects were found in 'a small vaulted chamber joining to the walls of a Temple in the lower part of Ancient Praeneste'. It is therefore not the case that the finds were made near the Temple of Fortuna Primigenia, a mistake originally made by Townley himself when annotating Skelton's engravings, and reiterated in various publications concerning the *cista mistica* (BAILEY p.132).

The other objects from the group are listed below: they are all discussed by BAILEY, together with the results of scientific examination and bibliography. Principal in the group is the cista, to whose significance Townley devoted much attention and hence its epithet.

Bronze cista and lid, GR 1814.7–4.703, BAILEY's no.VII, with bibliography: WALTERS *BMBronzes* no.743; G. BORDENACHE BATTAGLIA and A. EMILIOZZI, *Le ciste prénestine* I, I, Florence 1979, no.35; FÖERST *GPC* no.32; DE GRUMMOND 'Some unusual landscape conventions in Etruscan art', *AntK* XXV, 1982, p.7, n.26; TOUCHEFEU-MEYNIER in *LIMC* s.v. Andromache, p.773, no.58, fig.10. The lid is made from an ancient bronze bowl with a modern copper rim attached, and the ancient lid of a small vessel has been applied at the centre.

Two large bronze jugs. One has handles in the form of post-medieval naked male, bearded figures, GR 1824.4–89.5 (the vase), GR 1824.4–64.1-2 (the handles) BAILEY no.I, and was disposed of by Townley to Richard Payne Knight, who bequeathed it with the rest of his collection to the British Museum in 1824; the other, GR 1814.7–4.968, BAILEY no.II, has two cast handles, one of which originally belonged to the other jug and was probably attached to this one before being acquired by Byres, and the other made to match it. Both jugs are difficult to date, but may perhaps be late Etruscan or early Roman.

Bronze bowl with omphalos and two handles, GR 1814.7– 4.699, BAILEY no.III, perhaps of the 4th century BC.

Bronze ladle, GR 1814.7–4.700, BAILEY no.IV, perhaps of the 5th or 4th century BC.

Bronze knife, GR 1814.7–4.701, WALTERS *BMBronzes* no.2759; BAILEY no.V, 8th century BC; A.-M. BIETTI SESTIERI in SWADDLING (ed.) *IIAA*, no.16, p.5 (Caracupa type, end 9th/8th century BC, diffused in southern Lazio and Campania), cf. V. BIANCO-PERONI *Praehistorische Bronzefunde*, Abteil 7, 2, Munich 1976, *Die Messer in Italien*, p.41, nos 146–55 (advanced Early Iron Age, 8th century BC, perhaps towards the end).

Pair of bronze cymbals, GR 1814.7–4.702 and 702★, BAILEY no.VI, perhaps of the 3rd century BC if genuinely found with the cista but equally well of Roman Imperial date.

Pair of bronze bracelets, GR 1814.7–4.705-6, BAILEY no.IX, 9th century BC. A comparable find from

Pithekoussai suggests a slightly later date, c.750–700 BC: G. BUCHNER and D. RIDGWAY *Pithekoussai I, La Necropoli: Tombe 1–723 scavate dal 1952–1961*, MonAL Serie Monografica IV, Tomb 283, no.9, p.340, drawing pl.109g, photograph pl.149, 9. The type is diffused in Campania and further south.

Bronze spoon, GR 1814.7–4.707, BAILEY no.X; WALTERS *BMBronzes* no.2459. This is a composite piece, the bowl of 3rd-century AD type with the original handle replaced by a steering oar, around which is entwined a dolphin, from a bronze group of the 1st or 2nd century AD.

Bronze incense-burner, GR 1814.7–4.708, BAILEY no.XI. There are no published parallels and although this could belong to the 3rd century BC, like the cista, it could be as late as the Roman Imperial period.

Bronze figure of a warrior, GR 1814.7–4.709, BAILEY no.XII; WALTERS *BMBronzes* no.456; P.J. RIIS *Tyrrhenika*, Copenhagen 1941, p.36. The figure stands in frontal pose with left leg slightly bent, wearing a cuirass and pteryges, greaves and an Attic helmet with the cheek-pieces turned up, the crest now missing, as are the spear and shield; the shoulder-flaps of the cuirass are shown in prominent relief, and given a fur- or hide-like texture, almost as though the artist has misinterpreted them as part of an animal-skin. Again, there are few parallels: if ancient, the figure could perhaps be placed in the 3rd century BC, but the scientific examination places its authenticity in some doubt. The composition of a drilled sample from the calf was analysed by atomic absorption spectrometry by CRADDOCK (P.T. CRADDOCK *StEtr* 1984 p.243) and although the metal composition is acceptable for an ancient bronze, the copper content is slightly higher than in most Etruscan bronzes, and the nickel is also a little high. Most of the patina is artificial, much of the dark brown being resin, perhaps shellac, and over this are patches of green and blue malachite and azurite. Although these are normal corrosion products of bronze, they could not have formed naturally over the resin. Under the resin there is bright metal but there is some pitting and at least one area of cuprite, the normal red/brown corrosion product of copper. Genuine antiquities were not infrequently stripped and repatinated in accordance with the taste of 19th-century collectors such as Townley, but the stylistic anomalies of this piece, together with the rather unattractive and very deliberately deceptive nature of the patina suggest that the entire figure may be fake (technical information from British Museum Department of Scientific Research report, Project 6981, by Susan La Niece, 14 October 1997).

BAILEY concludes (pp.136–7) that the group comprises a heterogeneous collection of objects, but that the mirror and the cista (without its lid), the ladle, the incense-burner, the warrior, the jugs and the bowl (with or without handles) could have belonged to a tomb group of the 3rd century BC. We do not, however, have any firm evidence that they belonged together, and the new evidence about the warrior figure puts its authenticity in doubt.

34 [figs pp.178–80, 190–91]

Circular tanged mirror with extension and alien bronze handle

Menerva (Athena), Herkle (Herakles)

GR 1814.7–4.2869

Provenance. Said to be from Perugia. Second Townley collection; previously A. Ansidei collection, Rome, as noted on a print from the Townley collection, by DEMPSTER and in the *ES* entry.

Bibliography. DEMPSTER I 78, pl. 6 (illustrated without handle); GORI *Mus. Etr.* 2, p.411; PASSERI *Paralipomena ad Dempster* p.28; G.B. VERMIGLIOLI *Iscriz. Perugine*, Perugia 1804, pl.II, 2, p.52; A.L. MILLIN *Galérie Mythologique: Recueil de monuments pour servir a l'etude de la mythologie*, Paris 1811, II, pl.172 *bis*, p.249, no.436; LANZI *Saggio* II, 7, p.162, pl.11, no.1; HAWKINS III pp. 223–4, fig. 5; BYRES *Hypogaei*, pt.5, pl.7; MOSES *Greek Vases*, pl.67; GERHARD *ES* II pl.CXXXIV; III p.129; VAUX *BM Handbook* p.421; CII no.1063; CONESTABILE *Dei Monumenti di Perugia* IV, pl.77 = 103, fig.1, p.462, no.690; WALTERS *BMBronzes* no.544; BEAZLEY *JHS* 1949 p.4, fig.2; DE SIMONE *Entleh.* I p.71 n.9; A. BIRCHALL and P.E. CORBETT, *Greek Gods and Heroes*, London 1974, p.17, fig.22; PFISTER-ROESGEN *Spiegel* S 28, pp.48ff., 135–6 taf.30; FISCHER GRAF *Vulci* p.24, n.258; HAYNES *EtrBr* no.123, p.291; RIX *ET* p.353 Pe S.2.

Material and condition. Bronze. Lustrous, golden-coloured metal which has been abraded and polished. There is occasional black tarnish, and a few small pitted areas contain a malachite/cuprite layer, as found between the beads of the rim. The edge has been severely filed or abraded, and the upper profile of the beads on the obverse flattened. There is some smooth dark green patination around the beads and in the lines of the decoration and crevices of the reverse; this is of modern origin, and there is no original surface beneath it. Some slight roughening of the surface, perhaps due to corrosion which has been removed, occurs mainly over the diagonal upper left half of the obverse. Judging by the dendritic lines visible over much of the surface of the entire mirror, and in the lines of the decoration, the entire object has been etched to remove the original corrosion; the only ancient corrosion remaining is a green carbonate between the beads of the edge, and in some of the pitting. The object was then patinated artificially with the smooth dark green layer mentioned above, but it was apparently decided to remove this by abrasion to make the decoration more visible. Black pigment was then rubbed into the lines, and more recently the surface has been waxed, with some wax still remaining in the crevices. On the obverse motif, the upper palmette, the spirals and the bands linking them have been re-cut after etching, while the dolphins and spirals to the sides are worn or abraded (fig.33, p.191). Cracks occur around the disc, converging towards the centre, the deepest to the upper left of the obverse, also showing on the upper right of the reverse. Three circular cavities occur just above the waist of Menerva, and another is just over the left elbow of Herkle. The originally flat tang has been filed into a short, round stub and a small hole drilled through it. The beading ends about

1.0–1.5mm from each side of the stub and so the original tang could have been about 7.0mm wide. Attached to the stub are the remains of modern lead solder.

The handle was previously soldered to the stub and is evenly covered with a modern black patination; this has been applied over a partly abraded ancient corrosion layer (malachite has been abraded from the high spots, revealing cuprite). The collar has been lightly filed in modern times leaving a bright metal surface, but the basic shape is probably original. The hole at the top, into which the stub fitted, has been reamed out in modern times, and at the bottom of the hole can be seen the broken-off top of a corroded iron rod which, when tested with a magnet, was found to extend about 2.5cm into the handle. A small hole, 0.15cm in diameter, has been cut through on opposite sides of the hole, immediately below the collar, to correspond with the hole in the tang, to accommodate a pin.

Measurements. W. 15.9cm. H. 18.7cm. H. of tang 0.4mm. W. of extension at top 3.0cm. H. of handle 10.2cm. Wt. (without handle) 623g.

Type. Circular, thick, flat disc with vertical edge, made in one piece with an extension in the shape of a half-oval, and probably originally with a conventional, flat, tapering tang. The cast bronze handle is in the form of a Herakle's club tapering towards the extension, with a plain, round collar where it meets the extension, and terminating in a lion's head backed by a disc at a right angle to the handle. Centre point below Herkle's right thumb.

Decoration.
OBVERSE. The edge of the disc and also of the extension is beaded. The decorative motif on the extension and at the base of the disc consists of a five-lobed palmette above two addorsed spirals, the coils of the upper two bound by a band with a narrow, plain border along both edges, and the lower two by a band hatched diagonally and also with two narrow, plain borders. Beneath the lower pair is a double arc and above them a seven-lobed palmette. Beneath the upper spirals to either side emerges a semi-palmette with four lobes. Rising from the lower palmettes to either side is a long tendril which follows the contour of the disc, with one main coil and two more linked coils, surmounted by small dolphins drawn in outline only.

REVERSE. The border is formed by a deeply undulating ivy stem, whose two ends meet at the top in an irregular bunch of berries. An ivy leaf and normally a group of three berries grow in each loop of the wavy stem, and they are arranged so that each leaf faces outward save for the lowest which springs up vertically in the extra large loop at the base, and a smaller leaf above it. Below this loop is another stem coiled round in a circle with another upward-growing leaf within it which is decorated with a spiky bud formation. The circle is linked to the loop above by a curved stem to either side.

The exergue is formed by a band of zigzag with hatched triangles and below it eleven lobes or petals radiating from

a central point at the base, diminishing in width to either side in three-dimensional fashion.

The figured scene is formed by a group of Herkle, Menerva and a three-headed snake. The goddess is named to the left by the shoulder, right to left:

 menerva

and Herkle above his left upper arm, left to right:

 herkle

Both are striding to the left, with right foot advanced, their bodies shown frontally and heads in profile looking back to the right. Menerva, left, has both arms crooked up in front of her, gesticulating toward Herkle with her right hand, and grasping her spear, furnished with a number of horizontal struts (cf. no.24 in this volume) and a short loop midway, in her left. She has both feet in profile, while Herkle has his right leg and foot in profile and the left shown frontally, the foot overlapping the ivy of the border. He seems to have stepped to the left but is now turning, his torso frontal but head looking back, in profile to the right, his right arm crooked with the hand in front of the lion's face, possibly clasping two or three small spherical objects – the depiction is ambiguous here. Menerva is winged, the wings rising up and then branching outward, the longer coverts edged with hatched bands and the smaller ones shown as dotted scales, those of the right wing appearing to the left of her head. Her wavy hair hangs down at her back, with a fringe and several strands in front of the ears. She wears a plain diadem with a narrow plain border. The aegis is represented as a short mantle, fastened in front, as it were, by the gorgon's head, with a single, triple-headed snake rising to either side of it. The aegis has a plain wide border at the neck, and another border at the lower edge, decorated with circles; the scales are like the small coverts of the wings but inverted. Menerva wears two plain bracelets and what appear to be two armlets just below the elbows with circlets hanging from them. Her long garment has an overfold hanging to the hips at either side and rising to the waist at the front; this, the upper layer of the three-fold skirt of the garment, and the folds of a mantle emerging beneath her right forearm, have plain borders. All the layers of the garment hang in folds with zigzag edges and the central panel of the upper layer of the skirt has wavy diagonal lines branching upwards. Her feet appear to be bound with the thongs of sandals but no soles are indicated.

Left of Menerva is a three-headed snake, each head bearded, with a raised patch at the back and with a forked tongue and rows of regular teeth. The lower body is in a tight coil, the necks and upper sides of the bodies decorated with flame shapes and the undersides with a line divided into squares rather like the rows of teeth. The heads are arched menacingly towards Menerva. Herkle, following her closely, clutches his club in his right hand, and in his left what are presumably the golden apples of the Hesperides: if so, then the snake is presumably Ladon, guardian of the tree from which the apples were taken. He has short, curly hair and is naked apart from the lion-skin draped over his left upper arm, the mane rising up from the furrowed brow. Three paws and the tail dangle down behind. Between his feet lies his quiver, which he seems to have dropped – one side is decorated with scales and the other by curves, rather like a snake's body, the end curled round like a tail. It has a loop and a cloth lining showing at the neck.

HANDLE. The handle is round in section and tapers towards the top where the tang fits into a recess in a narrow plain collar; the recess is only 0.4cm deep. The handle is modelled three-dimensionally in the form of a wooden club, the knurls taking the form of hollowed-out, tear-drop shapes, with a globule at the base of each hollow. The handle terminates in a snarling lion's head also modelled three-dimensionally and at a right angle to it, backed by a saucer-shaped disc with a rope pattern around the edge, all cast in one.

Subject and interpretation. Herkle (Herakles), Menerva and a serpent-like creature with three heads, perhaps a version of the serpent, Ladon, guarding the tree bearing the Golden Apples of the Hesperides; this latter, however, seems unlikely, since Herkle and Menerva are hastening towards the creature, while Herkle may have the fruit already in his hand. Herkle is not shown attempting to cut off the heads of the creature, and there is no firm reason why it should be interpreted as the many-headed Hydra.

Characteristics of the decoration. The decoration appears to be chased. The lines are firm, and mostly of remarkably even depth and achieved with almost mechanical precision.

    There are a number of unusual features. *Obverse.* The double palmette motif is hard to parallel. The dolphins recall those leaping over waves which are found in the borders of wall-paintings ranging between the 5th and 3rd centuries BC, and also on a mirror in the Museum of Fine Arts, Boston, *CSE* USA 2, no.4, there dated no later than 450 BC. The lobes of the upper re-cut palmette are precise and regular while those of the other palmettes are irregular, and the dolphin on the left dips his nose down between the spirals while the head of the other remains nearer the horizontal, differing from archaic extension motifs which are usually symmetrical in intention.

    Reverse. Curious features of the decoration here are that every leaf is out-turned instead of alternating in direction; the U-shaped loops of the stem replace the normal milder undulations; the extension motif is illogical and merely an addition to the border (presumably an elaboration of the entwined stems occasionally found on mirrors such as nos 14 and 23 in this fascicule), the vertical duplication of the leaves within the loops recalling that of the palmettes on the obverse; the way in which the two stems meet at the top, in a kind of W, is also unparalleled; there are slight vari-

ations in the groups of berries, with a single one instead of three in one instance on the right, and a little above it a group of three without a stem, but such anomalies are not unusual in Etruscan art. Particularly surprising are the upstretched wings of Menerva, which are only otherwise paralleled by the Eros on the problematic mirror with figured handle (no. 33, this volume), and the scales of the aegis being simply inverted versions of the small coverts of the wings. Also uncharacteristic is the exergue with its three-dimensional petal decoration, perhaps intended to represent a phiale seen in profile. The hydra or serpent is a curious beast, not closely paralleled by any ancient representation. The mane of the lion-skin looks almost as though the artist has misunderstood it and made it into a plant-like feature (fig.32, p.191). The claws of the lion-skin are bird-like, with an unusual underside view of the paw to the right, and a kind of border around the skin itself. Nor is it clear what is intended by the two or three small discs in Herkle's left hand, which could be intended as the golden apples of the Hesperides, though in that case they are rather small; perhaps the artist has misunderstood the eye-sockets and muzzle of the lion-skin and made them into attributes.

Technical comment. See comments on the attachment of the handle in *Material and condition.*

Date. The mirror has until now, been traditionally dated in the publications as later 5th century, usually *c.*450–400 BC, which would thus make it early Classical but archaising, while the handle has long been acknowledged as alien and though it could be ancient, perhaps belonging to a small Roman utensil, the termination of the Herakles' club in a lion's head could be a relatively modern conceit (the alloy indicating only that it could be, but is not certainly, ancient). The mirror itself has a number of strange features, including those which are mentioned in *Characteristics of the decoration,* above. It is hard to parallel in style of decoration and in mirror type. For an Etruscan mirror with broader, semi-oval extension, however, see RICHTER *MMBronzes* no.813, pp.279–80, of unknown provenance, purchased in 1896, reverse undecorated but with palmette and addorsed spiral as extension motif on the obverse. The only convincing association of the mirror is with one from the Salting bequest acquired by the Victoria and Albert Museum in 1910 (E.A. LANE, *JHS* 57, 1937, pp.219–23, pl.VII), which has a scene of a satyr making advances to a maenad and is remarkably similar in style and spirit: most notable are the vigorous sideways movement of the maenad, which resembles that of Menerva, with arms bent up in similar pose and head turned back in profile, the details of the drapery, which likewise cannot be paralleled in Etruscan art (the swathes round the maenad's waist resemble the garment of Herkle on the Herkle and Mlacuch mirror, no. 20, this volume), and the zigzag hatched exergue, which resembles the British Museum mirror but is here – again unparalleled – manoeuvred to fill the entire exergue. The extension of the Victoria and Albert mirror is arc-shaped which, like the semi-oval of the British Museum example, is rare for an Etruscan mirror. Unfortunately no findspot or further history are attached to the Victoria and Albert mirror, and so we are no nearer to the origin of the British Museum mirror.

BEAZLEY has suggested that there may have been a three-figured original showing Menerva/Athena, Herkle/Herakles and Atlas, of which a mirror in the Vatican preserves the right half (PFISTER-ROESGEN *Spiegel* S 27, Mus.Greg.Etr. Inv. 12242) and the British Museum mirror the left half. The Athena on the Athena and Athanasia mirror in Paris, Cabinet des Médailles 1289 (REBUFFAT *Miroir* pp.68ff., 536, pl.7), with her cape-like aegis, layered drapery and outspread wings, also recalls the goddess here. The inscriptions on the British Museum mirror, however, are consistent with a date in the 5th century BC and, if copied from an ancient original, as Dr Pandolfini has pointed out (personal communication), must be a very faithful reproduction. Perhaps all three mirrors point back to an original Etruscan representation now lost.

The strongest possibility for the British Museum mirror is that it constitutes an ancient mirror, plain apart from the relief decoration of the edge, with the chased decoration added in relatively modern times (prior to 1723/4, when DEMPSTER's *De Etruriae Regali* was completed for publication, together with the addition of the plates, at the expense of Thomas Coke). This would have to have happened before the object was etched with some kind of acid, since the etchmarks traverse the chased lines. The piece then underwent a variety of treatments to achieve the desired effect (see *Material and condition*). The flat, stout and particularly heavy disc of even section indicates a date that cannot be much past the middle of the 5th century BC. The date of the Boston mirror quoted above as a parallel for the dolphin decoration (*Characteristics of the decoration*) would concur with this. If this assessment of the decoration is correct, this would be one of the earliest Etruscan mirrors with fake decoration, pre-dating Thomas Coke's publication of DEMPSTER's work in 1723 (see also, however, no.31 in this fascicule).

35   [figs pp.181–3]

Circular tanged mirror with extension
Hippocamp, two nereids

GR 1849.5–19.7

Provenance. Bought from John Doubleday, dealer and restorer, notably of the Portland Vase (see N. WILLIAMS *The Making and Breaking of the Portland Vase*, London 1989, pp.5–7), who acquired it at the Blayd sale, 13 February 1849. Previously Thomas Blayd collection; Pizzati collection, formerly in Florence.

Bibliography. INGHIRAMI *Etrusco Museo* I, pl.104, p.96 (with style improved upon and with border decoration not present on mirror); GERHARD *ES* I pl. LXV (reversed); III, pp.66–7.

Material and condition. Bronze. A small circular hole has been drilled through the top of the disc, either in antiquity or in modern times, prior to acquisition. It is not shown in GERHARD *ES*, but such a detail may have been thought unnecessary. Both sides of the disc and the edge have a thick, rough, green corrosion; the surfaces of the tang are smoother, with some cuprite, and its edges were filed in antiquity. On the tang, showing as slight vertical ridges, are traces of an organic material, probably remains from an original bone, ivory or wooden handle. The flanges on the reverse of the extension do not taper towards the base but end abruptly where the handle fitted on to the tang.

Measurements. W. 14.9cm. H. 18.3cm. W. across points 2.0cm. H. of tang 2.9cm. W. of tang at neck 1.8cm. Wt. 282g.

Type. Circular, flat mirror of even thickness, with thick, raised rim and slightly inturned edge, small, straight-sided extension and blunt-ended tang. No centre point visible.

Decoration.
OBVERSE. The edge of the disc and the sides of the extension are serrated in imitation of beading. The motif on the extension and base of the disc consists of a five-lobed palmette above two addorsed spirals with a single leaf on a stem to either side; the stems of the spirals branch out to either side, curving round at the ends with another stem extending beyond, terminating in a now indistinguishable design. Below the central spirals are two double V-shapes.

REVERSE. Two nereids, sitting facing each other, one on a hippocamp. Both are in similar positions in three-quarter view, heads in profile, with the arms nearest the spectator slightly behind them and resting their weight on the hand. Both have their hair swept back from the face, the one on the right with long hair down her back, the one on the left with shorter hair and a plain diadem. The latter sits 'side-saddle' on the hippocamp's back, slightly hunched; she is nude apart from the drapery around her left arm which is blown back behind her, giving the impression that she has just ridden up. Her left foot is shown in profile and the right foot probably frontal but incomplete. The hippocamp, keen-eyed and with ears pricked up, has a muzzle more like that of a dog or deer, or perhaps a long-snouted fish, than that of a horse. The front limbs are webbed and there is a spiky mane; the length of the body from below the jowl is decorated with a row of circles, while the underside of the body is marked off by roughly scalloped lines. The extremity of the tail is crude and lumpy. The nereid on the right sits on drapery, her right arm bent up holding a sceptre. A single line above her left ankle may indicate a shoe.

Characteristics of the decoration. What remains of the motif on the obverse is simple and careful, if somewhat basic, and achieved with a broader implement than that used on the reverse. It is filled with ancient, pale green patination, and is undoubtedly authentic, though it is now difficult to tell whether it was chased or engraved.

The entire decoration of the reverse, however, has been chased, and cuts through the patination, occasionally chipping it away to either side. If the drawing follows ancient lines, then they have been completely obliterated, but this is unlikely, since the scratchy, improvised nature of the cutting seems too spontaneous to be following an ancient original. The whole scene is somewhat sketchy, particularly the hair, faces and abruptly ending drapery of the figure on the left. The drapery on the right is somewhat schematic but there is an attempt to make it look more realistic. The sceptre of the right-hand figure is out of alignment above and below her hand, its finial is roughly drawn, and the feet of the figures are unfinished. The tail of the hippocamp, as already noted, is careless and clumsy, though the forepart of the animal is fairly convincingly portrayed and it has an alert expression, which cannot be said of the figures, who have a blank, pupil-less stare and minimal indication of the mouth. The nereid on the right has a prominent forehead with too short upper lip. The almond-shaped eyes are frontal in a profile face, the chins heavy and the necks short; the faces are in fact quite archaic-looking, with the eyes low at the sides of the nose. The anatomy on the other hand is more advanced, albeit somewhat crudely indicated, with the silhouettes fairly fluid and competent; the internal markings are nonetheless schematised, particularly that of the right-hand figure, with its vertical division of the rib cage and the common device of two horizontal lines above the navel, which is conventionally indicated by a hook. Both have too high, wide-apart breasts. On the plus side, there is an effective contraction of the front torso of the left-hand figure and the three-quarter views of the both are fairly successful.

Subject and interpretation. Two nereids, one riding a hippocamp, perhaps Thetis and Juno (cf. INGHIRAMI). For a similar rider on a hippocamp, see *CSE* BRD 4, no.36 (*ES* I pl.CXIX, p.119) described as Amor or Eros on his voyage to the Underworld; also ibid. n.249 for Odysseus in the Underworld. The decoration of the last mirror is, however, also suspect (see below).

Date. The mirror itself is without doubt ancient, with modern incised decoration on the reverse. The object is probably of the mid- to late 5th century BC, given the type, section and design of the motif on the obverse. For the theme of a nude rider on a hippocamp, see a mirror in Berlin, *CSE* BRD 4, no.36 (= *ES* pl. CXIX), here also 'side-saddle' but winged and holding a sword, on a mirror belonging to GERHARD, and said to be from Bomarzo. It is interesting that Gerhard's mirror has features similar to those of the modern decoration on a mirror in the British Museum (no.36, this volume), notably the spiral used to denote the shoulder muscle, here on the hippocamp and there on the dog, and the use of triple circles as a decorative motif, here on the hippocamp's body and there on the spearman's tunic. Though the decoration of this mirror, too, might therefore appear suspect, ZIMMER accepts it as authentic

and belonging to the latter part of the 4th century BC (*CSE* ibid., with comparanda), in which case it could perhaps have inspired the modern decoration both of the Berlin mirror and of no.36. The theme of hippocamp and rider is frequently found on the lids of Praenestine cistae, but as these cistae were so often in the 19th century either decorated with incised scenes, or the original scenes so completely re-incised that all trace of original decoration has gone, the designs on them cannot certainly be regarded as authentic. These observations are based on examination in the British Museum's Department of Scientific Research (for examples see WALTERS *BMBronzes* no.638 (= G.B. BATTAGLIA *Le Ciste Prenestine*, I, I, Rome 1979, pp. 112-15, no.29, pl. CXXXV-CXXXIX), 639, 640, 648).

36   [figs pp.184–6, 190]

Circular tanged mirror with rudimentary extension
Two warriors with dog

GR 1840.2–12.11

Provenance. Unknown. Bought at the sale of the collection of Samuel Butler, Bishop of Lichfield, 1840, lot 107 (see no.32 in this fascicule).

Bibliography. MS. Acquisitions pp.4a, 24.

Material and condition. Bronze. *Obverse.* Good condition, the bare metal showing with a dull sheen through a smooth even layer of red cuprite, partially overlaid by smooth green corrosion, with small pits bearing traces of a black substance. The green corrosion is rougher on the tang. Both sides of the disc appear to have been scraped and abraded, and patches of iridescence suggest that some chemical stripping has been carried out. The lines on the obverse contain mud and corrosion, while those on the reverse have only dirt and dust. Written in black ink left of the centre is 'B & M Lot 107 1840', referring to the sale of the Bishop of Lichfield's collection, though the significance of the letters B and M is uncertain. *Edge.* Bears similar patination to the that of the obverse, with green corrosion over red cuprite. *Reverse.* Again a layer of cuprite overlaid with green corrosion with the bare metal occasionally showing through; where it has been tooled, the entire decoration being a modern addition, the deep incision has chipped away the corrosion to either side, and further partial stripping has left rough, dark areas of metal similar to that of the incisions.

Measurements. W. 15.5cm. H. 22.4cm.

Type. Circular, flat disc mirror, thickening slightly towards the rim, with vertical edge and vestigial extension; made in one piece with a stout tang tapering minimally towards the base. Centre point midway between figures.

Decoration.

OBVERSE. The rim is beaded and at the base of the disc, continuing over the extension and on to the tang, is a palmette decoration. The lower part of the design is almost impossible to decipher, but included an inverted palmette; the upper palmette rests on a pair of horizontally placed double spirals, with leaf shapes springing from them.

REVERSE. The border consists of a continuous undulating stem with leaves alternating to either side, and two lines curve down from either side of the extension and on to the tang. The figured scene consists of two spearmen with a dog between, all faced to the left; they are perhaps intended to be moving forwards, but have come to a temporary halt, the two men with heads inclined, maybe looking down towards the dog. The man on the left has turned so that his torso is frontal and his face is shown in profile to the right. Both men wear high-crested helmets decorated with spirals on the domes, cuirasses with spiral decoration over the breasts and short tunics (that on the left decorated with two circles); the man on the right has greaves. They each carry a sheathed sword, a pair of spears and a pelta-shaped shield, that on the left fitted with an arm-band and handgrip, that on the right fitted with an arm-band only which is not in use. The dog, with pointed nose and rounded ears, is of indeterminate breed, but is probably meant to be a hound. The figures are unintelligibly inscribed, the words seemingly written from left to right going diagonally downwards.

Above the dog:

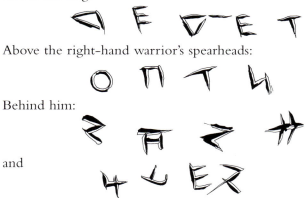

Above the right-hand warrior's spearheads:

Behind him:

and

Left of the left-hand warrior's legs:

Subject and interpretation. Two warriors with a dog. Most probably a genre scene; the inscriptions are nonsensical.

Characteristics of the decoration. Both sides are engraved, but the obverse motif was engraved in antiquity while the decoration on the reverse is modern (see also *Material and condition*). The motif on the obverse is cut with a fine tool using a light but firm touch, and the design has been carefully worked out using common, conventional elements. The engraving of the reverse, by a modern hand, cuts

through the adjacent corrosion and is deep, sharp and relatively clean. The border is executed with a certain degree of care and regularity, but the craftsman clearly has limited ability. For authentic early mirrors with continuous ivy leaf borders, see DE PUMA in *CSE USA* I, p.30. The lines are mostly broad and decisive, although finer and lighter in the area of the right-hand warrior's torso and upper shield, where bare metal shows and perhaps the craftsman thought it unnecessary to incise as deeply, not having any patination to cut through. There are a number of illogicalities in the armour, most noticeably the confusion between shields and breastplates, and the craftsman has not understood the function of the arm-band on the right-hand shield; the handgrip of the left-hand shield seems to be confused with the warrior's fingers. The pelta-type shields themselves are unusual to find on an Etruscan mirror, and as SASSATELLI has remarked (see below under *Date*), the archaic Greek vase-paintings which may have inspired this type of scene are numerous. The spiral motif of the warriors' breastplates, occasionally used in ancient representations as stylised decoration on the breasts of muscled cuirasses, is also used to indicate the dog's shoulder.

Technical comment. Both the extension and the tang are slightly off-centre. The raised rim has been smoothed flat in the region of the extension and upper tang. The mirror is undoubtedly ancient, as is the motif on the obverse, but the entire decoration on the reverse is manifestly modern.

Date. The mirror itself probably belongs to the late 5th or early 4th century BC, still being flat in section but with a slight recessing of the vestigial extension on the reverse; the motif on the obverse is of a general, fairly undistinguished type and difficult to use for dating purposes. The style of the drawing is very close to the fake decoration on a mirror in Bologna, Inv. It. 729, coll. Palagi No. 1820, *CSE Italia* I, I, 1, no.42: the heads have the same downward inclination and the faces have similar jutting profiles, frontal eyes and short horizontal lines for the mouth; the men all have two spears and similar tall helmet-crests, and circles – albeit on different scales – are used to decorate the tunics of the man on the Bologna mirror and one of the men on the British Museum mirror; lastly, similar spirals are used to represent the musculature of the dog's shoulder and the men's breastplates on the British Museum mirror and the horse's shoulder on the Bologna mirror. In compiling this entry, SASSATELLI concluded that the Bologna mirror itself was modern. The British Museum mirror now in question, however, is of disc type and undoubtedly authentic, on the grounds of style, analysis and technique. If decorated by the same hand, then the craftsman of the 19th century, as we may assume he was, was working on both ancient and modern mirrors. SASSATELLI concluded that the Bologna mirror was acquired by the Museo Civico in about 1840, the date when the British Museum acquired its mirror. Presumably both Palagi and the Bishop of Lichfield acquired the mirrors, directly or indirectly, from the same source.

APPENDIX:
THE COMPOSITION OF THE ETRUSCAN MIRRORS

P.T. Craddock and D.R. Hook
Department of Scientific Research, The British Museum

Introduction and analytical methods

Of the 36 mirrors published here, 19 were analysed quantitatively about 20 years ago as part of a general survey of the composition of Etruscan bronzes (CRADDOCK 1986; NB mirror no.7, of uncertain origin, was published as a Greek mirror in CRADDOCK 1977). Other analyses of Etruscan mirrors performed at the British Museum for the *Corpus Speculorum Etruscorum* have appeared in the first Danish fascicule (SALSKOV-ROBERTS 1981) and the Cambridge fascicule (NICHOLLS 1993) and other analyses will appear in the *CSE* fascicle devoted to Oxford. All of these mirrors were analysed by atomic absorption spectrometry (AAS). Details of the methodology are given in HUGHES *et al.* (1976) and the estimates of reproducibility and detection limits accompany the Table. During the more concentrated study of the mirrors for this project, analysis was carried out on the remainder of the mirrors that had not been previously sampled, either because the metal was too thin to be drilled or too badly corroded. They were all subjected to qualitative surface analysis by energy dispersive X-ray fluorescence (XRF) (COWELL 1998). Any of these that were of an apparently unusual composition, low tin or high lead for example, were drilled for quantitative analysis by inductively coupled plasma emission spectrometry (ICP) (HOOK 1998). For this first fascicule of the British Museum collection the XRF analysis of mirror no.35 showed a high lead content at the surface and a sample drilling was taken, which ICP analysis showed in fact to contain only traces of lead.

Discussion

The analyses of the mirrors published here show that they are of tin bronze with only small amounts of other metals (Table). Their tin contents cluster around 10% which is similar to the tin content of the contemporary Etruscan bronzes generally (CRADDOCK 1986). Mirror no.17 is the sole outlier with only 4.5% of tin. A tin content of 10% in a bronze represents the optimum composition for maximum strength and hardness with minimal embrittlement. The polished metal has an attractive golden hue.

The lead content of the mirrors is generally low, only no.12 has what could be considered a deliberate addition of lead (3.4%). The general absence of lead in these mirrors stands in marked contrast to the contemporary Etruscan cast bronzes, as exemplified by the statuettes for instance (CRADDOCK 1986). About 75% of the statuettes had more than 1% of lead, the lead content being quite evenly spread from 1% to 15%.

The reason for the absence of lead in the mirrors lies in the methods used to shape them. The metallographic examination carried out by PANSERI and LEONI on ten Etruscan mirrors (1956 and 1957–8) suggested that they had been cast as blanks, heated to homogenise the alloy, then cold-hammered to shape and annealed before being given a final hammering, as evidenced by the twinned and strained grains of alpha-phase bronze. This structure was also found in an Etruscan mirror by GOODWAY (1989), as well as in mirrors examined from the British Museum's collections (SWADDLING *et al.*), and PANSERI and LEONI's interpretation was broadly confirmed.

Lead does not dissolve in copper or bronze but remains separate, normally dispersed as fine globules. If, however, there is more than a few percent of lead then there is a danger that the globules may link up to form macroscopic 'lakes' of lead within the metal. These are potential sources of weakness, acting as if they were cracks in the metal and opening up if the metal is hammered. None of the mirrors analysed by PANSERI and LEONI or GOODWAY contained more than traces of lead, but several of the Etruscan mirrors analysed subsequently for the *CSE* project etc. do in fact contain several percent of lead and it must be supposed that only very light hammering, if any, was performed on these mirrors.

Both of the separate mirror handles published here were cast and were originally held to their mirror discs by solder, although some others were held by rivets. They are both of leaded bronze, no.33 with 13.2% and no.7 with 16.0% of lead. Some other mirror handles whose analyses have already been published were also found to be leaded. The handles of some of the later mirrors seem often to be quite heavily leaded, with lead contents of more than 20% (CRADDOCK 1986, MAES and GENIN 1978 and MAES 1987, for example) at a time when heavily leaded bronzes were in general use by the Etruscans (CRADDOCK 1986, and CRADDOCK and BURNETT 1998).

The handle of mirror no.33 is held in place by a hard solder of very similar composition to the handle itself.

The rivet from an ancient repair on mirror no.12 is of unalloyed copper. The rivet on mirror no.6, however, is of brass and is thus likely to be a recent repair.

The level of the trace elements in the mirrors is quite low compared to ancient bronzes generally, but similar to the levels found in other Etruscan bronzes (CRADDOCK 1986). A distinguishing feature found in these and in other Etruscan bronzes is the rather elevated cobalt content in the metal, which presumably reflects the composition of the Tuscan copper ores that the Etruscans are likely to have used.

References

COWELL, M. 1998 'Coin analysis by energy dispersive X-ray fluorescence spectrometry', in W.A. ODDY and M.R COWELL (eds), *Metallurgy in Numismatics 4*, Royal Numismatic Society, Special Publication 30, London, pp.448–60.

CRADDOCK, P.T. 1977 'The composition of the copper alloys used by the Greek, Etruscan and Roman civilisations, 2: the archaic, Classical and Hellenistic Greeks', *Journal of Archaeological Science* 4, pp.103–24.

CRADDOCK, P.T. 1986 'The metallurgy and composition of Etruscan bronze', *Studi Etruschi* 52, pp.211–71.

CRADDOCK, P.T. and BURNETT, A.M. 1998 'The composition of Etruscan and Umbrian copper alloy coinage', in W.A. ODDY and M.R. COWELL (eds), *Metallurgy in Numismatics 4*, Royal Numismatic Society, Special Publication 30, London, pp.262–75.

GOODWAY, M. 1989 'Etruscan mirrors: a reinterpretation', *MASCA* 6, pp.25–30.

HOOK, D.R. 1998 'Inductively coupled plasma atomic emission spectrometry and its rôle in numismatic studies', in W.A. ODDY and M.R. COWELL (eds), *Metallurgy in Numismatics 4*, Royal Numismatic Society, Special Publication 30, London, pp.237–52.

HUGHES, M.J., COWELL, M.R. and CRADDOCK, P.T. 1976 'Atomic absorption techniques in archaeology', *Archaeometry* 18, pp.19–36.

MAES, L. and GENIN, G. 1978 'Annexe: examens de laboratoire', in R. LAMBRECHTS, *Les miroirs étrusques et prénestins des Musées Royaux d'Art et d'Histoire à Bruxelles*, Brussels, pp.373–7.

MAES, L. 1987 'Annexe: examens de laboratoire', in R. LAMBRECHTS, *CSE* Belgique 1, Brussels, pp.172–4.

MASCA Journal of the Museum Applied Science Centre for Archaeology.

NICHOLLS, R.V. 1993 *CSE* Great Britain 2, Cambridge.

PANSERI, C. and LEONI, M. 1956 'Sulla tecnica di fabbricazione degli specchi di bronzo etruschi', *StEtr* 25, pp.305–19.

PANSERI, C. and LEONI, M. 1957–8 'The manufacturing technique of Etruscan mirrors', *Studies in Conservation* 3, pp.49–63.

SALSKOV-ROBERTS, H. 1981 *CSE* Denmark 1, Odense.

SWADDLING, J., CRADDOCK, P.T., LA NIECE, S. and HOCKEY, M. 2000 'Breaking the mould: the overwrought mirrors of Etruria', in M. PEARCE, D. RIDGWAY, F.R. SERRA RIDGWAY, R.D. WHITEHOUSE and J.B. WILKINS (eds), *Ancient Italy in its Mediterranean Setting: Studies in Honour of Ellen Macnamara*, Vol. 4, *Accordia Specialist Studies on the Mediterranean*, University of London, pp.117–40.

Table of analyses of mirrors in this fascicule

No.	Part	Cu	Pb	Sn	Ag	Fe	Sb	Ni	Co	As*	Bi	Zn	Total	Wt/mg	Technique
1		Cu,Sn,tr.Pb													XRF
2		Cu,Sn,tr.As,tr.Pb													XRF
3		Cu,Sn													XRF
4		Cu,Sn,tr.Pb													XRF
5		Cu,Sn,tr.As,tr.Pb													XRF
6	Mirror	Cu,Sn,tr.As,tr.Pb													XRF
	Handle	Cu,Sn,some Pb													XRF
	Rivet	Cu,Zn,Pb													XRF
7	Mirror	89.5	0.55	8.90	0.040	0.46	0.10	0.050	0.010	0.10 ★			99.5		AAS
	Cast handle (cf no.33 below)	77.5	16.0	5.50	0.050	0.03	0.10	0.040	0.060	0.50	0.15		100.0		AAS
8		87.5	0.02	12.9	0.060	0.10	0.20	0.040		0.10			100.9	9.88	AAS
9		Cu,Sn,some Pb													XRF
10		Cu,Sn,tr.As.tr.Pb													XRF
11		Cu,Sn,tr.As,some lead. Zinc found on surface – probably electro-chemically stripped													XRF
12	Mirror	87.5	3.40	7.90	0.015	0.80		0.045	0.015	<0.3 ★	<0.001		100.2	11.00	AAS
	Rivet	98.5	0.05	0.50	0.150	0.02		0.035		<0.1 ★		0.01	99.6	10.25	AAS
13		86.5	0.03	11.8	0.002	0.22		0.040	0.020	<0.1 ★			99.0		AAS
14		93.0	0.02	7.10	0.002	0.15		0.025	0.010	0.10			100.4	10.69	AAS
15		Cu,Sn,tr.Pb													XRF
16		89.0	0.05	9.40	0.010	0.02		0.030	0.020	0.30 ★			99.6		AAS
17		94.5	0.05	4.50	0.005	0.03		0.010		0.10			99.2	10.38	AAS
18		88.5	1.00	9.70	0.030	0.11		0.040	0.010	0.10			99.5	11.27	AAS
19		87.0	0.06	11.0	0.050	0.13		0.010		0.20			98.5		AAS
20		91.5	0.08	8.20	0.010	0.04		0.030	0.030	0.30			100.2	10.58	AAS
21		89.0	0.06	9.80	0.035	0.05		0.050	0.005	0.20			99.2	10.97	AAS
22		Cu,Sn,tr.As													XRF
23		92.0	0.20	9.00	0.030	0.11	0.03	0.020		0.10 ★	0.01	0.02	101.4	20.27	AAS
24		89.0	0.05	11.7	0.030	0.30	0.05	0.030	0.260	0.06	0.01		101.5	26.02	AAS
25		90.5	0.03	8.90	0.050	0.12	0.09			0.05	0.02		99.8	14.24	AAS
26		89.0	0.95	8.50	0.040	0.22	0.04	0.040	0.020	0.02	0.01	0.01	98.9	21.60	AAS
27		90.0	0.10	10.8	0.040	0.09	0.04	0.050	0.005	0.10	0.01	0.03	101.3	16.48	AAS
28		Cu,Sn,tr.Pb													XRF
29		92.0	0.10	7.70	0.040	0.02		0.040	0.015	0.20			100.1	10.66	AAS
30		Cu,Sn,tr.Pb													XRF
31		Cu,Sn. Arsenic possibly applied to surface to give black colour?													XRF
32		Cu,Sn,some Pb													XRF
33	Mirror	87.0	0.90	11.0	0.002	0.12		0.040	0.020	0.10			99.2	9.75	AAS
	Cast handle	75.5	13.2	11.5	0.050	0.02		0.030	0.010	0.20			100.5	11.29	AAS
	Joint	72.3	14.0	10.0	0.090	0.07	0.04	0.025	0.009	0.30		0.03		13.81	AAS
34		Cu,Sn,tr.As,some Pb													XRF
35		89.4	0.38	8.85	0.074	0.03	0.02	0.050	0.024	0.18	0.12	<0.02	99.2	10.22	ICP
36		Cu,Sn,tr.Pb													XRF

Notes:

The results are expressed as weight per cent. 'tr.' denotes trace; '<' denotes an element not present above the quoted detection limit. AAS = atomic absorption spectrometry; ICP = inductively coupled plasma atomic emission spectrometry; XRF = X-ray fluorescence. Wt/mg denotes the sample weight used for quantitative analysis. Low sample weights result in higher detection limits and poorer precision. Blank = element not looked for or an element not found by AAS. The following approximate detection limits for AAS apply: Ag, Co, Ni 0.005; Bi, Fe, Pb, Sb, Zn 0.01; As 0.04; Sn 0.2. Gold, cadmium and manganese were also sought in some cases. Both AAS and ICP have a precision of approximately ±2% for copper, ±5–10% for tin, zinc and lead when present in major amounts, the remaining minor and trace elements have a precision of between ±10–30%, deteriorating to ±50% at the detection limit. Most of the arsenic contents were reanalysed recently using XRF – an asterisk '★' denotes an XRF figure has replaced the previously published AAS determination made in the early 1970s, when the estimation of arsenic presented considerable problems.

LIST OF ABBREVIATIONS

AA   *Archäologischer Anzeiger*

ActaArch   *Acta Archaeologica*

ADAM   R. ADAM, *Recherches sur les miroirs prénestins*, Paris 1980

AJA   *American Journal of Archaeology*

AM   *Mitteilungen des Deutschen Archäologischen Instituts, Athenische Abteilung*

AnnFaina   *Annali della Fondazione per il Museo «Claudio Faina»*, Orvieto

AnnInst   *Annali dell'Instituto di Corrispondenza Archeologica*

Ann.Inst.Philol.et d'Hist.   *Annuaire de l'Institut de Philologie et d'Histoire Orientales, Université Libre de Bruxelles*

AntK   *Antike Kunst*

ArchNews   *Archaeological News*

ArchReports   *Archaeological Reports*

Art and Technology   S. DOERINGER, D.G. MITTEN and A. STEINBERG (eds), *Art and Technology, A Symposium on Classical Bronzes*, Massachusetts Institute of Technology 1970

AZ   *Archäologische Zeitung*

BABesch   *Bulletin van de Vereeniging tot Bevordering der Kennis van Antike Beschaving*

BALENSIEFEN   L. BALENSIEFEN, *Die Bedeutung des Spiegelbildes als ikonographisches Motiv in der Antiken Kunst*, Tübingen 1990

BAYET *Herclé*   H. BAYET, *Étude critique des principaux monuments relatif à l'Hercule étrusque*, Paris 1926

BCH   *Bulletin de Correspondance Hellénique*

BEAZLEY *ARV²*   J.D. BEAZLEY, *Attic Red-figure Vase-painters*, 2nd edn, Oxford 1963

BEAZLEY *EVP*   J.D. BEAZLEY, *Etruscan Vase Painting*, Oxford 1947

BEAZLEY *JHS* 1949   J.D. BEAZLEY, 'The world of the Etruscan mirror', *JHS* 69, 1949, pp.1–17

BIRCHALL and CORBETT   A. BIRCHALL and P.E. CORBETT, *Greek Gods and Heroes*, London 1974

BMQ   *British Museum Quarterly*

BONAPARTE *Catalogo*   L. BONAPARTE, *Catalogo di scelte antichità etrusche trovate negli scavi del Principe di Canino, 1828 a 1829*, Viterbo 1829

BONFANTE *EtrLife*   L. BONFANTE (ed.), *Etruscan Life and Afterlife: A Handbook of Etruscan Studies*, Detroit/Warminster 1986

BONFANTE *Etruscan*   L. BONFANTE, *Etruscan* (part of the series 'Reading the Past'), London 1990

BOTHMER *Amazons*   D. VON BOTHMER *Amazons in Greek Art*, Oxford 1957

BRENDEL *EA*   O.J. BRENDEL, *Etruscan Art*, Harmondsworth 1978; re-published with additional bibliography by F.R. Serra Ridgway, New Haven 1995

BROMMER *Denkmälerlisten*   F. BROMMER, *Denkmälerlisten zur griechischen Heldensage*, I–III, Marburg 1971–1976

BROMMER *Vasenlisten*   F. BROMMER, *Vasenlisten zur griechischen Heldensage³*, Marburg 1973

BullInst   *Bullettino dell'Instituto di Corrispondenza Archeologica*

BYRES *Hypogaei*   J. BYRES, *Hypogaei, or Sepulchral Caverns of Tarquinia, the Capital of Ancient Etruria*, London 1842

CAMERON *Hand-mirrors*   F. CAMERON, *Greek Bronze Hand-mirrors in Southern Italy*, British Archaeological Reports, International Series 58, Oxford 1979

CIE   *Corpus Inscriptionum Etruscarum*

CII   A. FABRETTI, *Corpus Inscriptionum Italicarum*, Augustae Taurinorum 1867

CII App.   G.F. GAMURRINI, *Appendice al Corpus Inscriptionum Italicarum*, Florence 1880

CII Suppl.   A. FABRETTI, *Primo, Secondo, Terzo Supplemento alla raccolta delle antichissime iscrizione italiche*, 1872, 1874, 1878

CONESTABILE *Perugia*   G. CONESTABILE, *Dei Monumenti di Perugia etrusca e romana, della letteratura e bibliografia Perugina*, I–IV, Perugia 1855–1870

COOK *Zeus*   A.B. COOK, *Zeus, A Study in Ancient Religion*, I–III, Cambridge 1914–40

CORSSEN *Sprache*   W.P. CORSSEN, *Über die Sprache der Etrusker*, I–II, Leipzig 1874–1875

CRISTOFANI *Dizionario*   M. CRISTOFANI (ed.), *Dizionario della Civiltà Etrusca*, Florence 1985

CRISTOFANI *Civiltà*   M. CRISTOFANI (ed.), *Civiltà degli Etruschi (catalogo della mostra, Firenze, Museo Archeologico, 16 maggio–20 ottobre 1985)*, Milan 1985

CSE   *Corpus Speculorum Etruscorum*

CSE Belgique 1   R. LAMBRECHTS, *CSE Belgique 1*, Rome 1987

CSE BRD 1–4   U. HÖCKMANN, *CSE Bundesrepublik Deutschland* 1; U. LIEPMANN –2; B. VON FREYTAG GEN.LÖRINGHOFF – 3; G. ZIMMER – 4; Munich 1987, 1988, 1990, 1995

CSE DDR I–II   G. HERES, *CSE Deutsche Demokratische Republik I–II*, Berlin 1986–7

CSE Denmark 1   H. SALSKOV-ROBERTS, *CSE Denmark 1*, Odense 1981

CSE France 1   D. EMMANUEL-REBUFFAT, *CSE France 1*, I–III, Rome 1988, 1991, 1997

CSE Great Britain 2   R. NICHOLLS, *CSE Great Britain 2*, Cambridge, Cambridge 1993

CSE Hongrie-Tchecoslovaquie   J.G. SZILÁGYI and, J. BOUZEK, *CSE Hongrie-Tchecoslovaquie*, Rome 1992

CSE Italia 1–3   G. SASSATELLI, *CSE Italia 1*, Bologna, Museo Civico, I–II, Rome 1981; A. FRASCARELLI, *CSE Italia 2*, Perugia, Museo Archeologico Nazionale I, Rome 1995; G. CATENI, *CSE Italia 3*, Volterra, Museo Guarnacci, I, Rome 1995; M.S PACETTI, *CSE Italia 4*, Orvieto, Museo Claudio Faina, Rome 1998

CSE The Netherlands   L.B. VAN DER MEER, *CSE The Netherlands*, Leiden 1983

CSE USA 1–3   R. DE PUMA, *CSE USA 1–2*, Iowa 1987, 1993; L. BONFANTE, *CSE USA 3*, Rome 1997

CSE Vaticano 1   R. LAMBRECHTS, *CSE Stato della Città del Vaticano 1*, Rome 1995

CVA   *Corpus Vasorum Antiquorum*

DA   C. DAREMBERG and E. SAGLIO, *Dictionnaire des Antiquités grecques et romaines*, I–X, Paris 1877–1919

DE GRUMMOND *Guide*   N.T. DE GRUMMOND, *A Guide to Etruscan Mirrors*, Tallahassee 1982

DE LA CHAUSSE   M.A.C. DE LA CHAUSSE *Museum Romanum sive thesaurus eruditae antiquitatis*, 2nd edn, 1707

DEMPSTER   T. DEMPSTER, *De Etruria Regali*, published and appended by F. Buonarroti, Florence 1723–1726

DE SIMONE *Entleh.*   C. DE SIMONE, *Die griechischen Entlehnungen im Etruskischen*, I–II, Wiesbaden 1968, 1970

DE WITTE *Description* — J. DE WITTE, *Description des antiquités et objets d'art qui composent le cabinet de feu M. Le Chevalier E.Durand*, Paris 1836

DUCATI *AE* — P. DUCATI, *Storia dell'arte etrusca*, Florence 1927

DUCATI *RM* — P. DUCATI, 'Contributo allo studio degli specchi etruschi figurati', *RM* 27, 1912, pp.243–85

EAA — *Enciclopedia dell'Arte Antica Classica e Orientale*

Etr.Culture — *Etruscan Culture, Land and People* (Archaeological research and studies conducted in San Giovenale and its environs by Members of the Swedish Institute in Rome), Malmo and New York 1962

FIESEL *Geschlecht* — E. FIESEL *Das grammatische Geschlecht im Etruskischen*, Göttingen 1922

FISCHER GRAF *Vulci* — U. FISCHER GRAF, *Spiegelwerkstätten in Vulci*, Berlin 1980 (*Archäologische Forschungen* VIII)

FÖERST *GPC* — G. FÖERST, *Die Gravierungen der pränestischen Cisten*, Rome 1978

FRIEDERICHS — C. FRIEDERICHS, *Berlins antike Bildwerke. II. Geräte und Broncen im Alten Museum, Kleinere Kunst und Industrie im Alterthum*, Düsseldorf 1871

FRIEDERICHS-WOLTERS — P.H.A. WOLTERS, *Die Gipsabgüsse antiker Bildwerke im Neuen Museum in historischer Folge erklärt ... von C. FRIEDERICHS, neu bearbeitet von P. WOLTERS*, Berlin 1885

GERHARD *Schriften* — E. GERHARD, *Gesammelte Akademische Abhandlungen und Kleine Schriften*, Berlin 1886–1888

GERHARD *Schmückung* — E. GERHARD, *Die Schmückung der Helena*, Winckelmannsprogramm 4, Berlin 1844

GERHARD *ES* — E. GERHARD, *Etruskische Spiegel* I–IV, Berlin 1840–1867

GIGLIOLI *AE* — G.Q. GIGLIOLI, *L'Arte Etrusca*, Milan 1935

GORI *Mus.Etr.* — A.F. GORI, *Museum Etruscum, exhibens insignia veterum etruscorum* 1–3, Florence 1737–1743

GUATTANI *Mon.ant.ined.* — G.A. GUATTANI, *Monumenti antichi inediti, ovvero notizie sulle antichità e belle arti di Roma, per l'anno*, Rome 1784(–89)

HAWKINS — E. HAWKINS, MS *Catalogue of the Bronzes in the British Museum* (probably compiled soon after 1837)

HAYNES *EBU* — S. HAYNES, *Etruscan Bronze Utensils*, London 1965 (revised 1974)

HAYNES *EtrBr* — S. HAYNES, *Etruscan Bronzes*, London 1985

HERBIG-SIMON — R. HERBIG, *Götter und Dämonen der etrusker*, herausgegeben und bearbeitet von E. SIMON, Mainz 1965

HINKS *BMPaintings* — R.P. HINKS, *Catalogue of the Greek, Etruscan and Roman Paintings and Mosaics in the British Museum*, London 1933

INGHIRAMI *Etrusco Museo* — D.VALERIANI and F. INGHIRAMI, *Etrusco Museo Chiusino dai suoi possessori pubblicato*, Poligrafia Fiesolana, Florence 1833

INGHIRAMI *MonEtr* — F. INGHIRAMI, *Monumenti etruschi o di etrusco nome* I–IV, Fiesole 1821–1826

JAHN *Arch.Aufs* — O. JAHN *Archäologische Aufsätze*, Greifswald 1845

JbZMusMainz — *Jahrbuch des Römisch-Germanischen Zentralmuseums, Mainz*

JdI — *Jahrbuch des Deutschen Archäologischen Instituts*

JHS — *Journal of Hellenic Studies*

KLÜGMANN-KÖRTE *ES* — A. KLÜGMANN and G. KÖRTE, *Etruskische Spiegel* V, Berlin 1897

KRAUSKOPF *Sagenkreis* — I. KRAUSKOPF, *Der thebanische Sagenkreis und andere griechische Sagen in der etruskischen Kunst*, Mainz 1974 (Heidelberger Akademie der Wissenschaften Kommission für antike Mythologie, Schriften zur antiken Mythologie II)

LAMB *Bronzes* — W. LAMB, *Greek and Roman Bronzes*, 1929 (reprinted with additions, Chicago 1969)

LAMBRECHTS, *Mir. Mus. Royaux* — R. LAMBRECHTS *Les miroirs étrusques et prénestins des Musées Royaux d'Art et d'Histoire à Bruxelles*, Brussels 1978

LANZI *Saggio* — L. LANZI *Saggio di lingua etrusca e di altre antiche d'Italia*², I–III, Florence 1824

LEROI *Catalogue* — P. LEROI, *Catalogue des objets d'art antiques du Moyen-Age et de la Renaissance, dependant de la succession Alessandro Castellani*, Vente à Rome, 17 Mars–

10 Avril 1884

LIMC — *Lexicon Iconographicum Mythologiae Classicae*, Zurich and Munich

MACNAMARA *Etruscans* — E. MACNAMARA, *The Etruscans*, London 1990

MANSUELLI *StEtr 1942* — G.A. MANSUELLI, 'Materiali per un supplemento al "corpus" degli specchi etruschi figurati', in *StEtr* XVI, 1942, pp.531–51

MANSUELLI *StEtr 1943* — G.A. MANSUELLI, 'Materiali per un supplemento al "corpus" degli specchi etruschi figurati II', in *StEtr* XVII, 1943, pp.487–521

MANSUELLI *StEtr 1946–47* — G.A. MANSUELLI, 'Gli specchi figurati etruschi', in *StEtr* XIX, 1946–47, pp.9–137

MANSUELLI *StEtr 1948–49* — G.A. MANSUELLI, 'Studi sugli specchi etruschi. IV. La mitologia figurata negli specchi etruschi', in *StEtr* XX, 1948–49, pp.59–98

MARSHALL *BM Finger Rings* — F.H. MARSHALL, *Catalogue of the Finger-rings, Greek, Etruscan and Roman, in the Departments of Antiquities in the British Museum*, London 1907 (reprinted 1968)

MARSHALL *BM Jewellery* — F.H. MARSHALL, *Catalogue of the Jewellery, Greek, Etruscan and Roman, in the Departments of Antiquities in the British Museum*, London 1911 (reprinted 1969)

MATTHIES *PS* — G. MATTHIES, *Die praenestinischen Spiegel*, Strasbourg/Göttingen 1912

MAYER-PROKOP — I. MAYER-PROKOP, *Die gravierten etruskischen Griffspiegel archaischen Stils*, Heidelberg 1967

MICALI *Mon.* — G. MICALI, *Monumenti per servire alla storia degli antichi popoli italiani*, Florence 1832

MICALI *Mon.Ined.* — G. MICALI, *Monumenti Inediti a illustrazione della storia degli antichi popoli italiani*, Florence 1844

MonInst — *Monumenti dell'Instituto di Corrispondenza Archeologica*

MonPiot — *Monuments et Mémoires, Fondation E. Piot*

MOSES *Greek Vases* — H. MOSES, *A Collection of Antique Vases, Altars, Paterae ...from various museums and collections*, London 1814

MS. Acquisitions — MS. Acquisitions, Greek and Roman Antiquities, British Museum 1840–1845

MURRAY *Handbook* — A.S. MURRAY, *Handbook of Greek Archaeology*, London 1892

MURRAY *Greek Bronzes* — A.S. MURRAY, *Greek Bronzes*, London 1898

Muse — *Muse* (Annual of the Museum of Art and Archaeology, Columbia)

Museum Bonaparte — *Museum Etrusque de Lucien Bonaparte Prince de Canino. Fouille de 1828 à 1829*, Viterbo 1829

NRIE — M. BUFFA, *Nuova raccolta di iscrizioni etrusche*, Milan 1935

NS — *Notizie degli Scavi di Antichità*

Öjh — *Jahreshefte des Österreichischen Archäologischen Instituts in Wien*

PASSERI *Paralipomena ad Dempster* — J.B. PASSERI in *T. Dempsteri libros de Etruria regali paralipomena, quibus tabulem eidem operi additae illustrantur ...* Lucca 1767

PFIFFIG *Religio* — A.J. PFIFFIG, *Religio etrusca*, Graz 1975

PFISTER-ROESGEN *Spiegel* — G. PFISTER-ROESGEN, *Die etruskischen Spiegel des 5.Jhs.v.Chr.*, Frankfurt 1975

Pulszky Memorial Exhibition — *Ferenc Pulszky (1814–1897) Memorial Exhibition*, Magyar Tudományos Akadémia, Múvészeti Gyújtemény, Budapest 1997

RALLO *Donne* — A. RALLO (ed.), *Le Donne in Etruria*, Rome 1989 (Studia Archeologica 52)

RALLO *Lasa* — A. RALLO, *Lasa. Iconografia e esegesi*, Florence 1974

RAOUL-ROCHETTE *Mon.Ined* — D.RAOUL-ROCHETTE, *Monuments inédits d'antiquité figurée, grecque, étrusque et romaine. Première partie, Cycle héroïque*, Paris 1833

RE — A. PAULI and G. WISSOWA, *Realencyclopädie der klassischen Altertumswissenschaft*

REBUFFAT *Miroir* — D. REBUFFAT-EMMANUEL, *Le miroir étrusque d'après la Collection du Cabinet des Médailles*, Rome 1973

RICHARDSON *Etruscans* — E. RICHARDSON, *The Etruscans: their Art and Civilization*, Chicago/London 1964

RICHTER *MMBronzes* — G.M.A. RICHTER, *The Metropolitan Museum of Art. Greek, Etruscan and Roman Bronzes*, New York 1915

Rix *ET*   H. Rix, *Etruskische Texte* 1–2, Tübingen 1991
RM   *Mitteilungen des Deutschen Archäologischen Instituts, Römische Abteilung*
Roscher   W.H. Roscher, *Ausführliches Lexikon der griechischen und römischen Mythologie*, I–VI, 1884–1937
Schneider   R. Schneider, *Die Geburt der Athena*, Abhandlung des Archäologisch-Epigraphischen Seminares der Universität Wien, hrsg. O. Benndorf u. O. Hirschfeld, Vienna 1880
Sprenger-   M. Sprenger, G. Bartoloni and M.
  Bartoloni   Hirmer, *The Etruscans*, New York 1983
Steingräber   S. Steingräber, *Etruskische Möbel*, Rome 1979
StEtr   *Studi Etruschi*
Swaddling (ed.) J. Swaddling (ed.), *Italian Iron Age Artefacts in the*
  IIAA   *British Museum; Papers of the Sixth British Museum Classical Colloquium 1982*, London 1986
Swaddling *et al.* J. Swaddling, P.T. Craddock, S. la niece and M. Hockey, 'Breaking the mould: the overwrought mirrors of Etruria', in M. Pearce, D. Ridgway, F.R. Serra Ridgway, R.D. Whitehouse and J.B. Wilkins (eds), *Ancient Italy in its Mediterranean Setting: Studies in Honour of Ellen Macnamara*, Vol. 4, *Accordia Specialist Studies on the Mediterranean*, London 2000, pp.117-40
Szilagyi   J.G. Szilagyi, 'Materiale etrusco e magnagreco in una collezione ungherese dell'ottocento (La collezione Fejérváry-Pulszky)', in *Scienze dell'Antichità: Storia Archeologia Antropologia* (Università degli Studi di Roma 'La Sapienza') 5, 1991, pp.483-572
Thes.L.E.I   *Thesaurus Linguae Etruscae. I. Indice Lessicale*

TLE   M. Pallottino, *Testimonia Linguae Etruscae*[2], Florence 1968
Touchefeu-   O. Touchefeu-Meynier, *Thèmes odysséens dans l'art*
  Meynier   *antique*, Paris 1968
Trendall *RVA*   A.D. Trendall, *The Red-Figured Vases of Apulia*, I, Oxford 1978
Trendall *RFSIS* A.D. Trendall, *Red-Figure Vases of South Italy and Sicily: A Handbook*, London 1989
van der Meer   L.B. van der Meer, *Interpretatio Etrusca, Greek Myths*
  Interpretatio *on Etruscan Mirrors*, Amsterdam 1995
Vaux *BM*   W.S.W. Vaux, *Handbook to the British Museum*,
  Handbook   London 1851
Walters   H.B. Walters, *Catalogue of the Bronzes, Greek,*
  BMBronzes   *Roman and Etruscan in the Department of Greek and Roman Antiquities, British Museum*, London 1899
Walters *BMGems* H.B. Walters, *Catalogue of the Engraved Gems and Cameos, Greek, Etruscan and Roman in the Department of Greek and Roman Antiquities, British Museum*, London 1926
Wiman *Malstria-* I.M.B. Wiman, *Malstria-Malena. Metals and Motifs*
  Malena   *in Etruscan Mirror Craft*, Studies in Mediterranean Archaeology XCI, Göteborg 1990
Zazoff *Skarabäen* P. Zazoff, *Etruskische Skarabäen*, Mainz 1968
Zimmer *Gerhard* G. Zimmer, 'Eduard Gerhard und das Corpus der etruskischen Spiegel', in *Dem Archäologen Eduard Gerhard 1795–1867 zu seinem 200. Geburtstag*, Winckelmann-Institut der Humboldt-Universität zu Berlin,2, hrsg. H.Wrede, Berlin 1995
Zimmer *Technik* G. Zimmer, *Etruskische Spiegel. Technik und Stil der Zeichnungen* 135. Winckelmannsprogramm der Archäologischen Gesellschaft zu Berlin, Berlin 1995

CONCORDANCE A

Corpus No.	Departmental Registration No.	WALTERS BMBronzes No.	GERHARD/ KLÜGMANN–KÖRTE
1	GR 1837.6–9.96	–	
2	GR 1975.9–1.4	–	–
3	GR 1975.9–1.5	–	–
4	GR 1867.5–8.379	–	–
5	GR 1997.9–12.18	–	–
6	GR 1814.7–4.1061	–	–
7	GR 1967.12–13.5	–	–
8	GR 1837.6–9.93	–	–
9	GR 1975.9–1.1	–	–
10	GR 1967.12–13.1	–	–
11	GR 1814.7–14.918	–	–
12	GR 1890.9–21.17	–	–
13	GR 1837.6–9.95	725	I, p.85
14	GR 1824.4–89.82	545	IV, p.21, pl.CCLXXXIX, fig.2
15	GR 1900.6–11.3	–	–
16	GR 1814.7–4.915	541	IV, p.74, pl.CDXIV, fig.2
17	GR 1884.6–14.56	543	V, pp.18–19, pl.12
18	GR 1873.8–20.110	546	V, p.20, pl.14
19	GR 1853.1–10.3	540	IV, p.8, Paralip.236a★;V, p.49, pl.38
20	GR 1772.3–4.7₄	542	III, p.147; IV, p.88, pl.CCCXLIV
21	GR 1847.9–9.2	621	V, p.122, pl.95
22	GR 1913.12–17.1	–	V, pp.151–2, pl.113
23	GR 1847.9–9.3	707	IV, pp.116–17, pl.CCCLXIV; V, p.64, n.1
24	GR 1873.8–20.103	617	V, p.12, pl.6
25	GR 1847.9–9.5	715	IV, p.40, pl.CCCXCII
26	GR 1868.5–20.55	724	IV, p.77, pl.CDXVII
27	GR 1888.11–10.1	620	V, p.221
28	GR 1847.9–9.4	622	IV, p.112, pl.CCCLIX
29	GR 1814.7–4.967	631	I, pl.XCIV, fig.2
30	GR 1966.3–28.13	–	IV, p.35, pl.CCCLXXXVI (reversed)
31	GR 1814.7–4.966	244	I, pl.CXX, fig.2; III, p.120
32	GR 1840.2–12.8	–	–
33	GR 1814.7–4.704	–	I, pl.CXVII; III, p.118
34	GR 1814.7–4.2869	544	II, pl.CXXXIV; III, p.129
35	GR 1849.5–19.7	–	I, pl.LXV (reversed); III, pp.66–7
36	GR 1840.2–12.11	–	–

CONCORDANCE B

GERHARD/ KLÜGMANN–KÖRTE		Corpus No.	Departmental Registration No.	WALTERS BMBronzes No.
I	p.85	13	GR 1837.6–9.95	725
I	pl.LXV, fig.2	35	GR 1849.5–19.7	–
I	pl.XCIV, fig.2	29	GR 1814.7–4.967	631
I	pl.CXVII	33	GR 1814.7–4.704	–
I	pl.CXX, fig.2	31	GR 1814.7–4.966	244
II	pl.CXXXIV	34	GR 1814.7–4.2869	544
IV	pl.CCLXXXIX, fig.2	14	GR 1824.4–89.82	545
	pl.CCCXLIV	20	GR 1772.3–4.7₄	542
	pl.CCCLIX	28	GR 1847.9–9.4	622
	pl.CCCLXIV	23	GR 1847.9–9.3	707
	pl.CCCLXXXVI (reversed)	30	GR 1966.3–28.13	–
	pl.CCCXCII	25	GR 1847.9–9.5	715
	pl.CDXIV, fig.2	16	GR 1814.7–4.915	541
	pl.CDXVII	26	GR 1868.5–20.55	724
V	pl.6	24	GR 1873.8–20.103	617
	pl.13	17	GR 1884.6–14.56	543
	pl.14	18	GR 1873.8–20.110	546
	pl.38	19	GR 1853.1–10.3	540
	pl.95	21	GR 1847.9–9.2	621
	pl.113	22	GR 1913.12–17.1	–

CONCORDANCE C

WALTERS BM Bronzes No.	Corpus No.	Departmental Registration No.
244	31	GR 1814.7–4.966
540	19	GR 1853.1–10.3
541	16	GR 1814.7–4.915
542	20	GR 1772.3–4.7₄
543	17	GR 1884.6–14.56
544	34	GR 1814.7–4.2869
545	14	GR 1824.4–89.82
546	18	GR 1873.8–20.110
617	24	GR 1873.8–20.103
620	27	GR 1888.11–10.1
621	21	GR 1847.9–9.2
622	28	GR 1847.9–9.4
631	29	GR 1814.7–4.967
707	23	GR 1847.9–9.3
715	25	GR 1847.9–9.5
724	26	GR 1868.5–20.55
725	13	GR 1837.6–9.95

CONCORDANCE D

Departmental Registration No.	Corpus No.	WALTERS BMBronzes No.
GR 1772.3–4.7₄	20	542
GR 1814.7–4.704	33	
GR 1814.7–4.915	16	541
GR 1814.7–4.918	11	
GR 1814.7–4.966	31	244
GR 1814.7–4.967	29	631
GR 1814.7–4.1061	6	
GR 1814.7–4.2869	34	544
GR 1824.4–89.82	14	545
GR 1837.6–9.93	8	
GR 1837.6–9.95	13	725
GR 1837.6–9.96	1	
GR 1840.2–12.8	32	
GR 1840.2–12.11	36	
GR 1847.9–9.2	21	621
GR 1847.9–9.3	23	707
GR 1847.9–9.4	28	622
GR 1847.9–9.5	25	715
GR 1849.5–19.7	35	
GR 1853.1–10.3	19	540
GR 1867.5–8.379	4	
GR 1868.5–20.55	26	724
GR 1873.8–20.103	24	617
GR 1873.8–20.110	18	546
GR 1884.6–14.56	17	543
GR 1888.11–10.1	27	620
GR 1890.9–21.17	12	
GR 1900.6–11.3	15	
GR 1913.12–17.1	22	
GR 1966.3–28.13	30	
GR 1967.12–13.1	10	
GR 1967.12–13.5	7	
GR 1975.9–1.1	9	
GR 1975.9–1.4	2	
GR 1975.9–1.5	3	
GR 1997.9–12.18	5	

Deities and heroes/heroines represented (Etruscan name, or Greek equivalent followed by Etruscan, if known)

Adonis ?18, ?31, ?33
Ajax/Aivas 25, 28
Amazon ?20, 22
Amphiaraos/Hamphiare 28
Anteros ?17
Antikleia ?26
Aphrodite/Turan 17, 18, ?32, 33
Athena/Menerva 24, 27, 34
Circe, see Kirke
Diomedes?/[Z]imite 22
Dioscuri ?16
Ectur/Hektor 25
Eros ?17, ?18, ?31, ?32, ?33
Eteokles/Evzicle 21
Ethauśva 24
Helen ?16
Helios/Usil ?14, 23
Herakles/Herecele/Herkle 20, 34
Hermes/Turms 27
Himeros ?17
Hippocamp 35
Hippolyta ?20
Hyakinthos ?31
Hyperion/Upriuś 23
Ixion 15
Juno ?35
Kirke ?26
Lasa 28
Maenad 19, 29
Medusa's head 27
Mlacuch 20
Nereid 35
Nike/Mean (Meanpe) ?32
Odysseus/Utuśe 22, ?26
Orion ?14
Peleus/Pele 30
Penthesilea/Pentasila 22
Perseus/Ferśe 27
Polyneikes/Fulnice 21
Satyr 19, 29
Thanr 24
Thetis/Thethis 30, ?35
Zeus/Tinia 24

Numbers refer to entries

Provenances

Atri/Viterbo/Vulci? 20
Bologna 12
Castiglione della Teverina,
(near Bolsena) 22
Chiusi 18
Perugia 27, 30, ?34
Praeneste 17, ?33
Vulci 1, 8, 13, ?23, 25, ?28

Inscriptions

aivas 25, 28
ectur 25
ethauśva 24
evzicle 21
[z]imite 22
hamphiare 28
herecele 20
herkle 34
thanc(.)vilus 26
thanr 24

thethis 30
lasa 28
menerva 24, 27, 34
mi 26
mlacuch 20
pele 30
pentasila 22
pupena 13
ramethas 13
tinia 24
turms 27
upriuś 23
usil 23
utuśe 22
ferśe 27
fulnial 26
fulnice 21

Etruscan owners' names

Rametha Pupena 13
Thancvil Fulni 26

Sources

Ansidei, A. 34
Blacas, Duke Peter Lewis John
Casimir de 4
Blayd, Thomas 35
Bonaparte, Lucien, Prince of
Canino 1, 8, 13
Braun, Dr Emil 23, 25, 28
Butler, Samuel, Bishop of
Lichfield 36
Byres, James 33
Campanari, Secondiano 23,
?25, ?28
Castellani, Alessandro 17, 18, 22,
24
Cureton, H.O. 19
Fejérváry-Pulszky collection
26
Ficoroni, Francesco 26
Fitzhenry, J.H. 22
Greville Chester, Reverend J. 12
Hamilton, Sir William 20
Hartwig, Dr.P 15
Helbig, Wolfgang 27

Magnini, P.A. Rolando 31
Martinetti collection 17
Museum of London (Gould
collection) 5
Knight, Richard Payne 14
Palm, Baron v. 26
Pizzati collection 35
Spencer Churchill, Captain E.G.
30
Townley, Peregrine Edward 33
Townley, Sir Charles (second
collection) 6, 11, 16, 29, 31,
33, 34
Tyszkiewicz, Comte Michel 24
Weightman, Mr 30

GENERAL INDEX

1a

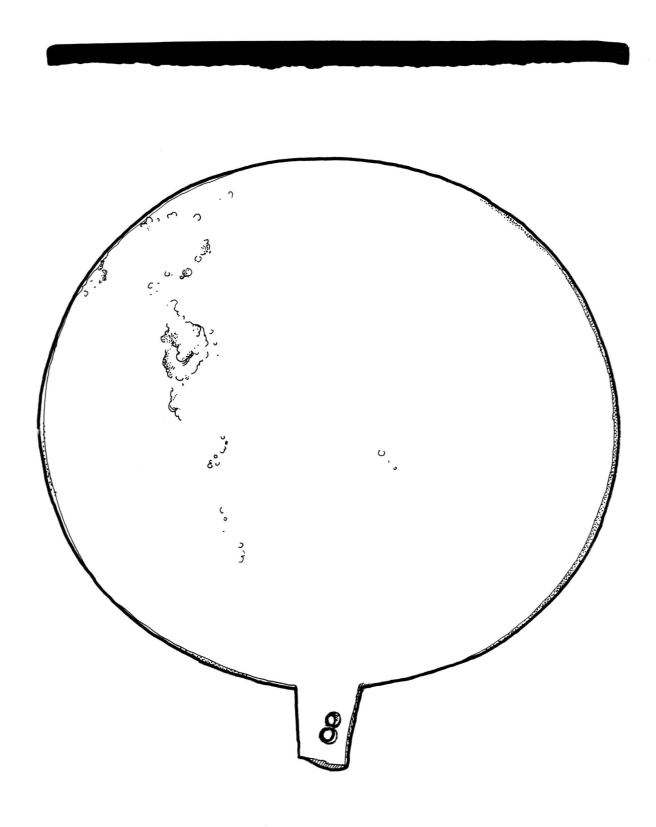

1b

2a

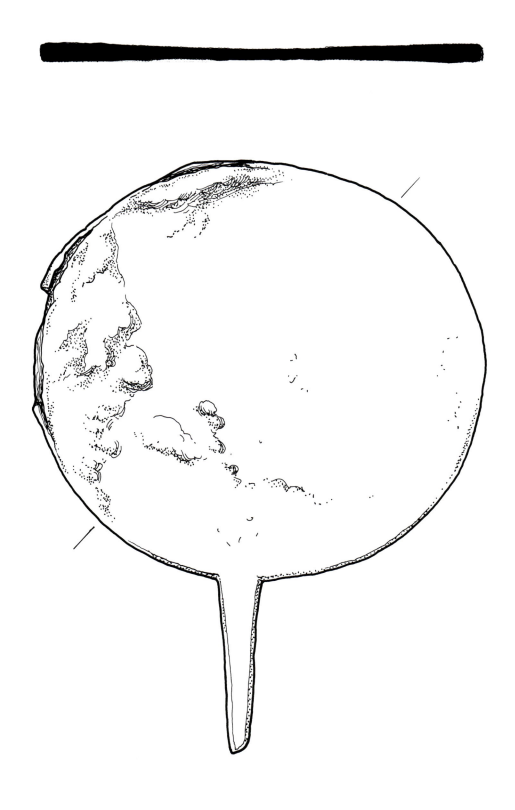

2b

3a

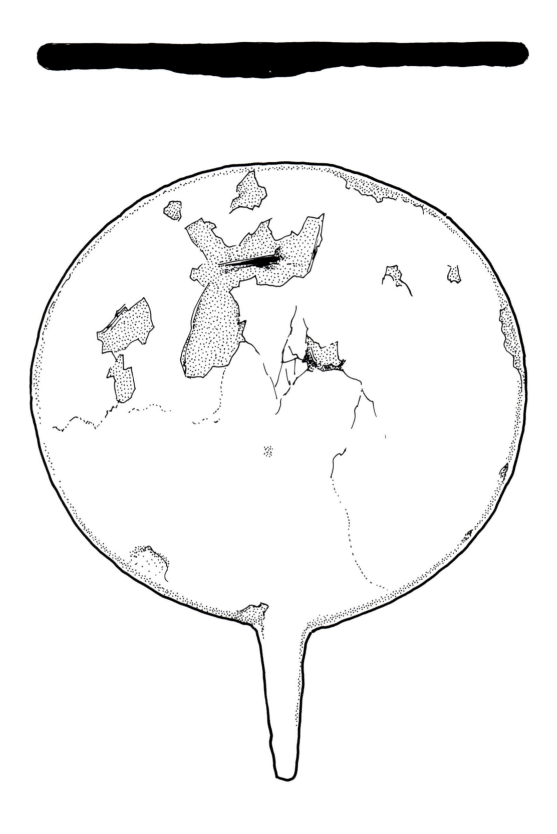

3b

4a

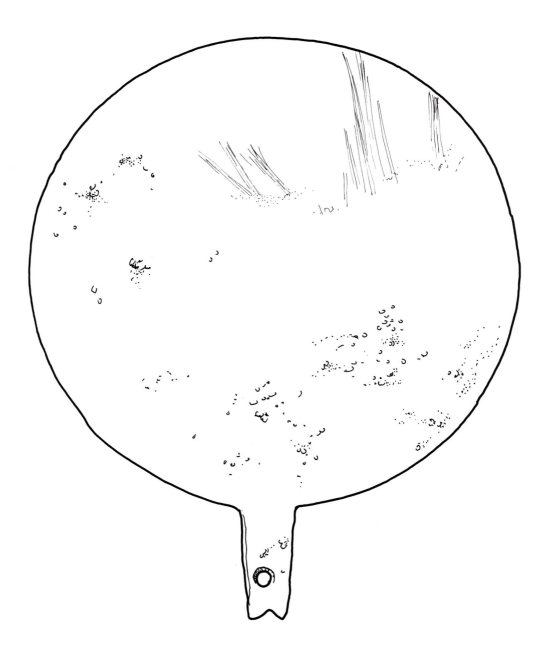

4b

4c

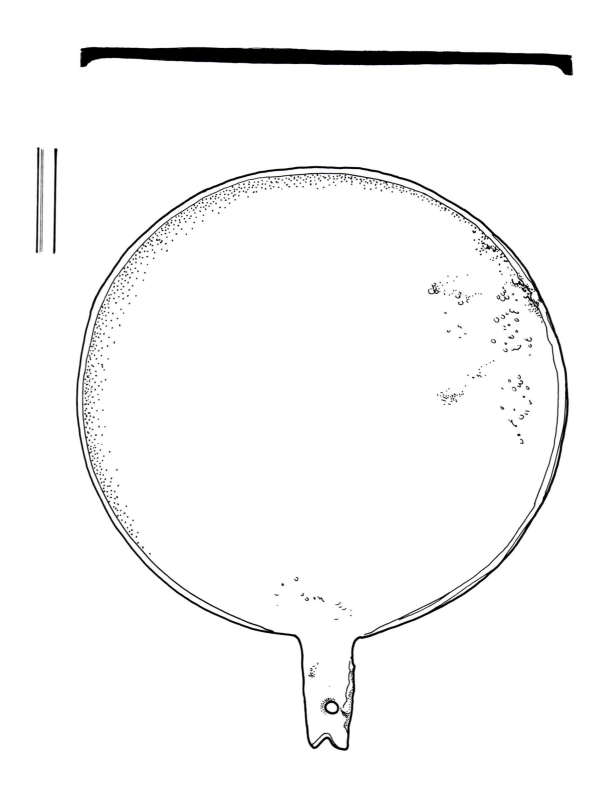

4d

5a

5a

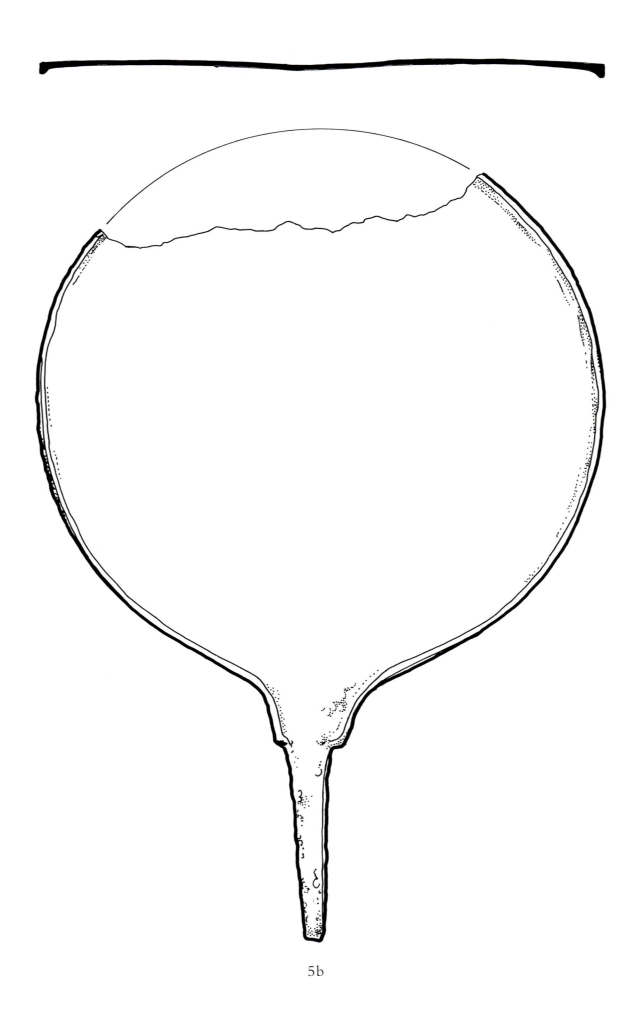

5b

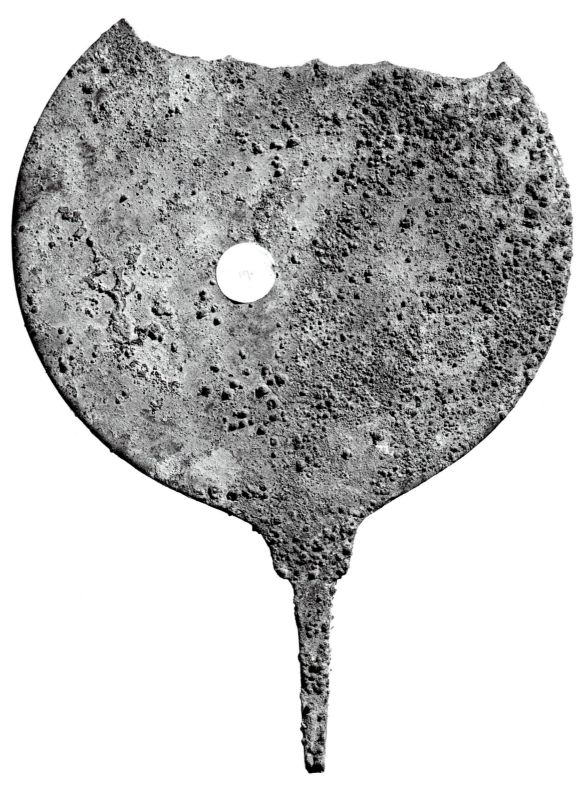

5c

5d

6a

6b

6c

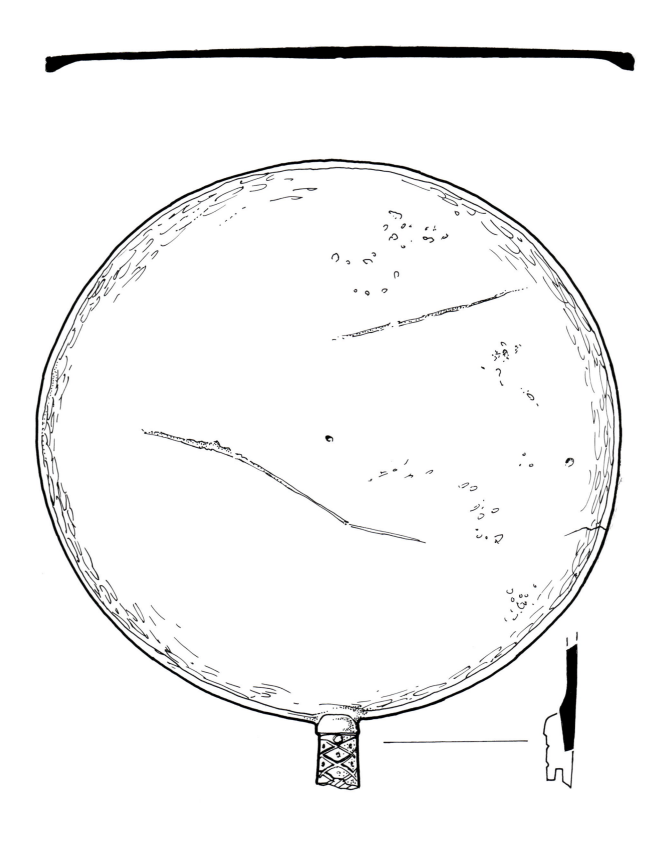

6d   6e

7a

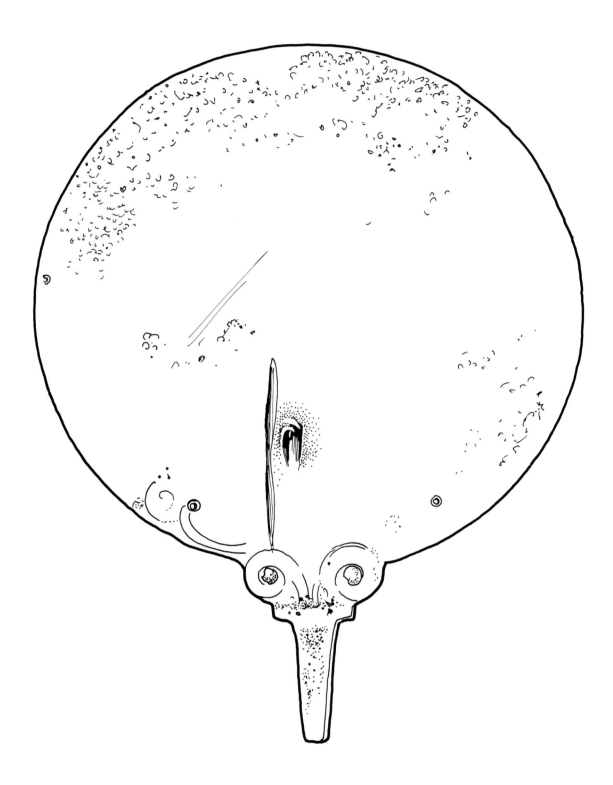

7b

7c

7c

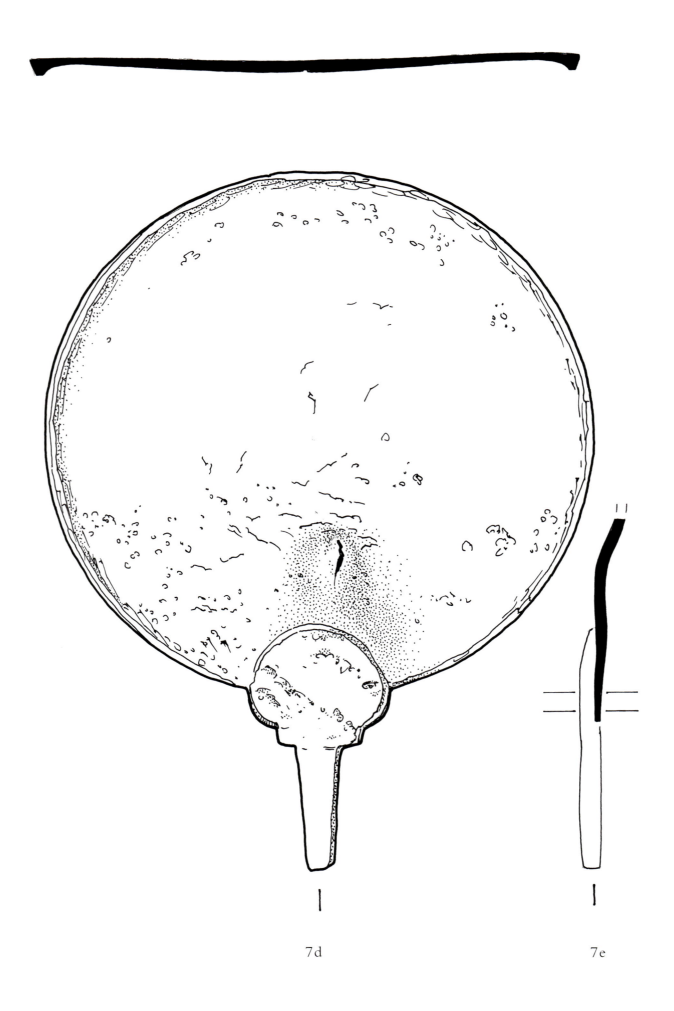

7d

7e

8a   8b

8c

9a

9b

9c

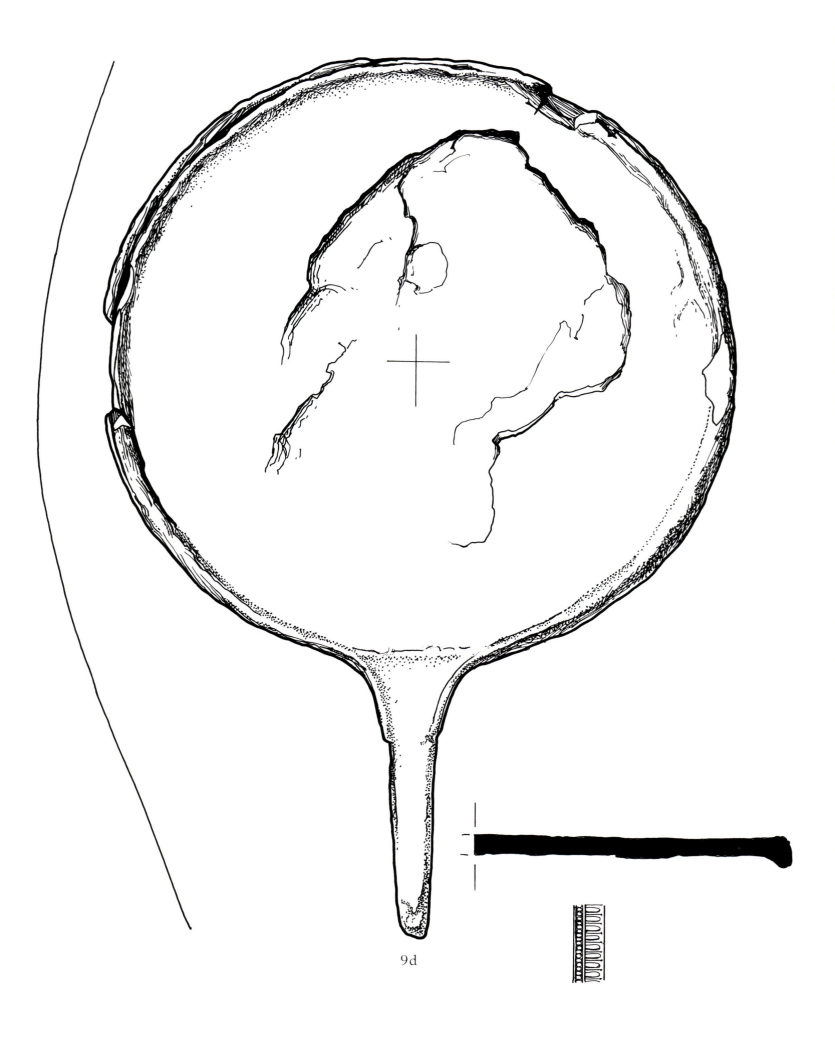

9d

10a

10b

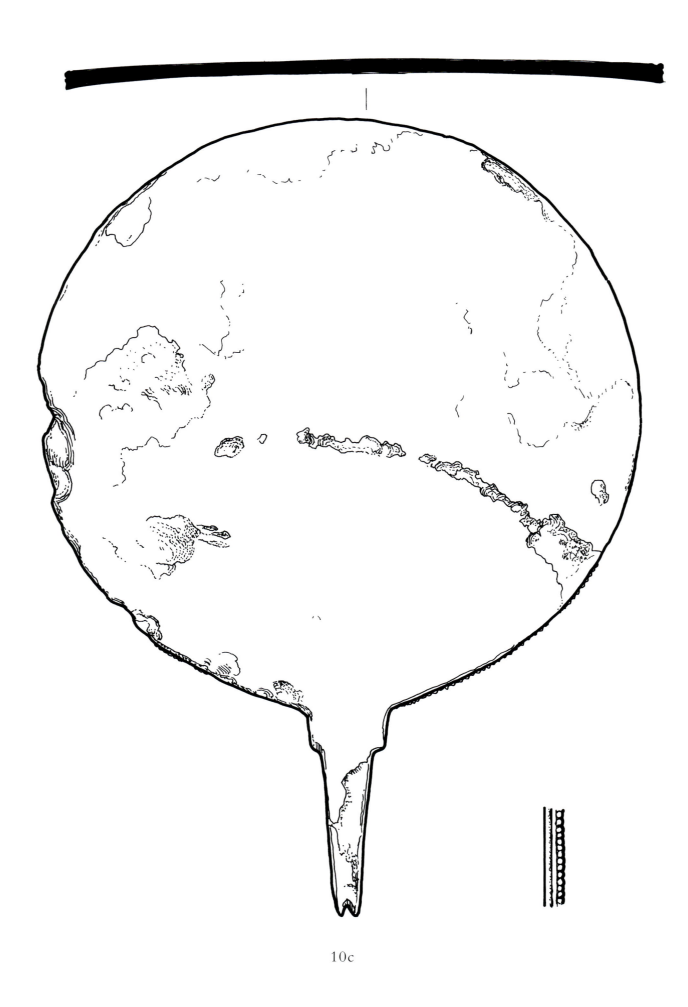

10c

11a

11b

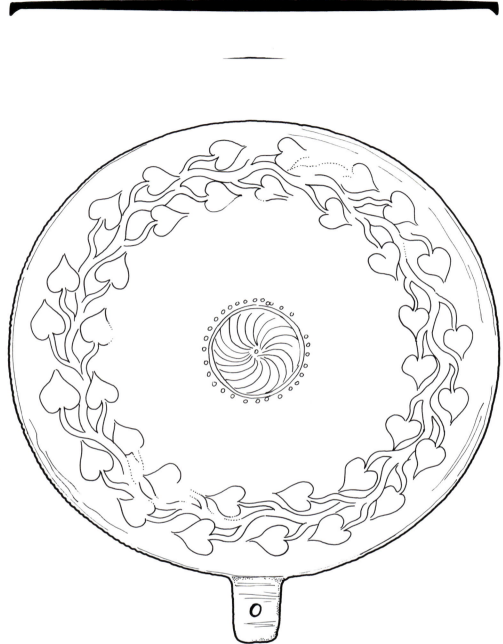

11c

12a

12b

12c

12c

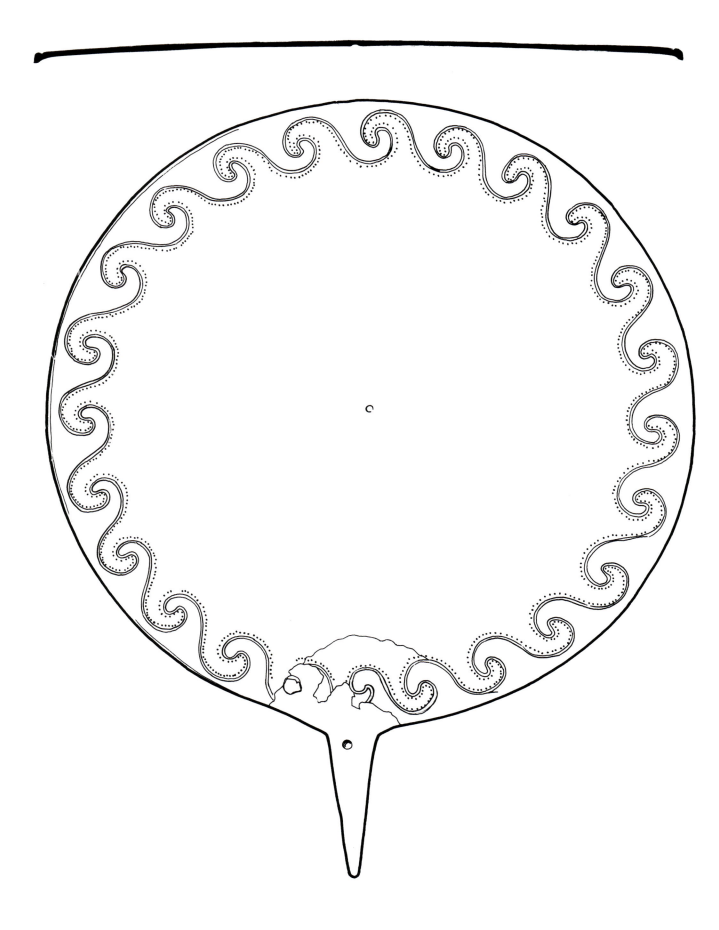

12d

13a

13a

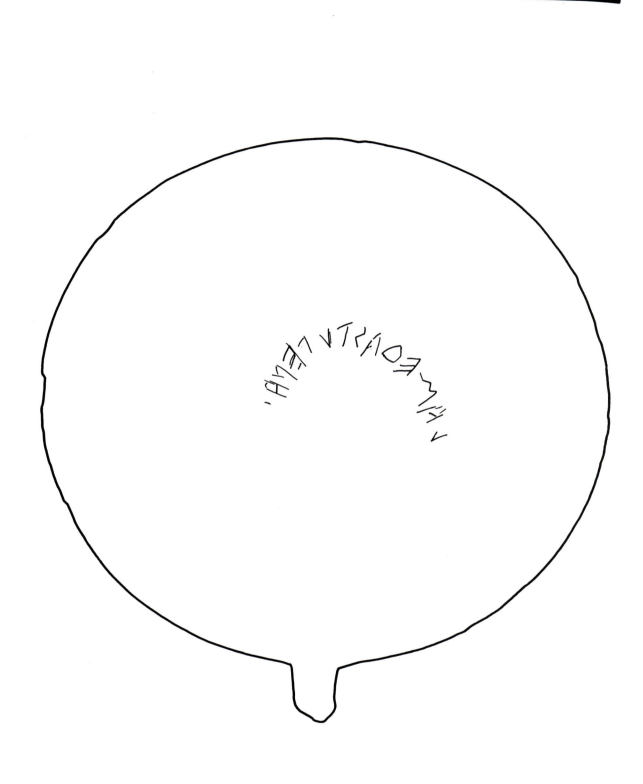

13b

13c

13c

14a

14b

14c

14c

14d

15a

15b

15c

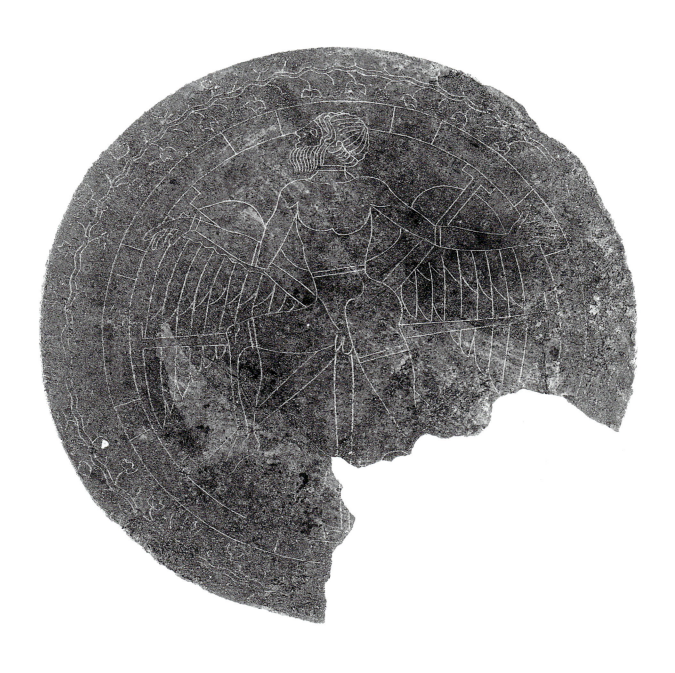

15c

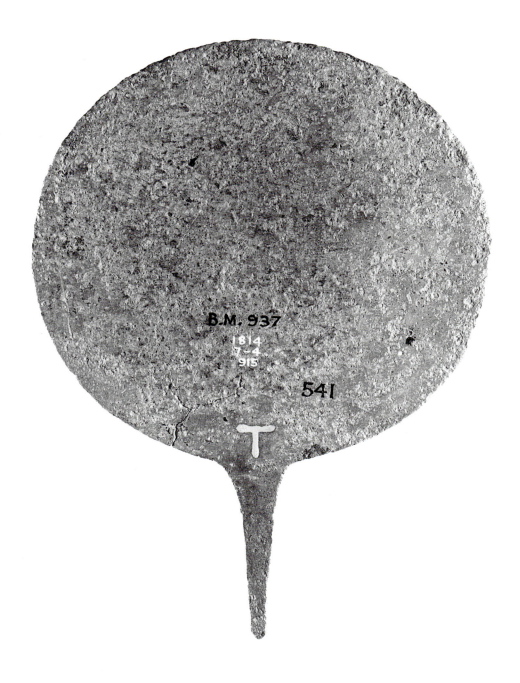

16a

16b

16b

16c

17a

17b

17c

17d

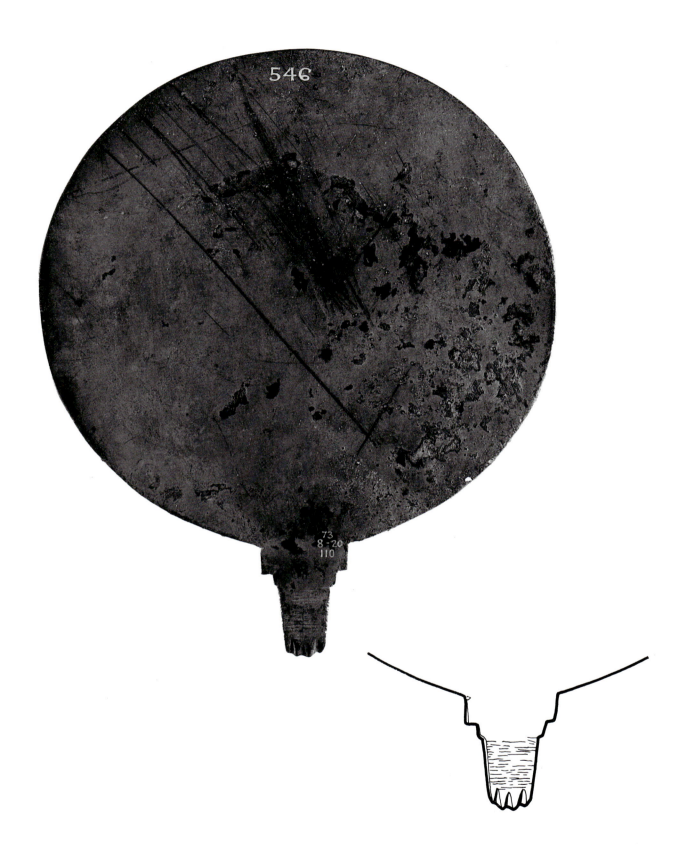

18a   18b

18c

18d

19a

19b

19c   19d

20a   20b

20c

20d

21a

21a

21b

21c   21d

22a   (both 95% actual size)   22b

22c   (95% actual size)

22d   (95% actual size)

23a   (90% actual size)

23b   (90% actual size)

23c   (both 90% actual size)   23d

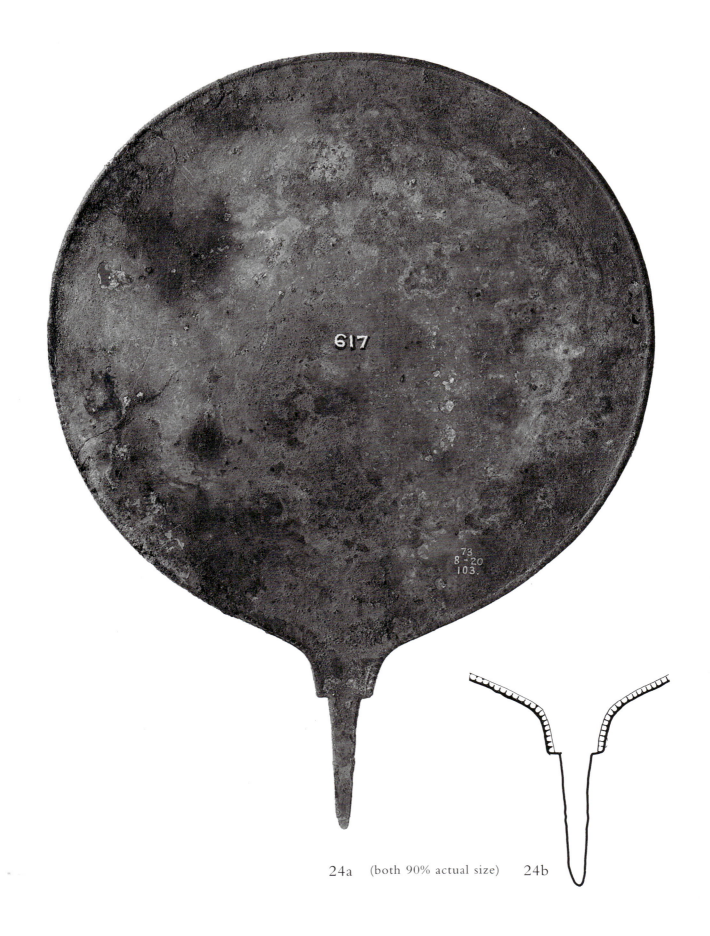

24a   (both 90% actual size)   24b

24c   (90% actual size)

24d (90% actual size)

25a

25a

25b

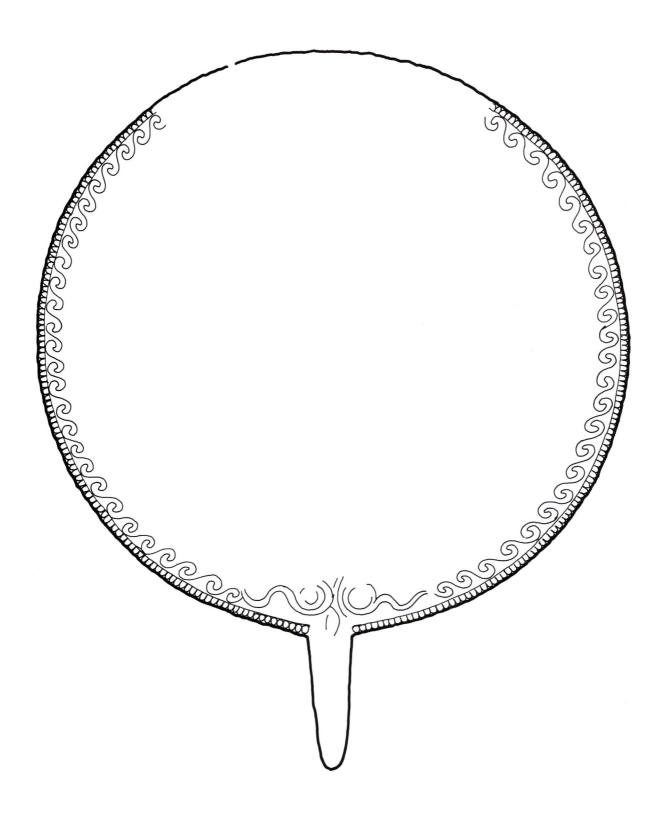

25b

25c

25d

26a

26a

26b

26c

26d

27a　　　　　(both 90% actual size)　27b

27c   (90% actual size)

27d

(90% actual size)

28a

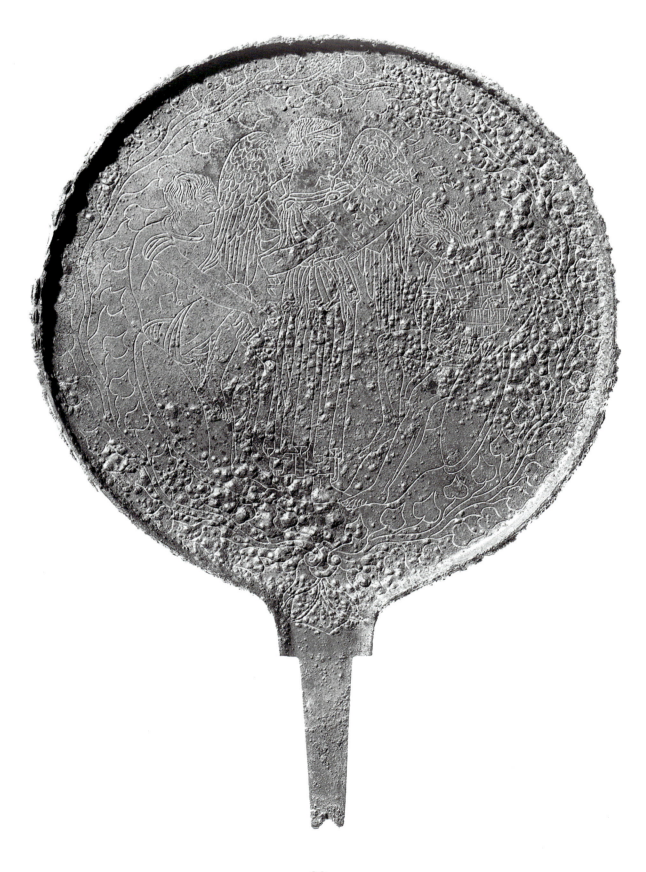

28a

28b

28c   28d

29a   29b

29c

29c

29d

30a   (75% actual size)

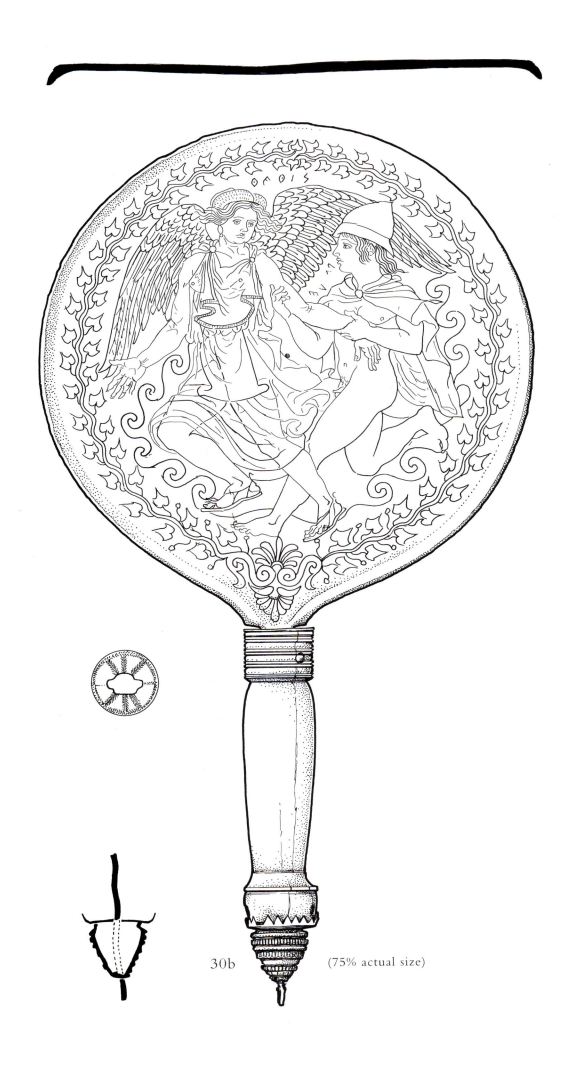

30b   (75% actual size)

30c　　　　　　　　　(both 75% actual size)　　　30d

30e (1:1)

31a

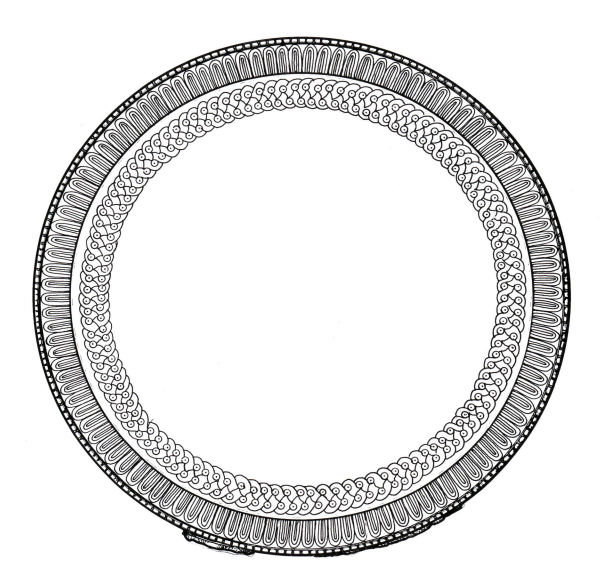

31b

31c

31c

31d

32a

32a

32b

32c   32d

33a   (80% actual size)   33b (1:1)

33c   (80% actual size)

33d   (80% actual size)

34a   (80% actual size)

34c   34d   34b   34e   (all 80% actual size)

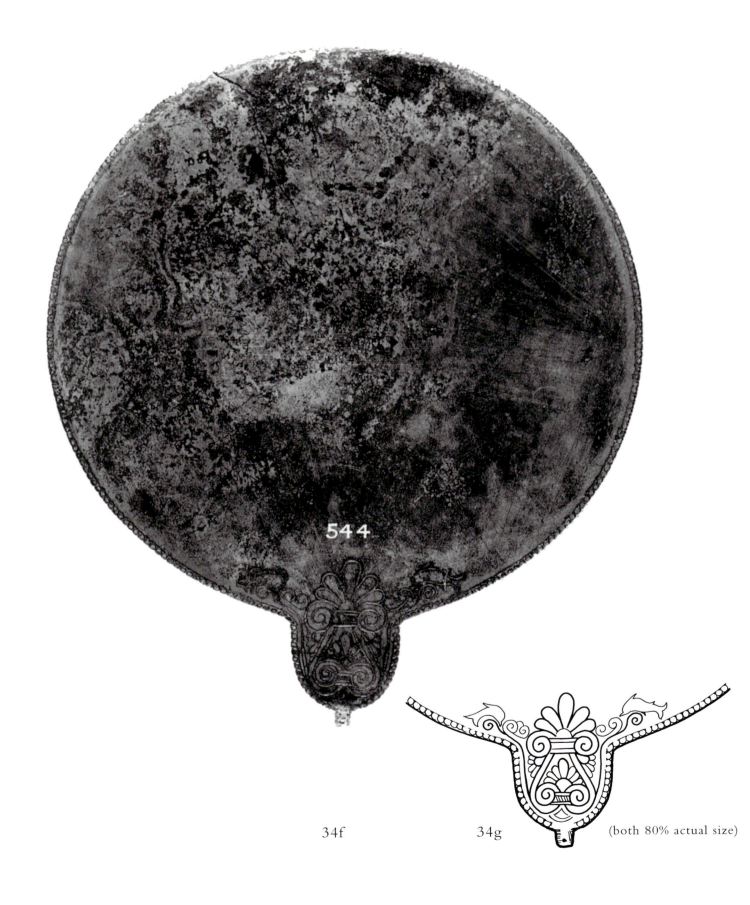

544

34f   34g   (both 80% actual size)

35a   35b

35c

35c

35d

36a

36b

36c   36d

No. 13

Fig. 1

No. 21

Fig. 4

Fig. 5

No. 20

Fig. 2

Fig. 3

No. 22

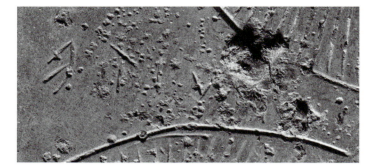

Fig. 6

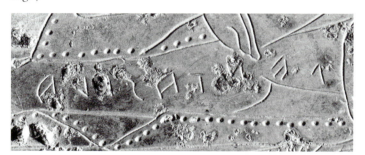

Fig. 7

Fig. 8

No. 23

Fig. 9

Fig. 10

No. 24

Fig. 11

Fig. 12

Fig. 13

Fig. 14

No. 25

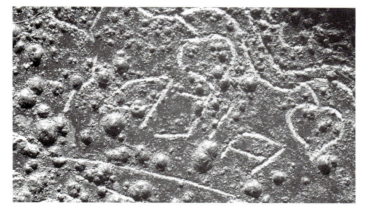

Fig. 15

Fig. 16

No. 27

Fig. 18

Fig. 19

No. 26

Fig. 17

No. 28

Fig. 20

Fig. 21

Fig. 22

No. 30

Fig. 23

Fig. 24

No. 34

Fig. 25

Fig. 26

No. 36

No. 34

Fig. 27

Fig. 28

Fig. 29

Fig. 30

Fig. 31

Fig. 32

Fig. 33

No. 30

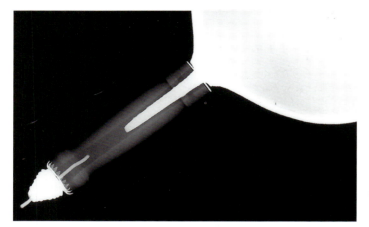

Fig. 34. Radiograph

No. 31

Fig. 35. After *de la Chausse* 11 pl. 19

No. 33

Fig. 36. Drawing of the 'cista mistica' group made for Charles Townley